T0305428

Corporate Strategy and Firm Growth

NEW PERSPECTIVES ON THE MODERN CORPORATION

Series Editor: Jonathan Michie, *Director, Department for Continuing Education and President, Kellogg College, University of Oxford, UK*

The modern corporation has far reaching influence on our lives in an increasingly globalised economy. This series will provide an invaluable forum for the publication of high quality works of scholarship covering the areas of :

- corporate governance and corporate responsibility, including environmental sustainability
- human resource management and other management practices, and the relationship of these to organisational outcomes and corporate performance
- industrial economics, organisational behaviour, innovation and competitiveness
- outsourcing, offshoring, joint ventures and strategic alliances
- different ownership forms, including social enterprise and employee ownership
- intellectual property and the learning economy, including knowledge
- transfer and information exchange.

Titles in the series include:

Corporate Governance, Organization and the Firm
Co-operation and Outsourcing in the Global Economy
Edited by Mario Morroni

The Modern Firm, Corporate Governance and Investment
Edited by Per-Olof Bjuggren and Dennis C. Mueller

The Growth of Firms
A Survey of Theories and Empirical Evidence
Alex Coad

Knowledge in the Development of Economies
Institutional Choices Under Globalisation
Edited by Silvia Sacchetti and Roger Sugden

Corporate Strategy and Firm Growth
Creating Value for Shareholders
Angelo Dringoli

Corporate Strategy and Firm Growth

Creating Value for Shareholders

Angelo Dringoli

Faculty of Economics, University of Siena, Italy

NEW PERSPECTIVES ON THE MODERN CORPORATION

Edward Elgar
Cheltenham, UK • Northampton, MA, USA

Published by
Edward Elgar Publishing Limited
The Lypiatts
15 Lansdown Road
Cheltenham
Glos GL50 2JA
UK

Edward Elgar Publishing, Inc.
William Pratt House
9 Dewey Court
Northampton
Massachusetts 01060
USA

A catalogue record for this book
is available from the British Library

Library of Congress Control Number: 2011931016

ISBN 978 0 85793 827 5 (Hardback)

Printed and bound by CPI Group (UK) Ltd, Croydon, CR0 4YY

Contents

Abbreviations

a	Expenses to increase resources
A	Depreciation and amortization
b	Rate at which the marginal labour hours decline as the cumulative number of units produced increases
C	Current operating costs
CFO	Cash flow from operations
Cu	Unit cost of product
$D(0)$	Value of debt at initial date 0
$E(0)$	Value of equity at initial date 0
$EBIT$	Earnings before interest and taxes
$EBITDA$	Earnings before interest, taxes and depreciation
EBT	Taxable income
$FCFO(t)$	Free cash flow from operations in period t
g	Growth rate of cash flows
$H(Q)$	Labour hours required for producing the Qth unit
I_E	Investment in a growth strategy
INT	Interest expenses
kd	Cost of debt
ke	Cost of equity
m	Unit margin
NI	Net income
P	Product price in period t
P_B	Price of firm B
Q	Quantity of product produced or sold
R	Revenues
R_j	Value of resource j
S	Period up to the structural change (years)
t	Period of time (year)
T	Process or product lifetime (years)

$TC(Q)$	Total cost of producing quantities Q
TV	Terminal value of the firm
$V(0)$	Firm value at initial date 0
V_A	Value of firm A
V_{AB}	Value of merger AB
V_{acq}	Value of acquisition
V_B	Value of firm B
V_S	Value of a growth strategy
V_{SA}	Value of an acquisition strategy
V_{SD}	Value of a product diversification strategy
V_{SH}	Value of a horizontal expansion strategy
V_{SV}	Value of a vertical integration strategy
V_{SY}	Value of synergy
WC	Working capital (difference between current assets and current liabilities)
α	Labour hours required for producing the first unit of product
γ	Rate of decay in resource value
ΔWC	Change in working capital
ΔI	Capital expenditures
μ	Rate of accumulation in resource value
ρ	Weighted average cost of capital ($WACC$)
τ	Corporate tax rate
τ^*	Adjusted corporate tax rate

Preface

In this book we study the growth of the firm and the conditions for growth which creates value for shareholders.

The approach of the first part of the book is normative; it uses a theoretical analysis to show what managers should do to maximize shareholders' value through growth strategies and what the conditions are for favouring one or the other type of strategy. With this aim in mind we focus the analysis on the main strategies adopted by enterprises for growth: horizontal expansion, vertical expansion and product diversification.

The order of presentation reflects the actual growth of many firms: expansion starts within a core industry and it is undertaken to enhance or protect a firm's position in that business (horizontal expansion). Then, a firm moves outside its initial industry integrating its activities or phases along its value chain (vertical integration expansion) until over the years it becomes increasingly more and more diversified, entering different related industries and finally unrelated industries (product diversification expansion).

Each growth strategy is viewed as a decision directed at creating value for shareholders, exploiting the various opportunities offered by the environment and the internal firm resources. Each growth strategy implies different changes in the firm's system and causes different effects on the firm's long-term cash flows. Therefore, defining a growth strategy which creates value requires examining the internal conditions of the firm to be analysed, evaluating the dynamics of the external environment in which the firm operates and estimating the expected effects on the value of the company.

In order for a defined strategy to create value, it is also necessary to adapt the firm's organizational structure so as to effectively manage the increased complexity of the new business system. To reach this aim the organizational structures which can offer the best solution with respect to each growth strategy are analysed.

To evaluate whether or not a growth strategy can create value, we present some analytical models capable of specifying the relevant conditions under which each type of strategy can create value, both in the case of internal development and in the case of acquisition of other companies. These analytical models also allow us to identify the limits regarding the firm's size both of an internal or external nature.

The book highlights the fact that growth does not necessarily produce an increase in the enterprise and in the shareholders' value; that clearly results only under particular conditions. Thus, top managers must carefully evaluate every growth alternative.

The book is based on established research traditions. In particular a number of insights are drawn from three distinct bodies of research: the resource-based view of the firm; the organizational economics –in particular transaction costs analysis– and the fundamentals of corporate finance. All these theoretical traditions made a substantial contribution to the arguments advanced here.

In particular, the resource based view of a firm is the fundamental theoretical reference for our analysis. We believe growth strategies have to rest both on the dynamics of industry structure and on the existing firm's system characteristics that is the firm's resources, assets and capabilities. Heterogeneity of resources and their firm-specific characteristics form the basis of diversity and the strategic variety of firms.

In the second part of the book four cases of successful companies are presented. These companies are characterized by a decade of continuous growth, accompanied by a systematic creation of value for shareholders. The growth strategies of these companies are examined and their characteristics and effects are described, using analyses from the companies' annual reports over a period of years. The purpose of these cases is to highlight how a firm chooses and implements a defined growth strategy. Thus the cases provide a link between theory and practice, making the analysis more real and interesting.

The book is mainly directed at researchers and students in economics and management. As it offers useful tools for managerial decisions, we think it can also be of interest to managers and consultants.

The book contains 11 formal chapters and supplementary appendixes on related topics or background information. In particular, the appendixes provide additional focus on the concepts and theories presented in each chapter.

Chapter 1 begins with an introduction to growth strategies, the fundamental bases of strategies and the principal patterns of firm development. Chapter 2 provides the essential theory concerning the firm value and the evaluation of a growth strategy. Chapter 3 examines the characteristics of horizontal expansion strategies and the conditions under which they can create value. Chapter 4 shifts the focus onto product diversification strategies, examining the conditions for which they can create value. Chapter 5 addresses the economic rationale for vertical integration strategies. Chapter 6 examines the appropriate organizational models for managing large and diversified companies and Chapter 7 discusses the limits to the firm's size.

In these chapters the theoretical exposition is often followed by numerical examples and simulation. Furthermore, some appendixes are dedicated to recalling topics and knowledge of particular interest for the analysis: scale economies, learning economies, transaction costs, and so on.

Chapters 8, 9, 10 and 11 analyse four successful companies L'Oreal, Campari, Luxottica and Geox, showing their different growth patterns and explaining their behaviour over a long period of time. They allow us to verify the results of the theoretical analysis developed in the first part and offer useful empirical material for further research.

This book is the result of some years of research developed at the School of Economics at the University of Siena and at the LUISS University of Rome. Outside school I have learned a lot from my experience as a management consultant and as a member of the board of directors of some industrial companies and banks.

Prof. Angelo Dringoli

Siena, April 2011

To Simonetta and Tommaso

PART I

GROWTH STRATEGIES AND FIRM VALUE

1. Growth strategies: types and fundamental bases

INTRODUCTION AND OBJECTIVES

In this chapter we define the main strategies for a firm's growth and we also choose the criteria for their evaluation. We distinguish among horizontal expansion, vertical integration and product diversification strategies, focusing the analysis on growth as a means for creating value for shareholders. We also explain why a firm's resources are the fundamental base for growth strategies and the ultimate source for obtaining a competitive advantage and creating value through expansion. Finally, the existence of a typical evolutionary model of firm is discussed, considering the results of some important empirical studies concerning the growth of large industrial corporations. In the appendix a model is presented for identifying the firm's resources which are the base of growth strategies.

GROWTH AS A STRATEGIC DECISION

First of all, what do we mean by growth? Common sense tells us that growth is a process through which the size of a firm becomes bigger, but how do we measure the firm's size – by the number of employees, the revenue, the capital invested or the added value?

Considering the pitfalls and incompleteness of other variables, we will use both invested capital and sales as the basic measures of a firm's size. Thus, the growth of a firm substantially means the increase in its investments and consequently in its production and selling capacity. Generally, the growth of investments also determines the growth of sales, but that is not a necessary consequence if investments are directed at realizing a superior vertical integration, so influencing the firm's added value but not revenue. In other cases, investments can determine an increase in sales but a reduction in the number of employees, due to the increase of labour productivity obtained from new plants and machinery. Finally, the growth of sales can be considerably larger than the growth of investments, due to the outsourcing of firm operations and production phases or the putting together of alliances and joint ventures.

In any case, the growth of a firm is not a natural and evolutionary process, but the result of managerial decisions which are directed at modifying the size of the firm in order to reach a precise objective.

The growth of a firm can be favoured, first of all, by the environment dynamics. Consider, for example, the opportunities for growth offered by a rise in population and by the corresponding increase in income per capita.

Important opportunities for growth can also derive from the introduction of new products and processes which meet latent customers' needs or even create new models in customers' behaviour. Finally, the growth can be realised in order to increase the market share, so reinforcing a firm's competitive position against its competitors.

The growth of a firm, whether it is favoured by external factors or driven by internal forces, requires the use of additional financial resources that must be rightly remunerated, in order to avoid destroying the value of the invested capital. For this reason decisions concerning the growth of a firm must have a reference picture represented by the long-term dynamics of the external environment, especially of industry, as well as of the firm's resources. They are strategic decisions because they are irreversible in the short term, as they concern changes in specific and not transferable assets.

Furthermore, since growth is not an evolutionary process but a consequence of a deliberate choice, this choice must be taken only if it creates value for shareholders. Therefore, a growth strategy must be carefully evaluated.

TYPES OF GROWTH STRATEGIES

The growth of a firm can follow different patterns, according to the opportunities offered by the environment and the disposable resources the firm has. Growth can be carried out through horizontal expansion processes in the business in which the firm is already operating. Moreover, growth can be realised through entrance into a different business, related or unrelated to the business in which a firm is already operating.

We will distinguish three different growth strategies:

- horizontal expansion strategy;
- vertical integration strategy;

- product diversification strategy.

We refer to horizontal expansion when a firm expands its production and sales capacity in the existing market or in different local or international markets, continuing to operate in the same industry or business with the same product. The extension to different market segments through new types and models of the same basic product is also considered as a horizontal expansion.

We refer to vertical expansion when a firm decides to make directly operations or phases of activity located upstream or downstream with respect to the present activity or to make directly components or services which before were acquired from other firms.

Finally, we refer to diversified expansion, when a firm enters into different industries or businesses with substantially different products, related or unrelated to the existing ones. In this case we will distinguish between:

- related diversification, when businesses are related either by markets or by product technologies;
- conglomerate diversification, when businesses are not related either by markets or by product technologies.

In our view, the introduction of different new models or types of a given basic product directed at different market segments (for example a new type or model of sunglasses) does not constitute a diversification strategy, but a horizontal expansion strategy.

The proposed classification goes into less detail than those proposed by other authors (Ansoff, 1965; Rumelt, 1974; Rispoli, 1998), because it aims principally at emphasizing the fundamental difference between the structural firm changes required by growth strategies involving entrance into different industries and those involving further expansion and penetration into the industry in which a firm is already operating.

In economic terms, a horizontal strategy determines an increase in the quantities produced and sold of a given product; a vertical integration strategy determines an increase in the added value of a firm; and a diversification strategy determines the production and sale of a different product (Table 1.1).

As will be clarified in the following chapters, each strategy implies different changes in the firm structure and requires different resources for it to be successful. Also the environmental conditions favouring one or the other strategy are very different. Therefore, the analysis of the firm structure and the environmental conditions form the bases for a coherent formulation of a growth strategy.

Table 1.1 Growth strategies and main economic effects

Growth strategies	Main economic effects
Horizontal expansion	
Expansion in domestic markets or entering in different geographical markets, producing the same product or new types or models.	Increase in quantities produced and sold and consequent increase in revenues and in costs.
Vertical integration	
Expansion along the value chain.	Increase in added value.
Product diversification	
Expansion entering different industries producing related or unrelated products.	Production and sale of a different product and consequent increase in revenues and costs.

MODES OF FIRM EXPANSION

The growth of a firm can be carried out in two different ways:

- internal or organic development;
- acquisition.

The first mode consists in building new production capacity through investment in a new plant, new sales network, new information and management system. The second mode for growth consists in the acquisition of firms already operating in the industry into which the firm is interested in entering.

The advantages and disadvantages of these two growth modes will be examined, with reference to each different growth strategy, in the following chapters.

A FIRM'S RESOURCES AND CAPABILITIES AS FUNDAMENTAL BASES OF GROWTH STRATEGIES

According to the resource-based theory (Barney, 1984, 1991 and 2001; Wernerfelt, 1984; Grant, 1991; Peteraf, 1993; Collis and Montgomery, 2005) we consider the firm as an organized set of resources (tangible and intangible) through which specific activities and processes are carried out so as to obtain products or services for markets.

A firm's resources[1] can be classified into three categories: tangible assets, intangible assets and organizational capabilities (Grant, 1998; Collis and Montgomery, 2005). Tangible assets are assets that can be seen and quantified. They are indicated in a firm's balance sheet and include production facilities, real estate, plant, etc. Intangible assets include brands, company reputation, technological knowledge, patents and trademarks.

Organizational capabilities represent the firm's capacity to deploy resources; they include the set of abilities incorporated in a firm's activities and processes from product development to manufacturing and to marketing. They are the result of the quality of people employed and their experience and accumulation of learning over time. The primary bases for the firm's capabilities are the skills and knowledge of its employees (the value of human capital).

The stock of resources a firm possesses at a certain date, especially intangible resources and capabilities, is a sedimentation of activities and processes carried out from period to period that slowly accumulate over time, according to rates specific to the type of resource. Think, for example, of a firm's reputation, brand image, brand loyalty or marketing expertise or R&D know-how, distribution network, etc.

Furthermore, the existing stock of resources depreciates over time, due to environmental changes and competition from rival firms, so it is necessary to plan appropriate expenditure flows for maintaining or increasing the stock level, also for externally acquiring the desired resources in a market transaction, for example purchasing an entire company or business unit.

A firm's resources are the fundamental basis of actual competitive advantage at the business unit level and thus of the level of income and cash flow. In fact, they are the durable stocks of resources that characterize the product being offered, the level of product differentiation and the costs of organization (Nelson, 1994).

Moreover, resources are the fundamental basis of growth strategies because they determine what a firm can do in the future. More precisely, resources define the acceptable domain of growth strategies a firm can pursue for creating value within the actual business and for entering into new businesses (Nelson and Winter, 1982; Wernerfelt, 1984; Winter, 1987; Hamel and Prahalad, 1994; Nelson, 1995) (Figure 1.1).

In fact, as many of a firm's resources cannot be accumulated instantaneously, because they are the result of a cumulative process developed over time, the choice of a strategy is limited by the current resource stock and by the speed at which a firm can acquire and accumulate new resources (Collis and Montgomery, 2005 p. 30).[2]

Roughly speaking, we can express the growth of a firm as a function of its specific resources and environmental variables, industry demand and supply, consumers' trends, etc. A list of resources and capabilities that generally are critical for growth strategies is shown in Table 1.2.

Therefore, if all firms in an industry cope with the same external variable, they nevertheless have different growth responses because each of them has a unique, specific set of resources.

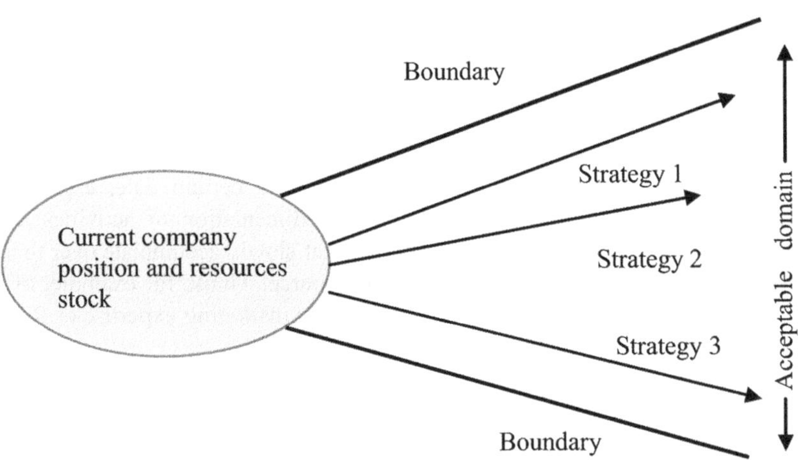

Figure 1.1 Resources stock and direction of growth

However, the growth of a firm cannot be determined once its internal structure is defined and the market variables have been estimated, because it is also influenced by casual variables. In this context, the value of resources, such as firm reputation, research and development (R&D) capabilities, advertising goodwill, etc., should be viewed as a capital good that is accumulated over time through an appropriate flow of expenses adding increments to an existing value, according to the efficiency of these expenses. But the asset value depreciates over time and needs maintenance. Thus, for example, advertising goodwill depreciates over time because consumers tend to forget brands and competitors operate to affirm their brands. Therefore, continuous advertising is needed to maintain a constant level of goodwill and a given rate of sales.[3] Similarly, the stock of knowledge depreciates over time and it is necessary to have a flow of R&D investments to maintain a firm's stock of knowledge.

Table 1.2 Critical resources for growth strategies

Types of resources	Resources for growth
Tangible assets	Plant production capacity Plant productivity and flexibility Distribution network Procurement logistic system Centralized R&D laboratory Administrative and support system
Intangible assets	Brand reputation Brand loyalty Patents
Core capabilities and competences	Production distinctive know-how Marketing and communication expertise R&D competences Coordination and control competences

In particular, we can consider that each resource value $R_j(t)$ (for example a brand) depreciates (decays) over time at a rate γ due to the competitive pressure of rival firms (innovation or imitation of product, etc.), but it can be renewed and also increased by current expenses $a(t)$, according to an accumulation rate μ. Thus the following analytical expression can represent this type of effect:

$$R_j(t) = R_j(t-1) + \mu\, a(\mathrm{t}) - \gamma\, R_j(t-1) \qquad (1.1)$$

where, in addition to the already known symbols, μ and γ are respectively the rates at which the resource accumulates and decays.

Expressing $R_j(t-1)$ as a function of $R_j(t-2)$ and so on, from the expression (1.1) the following is obtained:

$$R_j(t) = \mu_j a(t) + \mu_j a(t-1)(1-\gamma) + \mu_j a(t-2)(1-\gamma)^2 + $$
$$+ \mu_j a(t-n)(1-\gamma)^n \qquad (1.2)$$

In short, the actual value of the resource *j* is a function of the flows of expenses carried over from period to period during the life of the firm for increasing this specific resource *j* and of the rates at which the resource accumulates and decays. The entire stock of resources $[R_1(t), R_2(t), \ldots R_n(t)]$ characterizes the firm structure at every date *t* and makes it different from the other firms.

Because the value of resources deteriorates over time, it is necessary to upgrade these resources either internally by improving the existing resources, or externally by acquiring the desired resources in a market transaction, for example purchasing an entire company or business unit.

In conclusion, the stocks of resources of a firm and its knowledge, competences and capacities are the results of its history and they condition its planning and strategic capacity (Nelson, 1995). The heterogeneity of its resources and the consequent firm-specific characteristics are thus the basis of diversity and strategic variety of a firm, together with casual factors.

In this context, for defining a successful strategy it is of fundamental importance to understand which relevant resources are available in a firm and which can be acquired and internally developed over time (Wernerfelt, 1994; Hamel and Prahalad, 1994) (Table 1.2).[4] Growth strategies not only involve the exploitation of existing resources, but also the development of new ones. Therefore, it is necessary to investigate the ways in which a firm can grow its pool of resources.[5]

THE FUNDAMENTAL OBJECTIVE OF GROWTH: CREATING VALUE FOR SHAREHOLDERS

In order to evaluate a growth strategy, it is necessary to define a choice criterion which can generally be accepted and suitable. We assume a strategy is evaluated on the basis of effects produced on shareholders' equity value. More precisely, a growth strategy will be convenient only if it increases the equity value of a firm's shareholders.

On this subject, it is necessary to briefly recall the difference between the value of equity (*E*), that is the market value of shareholders' capital, the enterprise value (V), that is the market value of total assets, and the book value of assets (A), that is the value of assets as shown on the balance sheet. While the market value of assets will depend on the present value of expected operating cash flows, the book value of assets is simply the sum of the costs of a firm's assets according to accountancy principles.

The following relation is valid:

$$E = V - D \tag{1.3}$$

where D is the value of debt.

Having said that, it is necessary to clarify that the growth of a firm always implies an increase in total assets, as the book value, and in parallel it also determines an increase in liabilities or in equity, for the financing of the new assets. But it does not necessarily imply an increase in enterprise value, because this depends on the incremental operating cash flows, the investment and the costs of capital.

To clarify further, consider that a firm has invested in real estate capital equal to \$100 million and the market value $V(0)$ of this asset is equal to \$100 million. If the firm has no debt, the equity value $E(0)$ is also equal to \$100 million. We will have:

$$E(0) = V(0) - D(0) = 100 \tag{1.4}$$

Now, let us suppose that the same firm makes a further investment equal to \$50 million, borrowing this sum from a bank. If the market value of this investment is equal to \$50 million, there is no creation of value. The market enterprise value will be equal to \$150 million, the debt value equal to \$50 million and the equity value equal to \$100 million. Therefore, the investment determines an increase in enterprise value but also an equal increase of financing (debt). Thus, there is no creation of value for shareholders, due to the growth of the firm. In fact it will be:

$$E(1) = V(1) - D(1) = 150 - 50 = 100 \tag{1.5}$$

Note that the result would be the same if the investment had been financed with new equity from new shareholders. In this case, the total share value would increase like the enterprise value, but the equity value of the first shareholders would remain unchanged. Conversely, there will be an increase in the equity value of the shareholders if the market value of the new investment is equal to €70 million. In this case, the enterprise value results as being equal to \$170 million, with a creation of value equal to \$20 million for the shareholders. Precisely, it will be:

$$E(2) = V(2) - D(2) = 170 - 50 = 120 \tag{1.6}$$

In effect, the growth of the firm creates value for the shareholders only when the present value of the investment is greater than the capital required. This difference is the value of a growth strategy.

In the following chapters this subject will be analysed carefully, defining the specific conditions for how each growth strategy creates value for shareholders.

OVERCOMING THE DIVERGENCE BETWEEN MANAGERIAL AND SHAREHOLDERS' OBJECTIVES

The rationales discussed above for growth strategies presume the objective of enhancing shareholders' wealth. However, growth can also be pursued by managers for their own objective at the shareholders' expense, because it may provide increased career development opportunities and the pecuniary and non-pecuniary advantages of managing large firms.[6] In particular, diversification can be an easy strategy for pursuing growth, especially when it is achieved through mergers and acquisitions (M&A) instead of internal development.

But growth can progressively reduce the enterprise value and the shareholders' value when it is unprofitable and inefficient. So, shareholders have a clear interest in reducing the divergence between their own interests and management interests and in limiting the chance of managers to succeed with decisions which pursue their own interests rather than those of shareholders. A means for reducing the interest divergence with managers is represented by a management compensation structure and incentives capable of promoting management motivation to work for enhancing shareholders' wealth, so supporting both managerial and shareholders' goals.

In addition, as the probability of managers pursuing their own interests rather than those of shareholders is higher in an environment where incomplete and imperfect information exists, shareholders have to monitor management performance carefully and continuously verify the value of growth strategies. But shareholders must also create the conditions for vigorously replacing managers who operate to protect and expand their personal empires at the expense of shareholders. We will return to these topics in Chapter 7.

MODELS OF A FIRM'S EVOLUTION

Is there a model of firm growth? In other words, from a theoretical point of view is there a pattern of growth that a firm should follow over time in order to create value? And, what is the empirical evidence on the growth of enterprises?

From a theoretical point of view, the resource-based theory, which we have mentioned before, suggests that a growth strategy for being successful should be based on the firm's specific resources and tuned with the external conditions of industry demand and competition. Therefore, each growth strategy has to leverage on firm-specific resources and favourable external conditions: scale economies, transactions costs, economies of scope, learning economies, and so on.

All this suggests that each firm has its specific successful pattern of growth, according to the existing stock of resources and the ability to acquire and develop new resources (Norman, 1977; Teece, 1987, 2007; Teece et al., 1997).

However, considering the entire life cycle of a firm, a horizontal expansion generally should be the way that initially allows a firm to better leverage on its initial specialist resources; this first growth phase should be followed by a vertical integration expansion, either in manufacturing or in distribution activities to improve efficiency and market power. Finally, the further expansion should be based mainly on a related diversification, so as to exploit the accumulated set of multipurpose-excess resources. Unrelated diversification should not be realised because it is not an efficient strategy for the problems of uninformed central management, which simply cannot run R&D and investment-intense divisions, especially in high competitive environment.

What does the empirical evidence tell us? Examining the long period of history of the largest American corporations from the 1880s to the 1930s, Chandler (1962 and 1990) found that horizontal, vertical and diversified processes generally took place one after the other, during the life of corporations, both in relation to the firm's internal resources and the environmental conditions. The first two strategies were carried out in the initial phases of the growth of firms, in order to penetrate and consolidate their position on the existing markets, whereas diversification strategies were implemented in the subsequent phases of the firm's life, so as to better exploit the organizational capacities, as well as the accumulated know-how especially in marketing, distribution and R&D activities. Chandler (1962, p. 391) observes:

> As the market became more saturated and the opportunities to cut costs through more rational techniques lessened, enterprises began to search for other markets or to develop other businesses that might profitably employ some of their partially utilized resources or even make a more profitable application of those still being fully employed.

A further result was that while the diversification strategy permitted the continuing and expanding use of a firm's resources, it did not assure their efficient employment. In fact, expanding through diversification enlarged the range, number and complexity of entrepreneurial activities required of the senior executives, making it more and more difficult to efficiently administer different products and markets. For this reason, structural reorganization became necessary for rationalizing the use of expanding resources.

So, for Chandler the chapters in the collective history of the American industrial enterprises were characterized by phases in which resources were accumulated, then rationalized, then expanded and then once again rationalized.

After the Second World War the expansion of companies was characterized by the same model. In the 1960s the dominant trend was diversification and conglomeration (Shleifer and Vishny, 1994). In America and Europe the large enterprises progressively moved into other industries that appeared to have greater profit potential, even though their existing resources gave them little or no competitive advantage. Many firms entered distant or unrelated businesses by acquiring other firms already operating there (conglomerate diversification). This process continued in the 1960s and 1970s and it was characterized by waves of acquisitions and mergers. For the period 1973–1977 half of all assets acquired through merger and acquisition were in unrelated industries.

In the 1980s takeovers, in contrast, reversed this process and brought American corporation back to greater specialization (Shleifer and Vishny, 1994). These takeovers were followed by sell-offs of a substantial fraction of the target's assets to other firms. Restructuring was a major activity in American and European industry: the reduction in unrelated diversification was directed at recovering the efficiency necessary for sustaining continuing increasing competition (Hill and Hoskisson, 1987; Ravenscraft and Scherer, 1987; Shleifer and Vishny, 1994; Johnson et al., 1993).

Thus, a phase characterized by a re-focusing of activities on the firm's core business historically followed after a strong unrelated diversified growth, generally accomplished by a high number of M&A operations. This refocusing strategy became necessary in order to arrest the fall in efficiency of the organizational structure, often caused by over-diversified expansion that increased the firm size but reduced performance and destroyed value.[7]

In many cases a rapid expansion into distant or unrelated businesses had put an enormous strain on firm structure and reduced performance (Grant et al., 1988). The increase in the number of divisions administered, in some cases more than 50, and the wide variety of businesses in which some firms operated, created increasing difficulties in managing the firm because of a lack of information, a reduction in its quality and the inability of senior managers to evaluate it. In other cases too much diversification created significant problems because over time the firm produced less innovation. The resulting weakness in performance led firms to sell off many of their divisions and to concentrate on products and processes in which they had their strongest production, marketing and research capabilities to creating value. In the 1990s and the 2000s restructuring strategies were successfully carried out with strong reductions in the level of unrelated diversified activities by many enterprises.

In conclusion, empirical evidence confirms a basic pattern of growth over time, characterized by an initial phase of horizontal expansion in local and international markets, sometimes accompanied by vertical integration expansion up and down the value chain, followed by a phase of product-related diversification and sometimes a subsequent phase of unrelated diversification. This last phase is generally followed by a phase of restructuring, with strong reductions in the level of unrelated diversification and the return to core business activities where a firm's distinctive resources can be more efficiently exploited. Therefore, empirical evidence confirms that a growth strategy destroying value can be pursued, but it cannot be sustained over time; such a growth can be carried out in the short term, but it is not sustainable in the long term.

Empirical evidence also confirms that the model of growth for each firm remains unique and depends on the specific firm's resources in addition to the dynamics of industry structure. For each individual firm the various phases in the growth pattern vary in length, importance and impact and the different types of expansion have a very different relevance on growth and firm value. Some firms never attempted to expand through vertical integration, preferring to progressively outsource a large part of manufacturing activities; others expanded rapidly by moving overseas and developing a full line of comparable products to cover all market segments; others introduced new products, developed in research laboratories, to be sold to quite a different set of customers and markets; others maintained their existing lines of products intensifying their drive to cover the domestic and international market.

Obviously the influence of external conditions, especially the environmental and the industrial ones, are of fundamental importance in differentiating growth patterns.

In a number of cases that we examined during this research the growth pattern followed by companies had quite different results. The four cases presented in the second part of this book represent a limited but emblematic example. These successful companies belong to different industries and are not homogeneous regarding their initial firm structure and distinctive resources.

L'Oreal is characterized by simultaneous product diversification and horizontal expansion strategies realised both by organic development and acquisition of specialized firms and trademarks worldwide.

Campari has constantly followed a growth pattern based on product diversification and horizontal expansion strategies in different market segments and countries, mainly through acquisition of already existing firms and trademarks.

Luxottica has followed a growth model based on a combination of simultaneous strategies: a closely related product diversification, a horizontal expansion in different segments and geographical markets and a vertical integration in the retail distribution business.

Finally, Geox has followed a growth model mainly centred on horizontal expansion in different geographical markets, based on organic growth and a partial downwards vertical integration but with a total outsourcing of manufacturing.

Despite the differences in growth strategies, some constant characteristics are shown in the enterprises examined: a continuous growth and a constant creation of value. These companies and their growth strategies can be identified as models in competitiveness, efficiency and creation of value.

It would be very interesting to also compare the different growth patterns of the major companies competing in the same industry to clearly distinguish the influence of firm structure and thus of firm-specific resources from the influence of industry structure. That will be the objective of a further research.

APPENDIX A.1: USING THE VALUE CHAIN MODEL FOR IDENTIFYING A FIRM'S STRATEGIC RESOURCES FOR GROWTH

For identifying firm resources it can be useful to employ the value chain model proposed by Porter (1985 and 1991) (Figure A.1.1) or other models representing the firm system, for example the McKinsey model, or something similar (Abell, 1993; Dringoli, 2006).

Ansoff (1965 and 1988) propose organizing resources and skills along the major functional areas: research and development, operations, marketing, general management and finance. Within each of these functional areas he recognizes four categories of skills and resources: 1) facilities and equipment; 2) personnel skills; 3) organizational capabilities; and 4) management capabilities. In any case, it is a matter of analysing the organized set of activities and processes that are carried out by personnel application in order to obtain products or services for markets, identifying the relevant firm's resources.

Following Michael Porter (1985), we will distinguish between primary and support activities in the firm system. Among the primary activities there are: inbound logistics, operations, marketing and sales, outbound logistics and after sale service. Among the support activities there are: a firm's infrastructure (e.g. finance, accounting, etc.), human resource management, technology development and procurement.

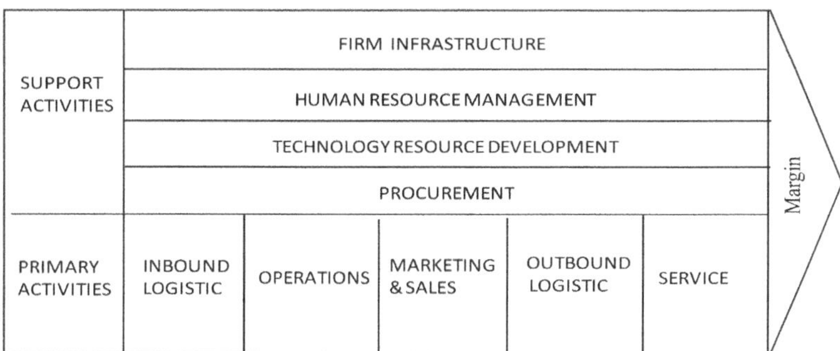

Note: The value chain depicts the firm as a collection of value-creating activities

Figure A.1.1 Michael Porter's value chain (1985)

As far as the primary activities are concerned, there are five generic categories of activities; each of them is dividable into a number of distinct activities that depend on the particular industry and the firm strategy.

1. *Inbound logistics*. These are activities associated with receiving and storing product inputs, such as buying, material handling, inventory control, etc.
2. *Operations*. These are activities concerning the transformation of inputs into the final product, such as machinery, assembly, packaging, equipment maintenance, etc.
3. *Marketing and sales*. These are activities associated with promoting and selling products.
4. *Outbound logistics*. These are activities concerning storing finished products, order processing and physically distributing the product to buyers.
5. *Service*. These are activities associated with providing after sale service to clients to enhance or maintain the value of the product such as installation, repair, part supply, etc.

Support activities can be divided into four generic categories, as shown in Figure A.1.1, each of which is dividable into a number of distinct activities that are specific to a given industry.

1. *Procurement*. These are activities associated to the function of purchasing inputs used in the production and selling of products. Purchased inputs include raw materials, energy and other supplies associated not only with primary activity but also with other support activities, as well as services.
2. *Technology development*. These are a range of activities that are directed at improving the product and the process; they take many forms, from basic research and product design to process equipment design, media research and servicing procedures.
3. *Human resource management*. These are activities that consist of recruiting, hiring, training, development and compensation of all types of personnel.
4. *Firm infrastructure*. These are a range of different activities including general management, planning, finance, accounting, legal, government affairs and quality management.

In using this representation it is possible to identify in detail, with reference to each different activity, the resources that determine the strengths and weaknesses of a firm. A chart for this analysis is shown in Table A.1.1.

Table A.1.1 A scheme for identifying firm strategic resources

Activities	Firm resources
Firm infrastructure	Tangible assets: Information system and technology platform; financial resources; etc. Intangible assets: Know-how in planning, finance, accounting, legal, government affairs and quality management. Capabilities: General management, etc.
Human resource management	Intangible assets: Firm reputation with employees and the community; educational, technical and professional qualifications of employees; the commitment and loyalty of employees; motivating empowering and retaining employees. Capabilities: HR management expertise; general management skills.
Technology development	Tangible assets: R&D laboratories; research facilities, etc. Intangible assets: Reputation in R&D activities; stock of technology: patents, trademarks, copyrights and trade secrets. Capabilities: R&D know-how, personnel expertise, etc.
Procurement	Tangible assets: Access to raw materials. Intangible: Firm reputation with suppliers. Capabilities: Buying expertise.
Inbound logistics	Tangible assets: Logistic machinery and plants. Capabilities: Inbound logistic expertise.
Operations	Tangible assets: Location and alternative uses for land and buildings; general and specialist machinery; plant capacity. Intangible assets: Technological knowledge; product and process patents; proprietary technology, copyrights, etc. Capabilities: Manufacturing expertise.
Marketing and sales	Tangible assets: Directed operating stores and franchising stores Intangible assets: Company and products brands; wholesalers and retailers network; sales organization; established relations; reputation for quality and reliability, etc. Capabilities: Marketing and selling expertise; effective brand management and brand promotion.
Outbound logistics	Tangible assets: Central and local stores. Intangible Assets: Level of service reputation. Capabilities: Logistic management expertise; efficiency and speed of distribution; effective use of logistic management techniques.
Service	Intangible Assets: Friendly service management. Capabilities: Quality and effectiveness of customer service

The value chain model is largely used for analysing firm resources. Collis and Montgomery (2005) propose the value chain for identifying the key success factors for a strategy. These authors suggest comparing the chain value of two businesses for revealing the differences in resources needed to support these businesses for a firm. The distinct success factors and the difficulty of a firm in transferring and sharing resources clearly point out that the company's profitability will decline when extending its activity instead of improving it.

Also Barney (2002) suggests using the value chain to identify the firm's resources. This author proposes a model of analysis of resources named VRIO (value, rarity, imitative and organization of resources) useful for defining the strengths and weaknesses of a firm. According to Barney, resources have to be valued on the basis of their value with respect to the environmental opportunities and threats; of their rarity, that favours the reaching of a competitive advantage, of facilities to be imitated and of firm organization capability in exploiting them. On the basis of the application of the VRIO framework it is possible to identify the key resources which make a firm a winner. In this context, Barney also presents an interesting application of the VRIO framework.

For evaluating the stock of resources and competences, Abell (1993) proposes representing the business system of a firm by the functional activities that characterize the way it works, emphasizing how each activity contributes to the added value of the firm. In particular, he rightly distinguishes between the internal resources, that is those specific to the business unit, and the external resources, that is those resulting from alliances and other similar agreements and relationships with other companies.

Hofer and Schendel (1978) consider five types of resources and competences at a business unit level: 1) financial resources; 2) material resources (such as plant, machinery, stores, inventories, etc.); 3) human resources; 4) organizational resources (quality control systems, financial control methods, etc.); 5) technological capabilities (high quality products, low cost production, high brand loyalty, etc).

NOTES

1. We use the term resource in its broad sense (Barney, 1991) and hence it includes activities, capabilities, etc. which allow the firm to generate rents.
2. From a conceptual point of view a firm's resources can be considered as state or level variables according to the concept of state used in system dynamics theory. A state or level variable is an accumulation, or integration over time, of flows or changes that come into and go out of the level. Conversely, a rate variable is a flow, decision, action or behaviour that changes over time as a function of influences acting upon it. The state

or level variables characterize a system at a certain date and influence the way the system works. Also the firm system can be represented by a set of state variables, according to the principle of system dyna ANFAO (2008).mics. For example, a firm's image is a state variable as it represents the customers' accumulation of intangible impressions stemming from information flows over an extended duration. Similarly, scientific knowledge is an information level variable and in a similar way so are a firm's employees, plants, and so on. On these topics, see the relevant theoretical contribution of Winter (1987). On the representation of the firm as a dynamic system, see: Forrester (1961); Simon (1981); Roberts (1999); Ceccanti (1996); Dringoli (2000 and 2006).

3. On this subject we refer to the classical papers on optimal advertising policy of Telser (1962) and Nerlove and Arrow (1962). For a critical review of these studies see Dringoli (1973). On the process of resource accumulation and decay see also Dierickx and Cool (1989).
4. According to Wernerfelt (1984) this analysis can be conducted through what is called a resource-product matrix in which the checked entries indicate the importance of a resource in a product and viceversa. In this context, a firm acquisition can be seen as a purchase of rare resources in a highly imperfect market.
5. On the importance of developing existing resources and also changing them when it is necessary in order to sustain the growth, see the classic study of Norman (1977). The capacity of a firm to create, extend or modify its resource base for sustaining the growth and creating value in rapidly changing environment is what recent literature calls dynamics capabilities (Helfat et al., 2007). On the studies for investigating dynamics capabilities see: Teece, et al., (1997); Eisenhardt and Martin (2000); Zollo and Winter (2002); Winter (2003); Helfat and Peteraf (2003); Teece (2007); Ambrosini et al., (2009); Easterby-Smith et al., (2009).
6. On this topic there are numerous theoretical and empirical studies (see Marris, 1964; Jensen, 1986; Jensen and Murphy, 1990). Among the empirical studies we cite in particular Seth et al., (2002). They investigated a sample of US cross-border acquisitions and found indication that 26% were accomplished by managers for their own utility rather than shareholders' interest. In addition, they established evidence of hubris in cases where managers overvalued the target firms by mistake.
7. A study by Rumelt (1974) found that firms that diversified into businesses closely related to their core business were significantly more profitable than those that pursued unrelated diversification. Subsequent researches confirmed Rumelt's findings both for the USA and for the other countries (see Peters and Waterman, 1982 and Grant, 1988). At the same time the problems associated with wide-ranging unrelated diversification were highlighted by the poor performance of conglomerates. Other studies have less consistent results. See, for example: Christensen and Montgomery (1981); Luffman and Reed (1984); Michel and Shaked (1984).

2. Analytical models for evaluating growth strategies

INTRODUCTION AND OBJECTIVES

In this chapter we analyse the conditions for creating value for shareholders either with organic growth strategies or growth strategies based on M&A operations. With this aim in mind, growth strategies are conceived as investment decisions directed at modifying the firm's structure and reshaping the business system. Thus, the appraisal of the financial effects of a strategy is of fundamental importance for evaluating the suitability of a strategy for creating value for shareholders.

After a reminder of the general model of firm value and of the fundamental variables on which it depends, the effects of growth strategies are analysed, defining a quantitative model for evaluating the conditions in which they can create value for shareholders. In this context, growth strategies both through organic development and through acquisition of firms that are already operating are considered.

As the growth of a firm can be driven by objectives which are different from the creation of value for shareholders, a discussion on this topic is developed in the final sections of the chapter. In the appendix an application of the model is presented to determine the value of an acquisition strategy and the value of synergies.

THE VALUE OF THE FIRM: THE GENERAL MODEL

Corporate finance literature has emphasized that the value of a firm is obtained by discounting expected free cash flows from operations $FCFO(t)$, realised in the lifetime of a business, at the weighted average cost of capital ρ (Levy and Sarnat, 1986; Copeland and Weston, 1988; Copeland et al., 1995; Brealey and Myers, 1996; Ross et al., 1999).

Considering an unlimited lifetime period, the value of the firm $V(0)$ can be expressed as follows:

$$V(0) = \sum_{t=1}^{\infty} \frac{FCFO(t)}{(1+\rho)^t} \tag{2.1}$$

with *FCFO*(*t*) being free cash flows from operations in period *t* (year), equal to cash flows from operations *CFO*(*t*) minus working capital change $\Delta WC(t)$ and the capital expenditures $\Delta I(t)$ necessary for maintaining the efficiency of the firm and favouring the operating cash flows; and ρ the weighted average cost of capital, that is the cost of the different components of financing used by the firm, weighted by their market value proportions (*WACC*).

In practice, for determining the value of a firm some assumptions must be introduced regarding the dynamics of *FCFO*(*t*) and this means prefiguring a credible scenario about future environmental conditions and a firm's competitive advantage.

If the existing firm positioning can be maintained over time and the free cash flow from operations, *FCFO** as an average value of flows realised in a defined period of time, can be maintained constant for an unlimited period of time by sustaining a flow of investments $\Delta I(t)$ (steady state hypothesis), the value of the firm will be:

$$V(0) = \frac{FCFO^*}{\rho} \tag{2.2}$$

In the case of a more favourable scenario, represented for example by a sustained growth of the economy or of the industry, we can assume that the *FCFO*(*t*) will increase at a constant rate *g*, for an unlimited period of time, by sustaining a flow of increasing investment $\Delta I(t)$. Such being the case, the value of the firm will be:

$$V(0) = \frac{FCFO(1)}{\rho - g} \tag{2.3}$$

where *FCFO*(1) is the free operating cash flow at the end of the first year.

Finally, the value of a firm can be determined by estimating analytically the *FCFO*(*t*) that a firm will gain according a defined business plan over a credible time horizon *S*, say three to five years (short term cash flows), and by assuming that the free cash flows of the following periods (long-term cash flows) remain constant and equal to an average value *FCFO** for an unlimited period of time. This can be a credible scenario if a firm can maintain the competitive position obtained at the end of the plan horizon *S*.

In this case we will have:

$$V(0)=\sum_{t=1}^{S}\frac{FCFO(t)}{(1+\rho)^{t}}+\left[\frac{FCFO*}{\rho}\frac{1}{(1+\rho)^{S}}\right] \tag{2.4}$$

If *FCFO*(t), after the first period S, grows at a constant rate g for an unlimited period of time, the value of the firm will be:

$$V(0)=\sum_{t=1}^{S}\frac{FCFO(t)}{(1+\rho)^{t}}+\left[\frac{FCFO(S+1)}{(\rho-g)}\frac{1}{(1+\rho)^{S}}\right] \tag{2.5}$$

The choice of one or the other model will depend on the different credible scenarios for the firm and on the purpose of valuation.

As for the cost of capital (*WACC*), we use the general formula for estimating:

$$WACC=\rho=kd\frac{D}{V}+ke\frac{E}{V} \tag{2.6}$$

where kd is the cost of debt and ke the cost of equity, D the value of debt and E the value of equity.

The equity value E is equal to the difference between the value of the firm V, as the value of whole of activities, and the value of financial debts D:

$$E(0) = V(0) - D(0) \tag{2.7}$$

The following description shows the determinants of free cash flows from operations, *FCFO*, in each period t:

+	Revenues	R
–	Current operating expenses	C
=	Earnings before interest, taxes and depreciation	*EBITDA*
–	Depreciation and amortization	A
=	Earnings before interest and taxes	*EBIT*
–	Interest expenses	*INT*
=	Taxable income	*EBT*
–	Taxes	*EBT tc*
=	Net income	*NI*
+	Interest expenses	*INT*

+	Depreciation and amortization	A
=	Cash flow from operations	CFO
–	Working capital change	ΔWC
–	Capital expenditures	ΔI
=	Free cash flow from operations	$FCFO$

where tc is the tax rate on taxable income (corporate profit).

That is:

$$FCFO = (EBITDA - A - INT)\,(1 - tc) + INT + A - \Delta WC - \Delta I \qquad (2.8)$$

$$FCFO = EBITDA\,(1 - tc) + A\,tc + INT\,tc - \Delta WC - \Delta I \qquad (2.9)$$

Note that in the leveraged firm the $FCFO$ is increased by the tax benefit ($INT\ tc$) deriving from the application of corporate tax to earnings after interest.

Also note that the capital expenditure ΔI affects operating cash flow. In a finite-lived asset, the capital expenditure ΔI is the investment needed to maintain the assets' cash flows until the end of its life time, while in an infinite-lived asset, capital expenditure is the investment needed to maintain cash flows for ever. Therefore, the higher the projected future growth of cash flows (g), the greater the capital expenditures ΔI will be (Damodaran, 1994).

THE VALUE OF THE FIRM AS A FUNCTION OF MANAGERIAL ECONOMIC VARIABLES

In order to determine the value of the firm, we prefer to disregard the financial tax benefits, rightly reducing the cost of debt by tax rate, $k_d\,(1 - tc)$, in the expression of weighted average cost of capital ($WACC$), as the majority of financial literature does (see, for example, Copeland et al., 1995). That is:

$$FCFO(t) = EBITDA(t)\,(1 - tc) + A(t)\,tc - \Delta WC - \Delta I(t) \qquad (2.10)$$

$$WACC = \rho = kd\,(1 - tc)\frac{D}{V} + ke\frac{E}{V} \tag{2.11}$$

The *WACC* depends on the cost of funds, *kd* (debt), *ke* (equity) and the capital structure of the firm (*D*/*V* and *E*/*V*).

To simplify the analysis, we also consider the tax benefits from depreciation through an appropriate reduction of the tax rate on *EBITDA* (with $\tau^* < tc$). Considering the complexity in estimating the relevant variables precisely, this expedient may be accepted for an analysis aimed at ascertaining the conditions for a profitable strategy, in terms which cannot be reduced to a marginal analysis.[1]

The expression (2.10) becomes:

$$FCFO(t) = EBITDA(t)\,(1-\tau^*) - \Delta WC(t) - \Delta I(t) \tag{2.12}$$

The *EBITDA*(*t*) depends on the quantities of product sold $Q_v(t)$, the sale price *P*(*t*) and the current unit operating expenses *Cu*(*t*). Therefore, we will express *EBITDA*(*t*) as:

$$EBITDA(t) = [P(t) - Cu(t)]\,Q(t) \tag{2.13}$$

and *FCFO*(*t*) as:

$$FCFO(t) = [P(t) - Cu(t)]\,Q(t)\,(1-\tau^*) - \Delta WC(t) - \Delta I\,(t) \tag{2.14}$$

This solution is very useful, because it enables the representation of the *FCFO* (and consequently of the firm value) as a function of the most relevant economic variables of the business management: the product price *P*(*t*), the operating costs *C*(*t*), the quantities sold *Q*(*t*) and the capital expenditure $\Delta I(t)$. These are the variables under the evaluation and control of the management.[2]

Figure 2.1 shows the determinants of value: benefits provided by the product, unit margin, costs and volumes (number of units sold) (Ghemawat 1991; Dringoli, 2009). Margins (*P* – *Cu*) depend basically on the differential benefits provided to consumers. Volumes (*Q*) depend on the organization size and costs which in turn reflect on price. Costs to the organization and benefits (the advantages which products may provide to consumers compared with those of competitors) determine the unit margin that is the difference between price and cost. However, benefits and costs also influence production volumes and consequently the total margin.

Within the industry, the firm may create value in many different ways in relation to the importance given to each of the four value determinants: product benefits, organization costs, unit margin and sale volumes. Each strategy tends to leverage on one of these factors (Porter, 1980).

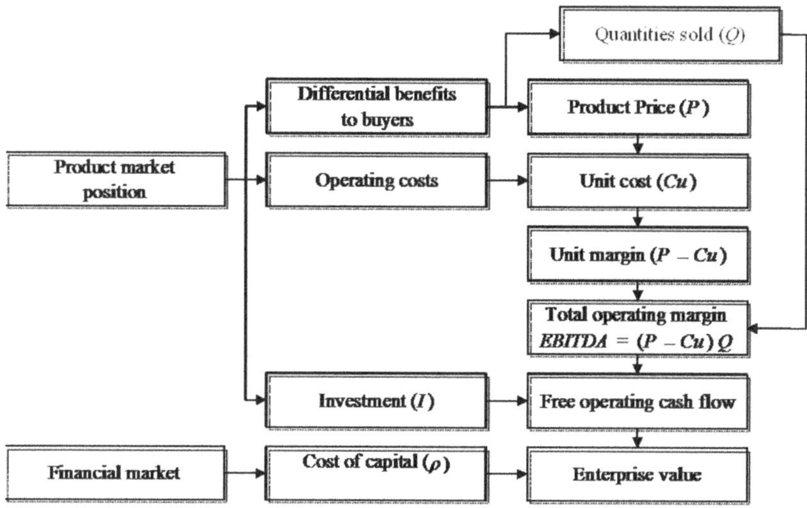

Figure 2.1 Framework for the analysis of firm value

ANALYTICAL MODELS FOR EVALUATING GROWTH STRATEGIES

Evaluating growth strategies carried out through organic development

The analytical models explained above allow clarification of the fundamental variables that influence the firm value and offer practical frameworks for evaluating growth strategies.

As a defined growth strategy is addressed at producing relevant discontinuities in sales and operating cash flows, it is necessary to evaluate in detail the effects of this strategy on the firm value, in order to verify if it creates value for shareholders.

To this purpose, the incremental operating cash flows produced by the growth strategy and the necessary investment must be estimated analytically. With this approach in mind, different models can be used for evaluating a growth strategy.[3]

A first model consists in supposing that the average increase of operating cash flows produced by the expansion $\Delta FCFO^*$ can be maintained constant for an undetermined period of time by a flow of capital expenditures $\Delta I(t)$. That means that the firm, after the expansion, remains in a stationary state for an unlimited period of time. In this case, the value of a growth strategy will be:

$$V_S(0) = \frac{\Delta FCFO^*}{\rho} - I_E \tag{2.15}$$

where: $V_S(0)$ is the net value of the growth strategy at time 0; $I_E(0)$ is the total investment required by the expansion strategy, which includes the investment in plant, distribution network, marketing and working capital; $\Delta FCFO^*$ is the incremental free operating cash flow determined by the expansion investment $I_E(s)$ and ρ is the cost of capital.

A different model for evaluating an expansion strategy consists in estimating analytically the increase of free cash flow, $\Delta FCFO(t)$, for a certain period (three to five years) as a consequence of expansion and adding to the present value of these cash flows the value of the strategy at the end of the period considered that is the terminal value $TVs\ (T)$. In this case the value of the strategy will be:

$$V_S(0) = \sum_{t=1}^{T} \frac{\Delta FCFO(t)}{(1+\rho)^t} + \frac{TVs(T)}{(1+\rho)^T} - I_E(0) \tag{2.16}$$

Since the terminal value of the strategy at time T is the present value of the future $FCFO$ after time T, the determination of terminal value requires to making credible forecasts on the $FCFO$ over a long period.

A simple way to cope with the difficulties of a reliable estimate of $FCFO$ after time T consists in assuming that these flows are equal to the last estimated cash flow $FCFO(T)$ and remain constant for an unlimited period. Under this assumption the terminal value will be:

$$TV_S(T) = \frac{FCFO(T)}{\rho} \tag{2.17}$$

If we consider that *FCFO* after *T* grow at a constant rate *g*, the terminal value will be:

$$TV_S(T) = \frac{FCFO(T+1)}{(\rho - g)} \tag{2.18}$$

Instead of making long-term forecasts on the *FCFO*, some authors suggest assuming the terminal value $TV_S(T)$ to be equal to the liquidation value of assets. That can be justified as a precaution or as a way to avoid the pitfalls of looking over too long a period. Accurate accounting or market measure of assets can be more robust and reliable over a limited period of three or five years than an infinitely discounted series of future cash flows.[4] In the case where the terminal value is expressed by the liquidation value of all assets that characterize the expansion, it will be:

$$TV_S(T) = \sum_{j=1}^{n} \frac{ASSETS_j(T)}{(1+\rho)^T} \tag{2.19}$$

For evaluating the growth strategies we will use, in this study, the model represented by expression (2.15), assuming that the average free cash flows from operations produced by the expansion $\Delta FCFO^*$ can be maintained constant for an undetermined period of time by a flow of capital expenditures ΔI(t). Therefore, the value of a growth strategy will be:

$$V_S(0) = \frac{\Delta FCFO^*}{\rho} - I_E \tag{2.20}$$

We believe that this model is based on credible assumptions and it is able to offer a quantitative framework suitable to guide managerial decisions in a context that suffers the problems of horizon, uncertainty and complexity.

In spite of the limits of the proposed model, nevertheless we believe that they can be accepted because of the magnitude of the inevitable imprecision in strategy valuation. Furthermore, the proposed model has the merit of being easily usable and providing practical help to managers, focusing the analysis on the fundamental variables that influence the value of a growth strategy: investments, prices, quantities and costs.

As we have explained above, it is:

$$\Delta FCFO = \Delta EBITDA\ (1 - \tau^*) - \Delta I(t) \tag{2.21}$$

Thus the incremental operating cash flow will depend on the product unit margin and the incremental quantities sold, in accordance with the expression (2.12).

Therefore, a growth strategy will create value only if the present value of the incremental net operating cash flows is greater than the required investment for the programmed expansion (however it is financed):

$$V_S(0) > 0 \tag{2.22}$$

where:

$$V_S(0) = \frac{\Delta FCFO^*}{\rho} - I_E$$

According to the proposed model, the value of a growth strategy will depend on the variables I_E, ρ and $\Delta FCFO^*$. In order to estimate these variables, it will be necessary to analyse carefully the long-term environmental tendencies and particularly the dynamics of competitive forces in industry.

In conclusion, we will evaluate an expansion strategy as a complex one-stage investment, which can be accepted or rejected according to its contribution to value creation for shareholders. Nevertheless, we are aware that an expansion strategy can take the form of a sequence of investments to be realised at future stages of a firm's development. In this case, it will be a matter of evaluating, at each stage, if the investment required for implementing the desired expansion will create value for shareholders.

It is also possible that an expansion strategy can be represented immediately by a chain of subsequent investment decisions, where today's decision will depend on what we plan to do tomorrow and vice versa. In this case, the evaluation of a growth strategy becomes a sequential decision problem that can be treated by the decision tree analysis. It is a matter of estimating the investments and the expected *FCFO* at each stage of growth, taking into consideration the risks of alternative patterns and then summarizing the cash flow consequences in terms of net present value (Copeland et al., 1995; Brealey and Meyers, 1996).

However, the trouble with the decision tree analysis is clear: it requires an explicit definition, at an initial time, of possible future events and decisions and on the basis of this information it indicates whether the expansion strategy can create value. Furthermore, decision tree analysis does not consider that a subsequent investment can be abandoned before its realization, so reducing risk, if future events no longer make it convenient. In other words, it does not consider that, as time passes, new information can be acquired and the market scenario can be changed towards new growth perspectives and thus also the decision of the subsequent investment. In brief, the decision tree analysis does not consider the value of flexibility in sequential investment decisions. For these reasons we believe our approach is more correct and easier to be used by managers.

Finally, we express severe doubts on the possibility of using the real option theory (Dixit and Pyndick, 1994; Dixit, 1995; Copeland et al., 1996; Hull, 1997; Amran and Kulatilaka 1999; Kogut and Kulatilaka, 2006) for evaluating growth strategies;[5] these doubts arise not only from the difficulties in its practical application, but also because an expansion investment can be considered a valuable real option only under particular circumstances. To be precise, this is true only if a firm is favoured for the further expansion investment in the business, paying a price for it (*strike price*) that is lower than that required if the initial investment had not been made.

Evaluating growth strategies carried out through acquisition of firms

For a growth strategy through acquisition to create value for shareholders it is necessary that the increase in value of the combined firm, with respect to the value of the acquiring firm before the acquisition, is larger than the negotiated value (price) for the acquired firm. More precisely, the acquisition will create value for shareholders of firm A if:

$$(V_{AB} - V_A) - P_B > 0 \tag{2. 23}$$

where: V_A and V_B respectively are the market value of firm A (the acquiring firm) and the market value of target firm B, when they operate independently; V_{AB} is the value of the combined firm after the acquisition and P_B the negotiated value (price) for firm B, that is the investment made by firm A for acquiring the assets of B.

Therefore the net value of the acquisition strategy, V_{SA}, will be:

$$V_{SA} = (V_{AB} - V_A) - P_B \tag{2.24}$$

In particular the value of acquisition of B is given by:

$$V_{acq} = V_{AB} - V_A \tag{2.25}$$

Therefore, the value created by the acquisition, or value of synergy, V_{SY}, is given by:

$$V_{SY} = V_{AB} - (V_A + V_B) = V_{acq} - V_B \tag{2.26}$$

As is well known, synergy is described in business literature as the 2 + 2 = 5 effect, to denote the fact that the performance of combined activities or resources is greater than the sum of its parts.[6]

The value of the acquisition can be also expressed as follows:

$$V_{acq} = V_B + V_{SY} \tag{2.27}$$

Note that, in order for the acquisition to be profitable for the shareholders of firm A, it is not sufficient that the value created by the merger, V_{SY}, that is the value of synergies, is larger than zero. It occurs that at least a part of this value remains to the shareholders of the acquiring firm. For this to happen, the value created by the acquisition must not be entirely distributed to the shareholders of firm B. In other words it occurs that the price for the firm B to be lower than the value of acquisition:

$$P_B < V_{acq} \tag{2.28}$$

That is:

$$P_B < V_B + V_{SY} \tag{2.29}$$

If $\Delta FOFO^*$ is the increase of cash flow obtained by firm A after the acquisition of firm B and this is constant in time (such as perpetual annuity), the value of the acquisition will be:

$$V_{acq} = \frac{\Delta FCFO^*}{\rho} \tag{2.30}$$

Consequently, the value created for the shareholders of firm A by the acquisition, that is the net value of the acquisition strategy, will be:

$$V_{SA} = \frac{\Delta FCFO^*}{\rho} - P_B \tag{2.31}$$

In other words, a growth strategy will create value for the present shareholders if the value of the acquisition is larger than the price negotiated for the acquired firm P_B. Generally, it will be:

$$P_B = V_B\,(1+p) \tag{2.32}$$

with p being the premium rate over the market value of firm B before acquisition transferred by the bidding firm to the shareholders of the target firm.

Note that the value of synergy is:

$$V_{SY} = \frac{\Delta FCFO^*}{\rho} - V_B \tag{2.33}$$

Therefore the maximum price to be paid for the assets of firm B will be:

$$P_B(\max) = \frac{\Delta FCFO^*}{\rho} \tag{2.34}$$

The price paid for the target firm will define the sharing of synergy benefits. In effect, when it is a matter of acquiring a firm the problem is who gets the benefits of synergies, the shareholders of firm A or the shareholders of firm B, or both of them? That will depend on the price paid for the target firm B. Since the acquiring firm and the target firm are contributors to the creation of synergies, the sharing of the benefits of synergies among the two firms will depend on the possibility that the bidding firm can be replaced by other firms. Generally, if there are multiple bidders interested in the acquisition, the shareholders of the target firm will get the large part of synergy gains.

It is useful to point out that the acquisition price of target firm B, P_B, is the value contractually defined by parties for firm B, as the value of its operating assets on the basis of asset side valuation method. Therefore, the resulting value of shares of firm B, E_B ,will be:

$$E_B = P_B - D_B \tag{2.35}$$

Obviously, the premium obtained over the market value of firm B before acquisition will be gained by the shareholders of B.

While we propose analytical models for estimating the value created by growth strategies, we are also aware of their limits, principally deriving from the difficulties in correctly evaluating risk and the terminal value of strategies. However we believe that these difficulties are inherent to the object of analysis rather than the proposed methodology. Obviously, the models must be used with great care both considering that the evaluation regards strategies and not simply projects and taking into consideration the sensitivity of value to different variables.

However, we believe that the advantages of the methodology proposed are relevant with respect to other traditional methods of strategy valuation, such as return on investment (*ROI*), payback period, etc.[7] In fact, the proposed methodology forces managers to consider the true determinants of economic value and their relationships, helping them to return to fundamentals of growth strategies.

In the following sections we will examine analytically the sources of value in the different growth strategies taken into consideration.

THE CHOICE BETWEEN ORGANIC DEVELOPMENT AND GROWTH THROUGH ACQUISITIONS

The choice between organic (or internal) development and growth through acquisition requires comparing the value created by the two alternatives (Table 2.1).

Growth through organic development offers the following advantages:

- the investment can be defined precisely in relation to the actual needs and objectives of the firm;
- the investment can be made gradually in relation to the disposable resources.

The disadvantages of this alternative are the following:

- the investment determines an increase of production capacity in the industry with the risk of overcapacity if aggregate demand does not grow adequately; overcapacity in an industry can cause a price war among the competing firms with a consequent fall in margins and cash flows;
- the expansion of production can take a long time as it requires building plants and obtaining the right machinery.

Alternatively, growth through acquisition presents the following advantages:

- a greater rapidity in implementing the production expansion;
- a more rapid increase in customers' portfolio, sales and market share;
- an easier entry into a market or business;
- no increase in the aggregate supply of industry;
- the exploitation of synergies and new competences and know how.

Conversely, growth through acquisitions has the following disadvantages:

- difficulty in correctly evaluating the target firm, because of limited information;
- difficulty in estimating the integration time and costs of target firms.

Generally, a firm prefers growth through acquisition when the industry demand is relatively stable and the competitive pressure is high. In these situations, through acquisition, a firm can rapidly realise a relevant increase in size, reducing the number of competitors and increasing its market share and bargaining power.

Table 2.1 Comparing internal development with acquisitions.

	Internal expansion	Acquisition
Benefits	Right dimension of the investments Efficiency in investment location Use of new technologies Quick integration of the investments into the existing firm structure Simple and easy decisional processes	Objective rapidly reached Easily overcoming the barriers to entry Rapid increase of the market share Opening of strategic windows Positive effects on the firm image Exploiting fiscal advantages
Drawbacks	Increase in production capacity and negative effects on product prices	Difficulties in integrating firms' organizations Acquisition costs and uncertainty in asset values

However, management must not underestimate the costs of integrating different organizational structures. Empirical evidence shows that mergers and acquisitions frequently bring positive short-term return for shareholders of target firms but more questionable long-term benefits to investors in acquiring firms. Even though empirical studies highlight the wide variation in the results of acquisitions at the firm level, at the aggregate level they show that only 40–50% of acquirers do achieve positive returns in the two to three year period following acquisition (Kitching, 1974; Gregory, 1997; Agrawal and Jaffe, 2000; Capron and Pistre, 2002).

Since the stock prices of the target firms on average rise significantly when acquisitions are announced, in contrast to the decline in stock price value of the acquiring firm, this suggests that the value created in most mergers is often captured by the shareholders of the acquired firms (Andrade et al., 2001).

THE RELIABILITY OF A GROWTH STRATEGY

A growth strategy is a strategy that determines the structural change of a firm, a change of the fundamental characteristics of the business system (production and distribution capacities, logistic system, organizational structure, etc.). These represent changes that are not reversible in the short term, because they modify some distinguishing and specific features of a firm (tangible and intangible assets) (Dringoli, 2000).

Consequently, this decision must be taken by evaluating the long-term dynamics of demand and competitive forces. In other words, it is the irreversibility of structural changes that makes it necessary to look at the long-term future.

In particular, a growth strategy must be defined correctly by considering not only the internal characteristics of the firm's business system, but also the dynamics of the external environment and particularly of the industry. In fact, it is customers' behaviour and competitors' reactions that can prevent a firm from reaching the planned objectives, as happens in a competitive game.

For a growth strategy to be reliable, it has to be consistent with the environment trends and with the firm's structure and its distinguishing resources. In particular, management must choose a strategy which exploits the firm's specific culture and exclusive know-how. That will allow the firm to control its operating costs and to reduce the risk of investment, thereby obtaining a competitive advantage over its competitors

The in-depth knowledge of a firm's structure and its distinguishing resources also means correctly understanding the actual limits of the firm. This allows the opportunities to be exploited to be clearly defined, as well as the new resources that need to be acquired in order for the growth to be sustainable.

MANAGERS' POWER, GROWTH AND FIRM'S VALUE

The growth of a firm can be driven by objectives which are different from the creation of value for shareholders: for example greater prestige, more power or higher wages for managers. All these objectives, frequently pursued by managers, are generally reached when the firm is larger.

According to the managerial economics theory of firms (Marris, 1964), the prevalent power of top managers over shareholders, especially in large public companies, often makes the manager's interest prevail over the shareholders' one. That consequently favours expansion strategies which are not coherent with the objective of creating value for shareholders.[8] Also if that often happens in actual markets, we do not consider the growth of the firm as a final objective to pursue and as the right criterion for choosing a strategy. In fact, a growth strategy driven by an objective which is different from creating value for shareholders does not allow an efficient use of capital and therefore it is not sustainable in the long run.

To be precise, where capital markets are efficient, this strategy is ultimately punished by the financial markets through a progressive fall in the value of the shares until a takeover of the firm is launched from a new property. Existing managers are then removed and replaced by managers capable of developing strategies which create value for shareholders.

If the capital markets are not efficient, the growth of the firm can continue for a longer time but it will eventually come to an end, since the progressive reduction in incomes and cash flow will increase the leverage of the firm (that is the debt/equity ratio) to a level where the capacity for further funding of the investments will be severely reduced and eventually cancelled.

APPENDIX A2: EVALUATING AN ACQUISITION STRATEGY: AN EXAMPLE

To further clarify, let us consider the following example. A firm A is evaluating the acquisition of firm B operating in the same industry. The relevant data about the two firms are shown in Tables A2.1 and A2.2. In particular, the estimated *FCFO* for firms A and B standing alone prior to merger are respectively equal to €30 and €10 million and the incremental free cash flow that firm A estimates to obtain from the acquisition of B is equal to €20 million; the cost of capital ρ is supposed equal to 10 per cent for the all firms. The acquisition is supposedly financed by debt.

We consider that the value of firms is determined by applying the following model:

$$V(0) = \frac{FCFO^*}{\rho} \tag{A2.1}$$

We also consider valuing the acquisition strategy V_{SA} according to the proposed model, as the following formula:

$$V_{SA} = \frac{\Delta FCFO^*}{\rho} - P_B > 0 \tag{A2.2}$$

where the first addendum is the value of acquisition for the acquiring firm A and the second the price to be paid for the firm B. The difference is the value created by the acquisition strategy.

On the basis of these data and assumptions the values of firm A and B standing alone and the value of merger AB are calculated, as well as the value of synergies and of acquisition strategies, firstly considering a price of acquisition of firm B equal to €130 million (Table A2.1, case one) and then assuming a price equal to € 200 million (Table A2.2, case two).

The values of firms A and B standing alone are equal to €300 and €100 million, while the value of the combined firm AB is equal to €500 million and the value of synergies is equal to €100 million.

In case one, the price paid for the target firm, P_B, is €130 million, the net value of the acquisition strategy is €70 million, while the premium paid to the shareholders of B is €30 million; therefore the synergies gained by the shareholders of A and B are, respectively, equal to €70 and €30 million.

Table A2.1 Growth through acquisition: acquisition value, value of synergies and the value of strategy. Case one.

(€mill.)		Firm A stand alone	Firm B stand alone	Firm AB combined
Free cash flows	$FCFO^*$	30	10	50
Incremental free operating cash flows	$\Delta FCFO^*$	0		20
Cost of capital (%)	ρ	10	10	10
Firm value	V	300	100	500
Debt value	D	200	50	330
Equity value	E	100	50	170
Acquisition value	V_{acq}			200
Price of firm B	P_B			130
Value of acquisition strategy	V_{SA}			70
Value of synergy	V_{SY}			100
Assigned value to shares B	S_B			80
Premium paid to shareholders of firm B				30
Increased debt of firm AB after acquisition				130
Increased value for shareholders of firm A				70

Note: €130 million is the increase of total debt for firm AB with respect to debt that A had standing alone. As firm B had an initial debt equal to €50 million the new debt for the merger will be €80 million.

Table A2.2 Growth through acquisition: acquisition value, value of synergies and the value of strategy. Case two.

(€mill.)		Firm A stand alone	Firm B stand alone	Firm AB combined
Free cash flows	$FCFO^*$	30	10	50
Incremental free operating cash flows	$\Delta FCFO^*$	0		20
Cost of capital (%)	ρ	10	10	10
Firm value	V	300	100	500
Debt value	D	200	50	400
Equity value	E	100	50	100
Acquisition value	V_{acq}			200
Price of firm B	P_B			200
Value of acquisition strategy	V_{SA}			0
Value of synergy	V_{SY}			100
Assigned value to shares B	S_B			150
Premium paid to shareholders of firm B				100
Increased debt of firm AB after acquisition				200
Increased value for shareholders of firm A				0

Note: €200 million is the increase of total debt for firm AB with respect to debt that A had standing alone. As firm B had an initial debt equal to €50 million the new debt for the merger will be €150 million.

In case two, the negotiated value (price) for the target firm, P_B, is €200 million, the value of the acquisition strategy is equal to zero, while the premium paid to the shareholders of B is €100 million; therefore the synergies gained by the shareholders of A and B are respectively equal to zero and €100 million (Table A2.2).

Tables A2.1 and A2.2 also indicate the values of shares B and shares A as well as the value of debt of firm A before and after the acquisition.

NOTES

1. Rappaport (1986) introduces more drastic simplifications: a constant unit operative margin (the ratio between the operating income and the sales), a constant rate of sales growth, etc.
2. Many authors underline the opportunity, from a practical point of view, to express cash flow on the basis of the most relevant economic variables used in the operating management of the firm. See, for example, Rappaport, (1986); Copeland et al., (1995); Grant (1998).
3. On the analytical methods for evaluating strategies see, in particular: Rappaport (1986); Day (1990); Johnson (2006).
4. See Johnson (2006). In order to determine the terminal value, this author suggests searching for a value that likely investors will attribute to the company, given the performance trajectory of the company in the last years. According to Johnson, if the accounting is done on the basis of market prices and accurate replacement values, accounting measures can be robust and reliable. He calls this alternative approach scenario-based retrospective valuation or alternatively the CV view of valuation (p. 190).
5. In synthesis, with an expansion investment a firm can acquire a real option that is an opportunity to further expand the investment or to postpone it over time when the scenario is more definite, so reducing the risk. This flexibility has a value that can be determined. Following the methodology developed for financial options, an expansion investment can be considered the price of an option, the further investment – required to capitalize the new opportunities – is the exercise price of the option (strike) and the present value of expected cash flows is the market value of this future investment. So, the value of this option, at expiration, will be positive if the value of the expected cash flows rises above the exercise price and it will be precisely equal to the value of investment minus the exercise price. Conversely, if the value of the future investment is less than the exercise price, at point of expiration, the option value will be equal to zero. Because of uncertainty in cash flow trajectories, the option is valuable as the buyer (investor) can wait for a favourable scenario to happen before making its subsequent investment. As the option theory proves, options are valuable where uncertainty is high and the expiration time for decision is located in the distant future. See Dixit and Pyndick (1994); Amran and Kulatilaka (1999).
6. On this subject see: Ansoff (1965 and 1988); Porter (1985); Campbell and Sommers Luchs (1998).
7. For a systemic review of the impact of accounting policy see Edwards et al. (1987).

3. Horizontal expansion strategies

INTRODUCTION AND OBJECTIVES

The horizontal expansion strategy is a course of action that allows a firm to increase its own production capacity and thus its supply, while continuing to produce the same basic product. The increased production can be offered in existing markets, in new geographical markets or in new markets for different applications and uses of the same products. Horizontal expansion strategies can differ according to the objectives pursued and the different size of the capacity jumps.

In this chapter we will analyse the conditions for a horizontal expansion strategy creating value; the relevant variables are also analysed in their fundamental relations through a quantitative model, in order to offer a useful guide for decision making.

In the appendix the background information on economies of scale and on economies of experience is presented, underlining their importance for successful horizontal expansion strategies.

HORIZONTAL EXPANSION FORMS AND MAIN LEVERS FOR CREATING VALUE

A firm's horizontal expansion strategy can take the following forms:

- expansion with the existing product or line in the existing markets (market penetration) or in different market segments with new types or models of the same basic product (Figure 3.1);
- expansion with the existing product or line in new geographic markets, included foreign markets (international development) (Figure 3.2);
- expansion with the existing product or line in new markets characterized by different uses and applications of products (increase in uses and applications of existing products).

Horizontal expansion strategies have been adopted by many successful firms such as Luxottica (see Chapter 10), L'Oreal (see Chapter 8), Volkswagen, Italcementi, Eni, etc.

The levers for creating value are the following:

- the increase in production and sale quantities;
- the reduction in unit production, procurement and selling cost, due to the larger scale of activity and the sharing of common activities and resources;
- the increase in bargaining power towards customers and the consequent increase in product price.

Buyers/product varieties	Market segment A	Market segment B	Market segment C
Model A	➡		
Model B		➡	
Model C			➡

Figure 3.1 Horizontal strategy: expansion in different market segments

INTERNATIONAL HORIZONTAL EXPANSION STRATEGIES

Where a horizontal expansion strategy is implemented through internationalization it is a matter of evaluating the investments to make and the dynamics of sales and prices in the foreign markets. Obviously, the investment and the costs will take different values according to the different modes of implementing the international expansion strategy: indirect export, direct export, production in foreign countries and cooperation with local firms.

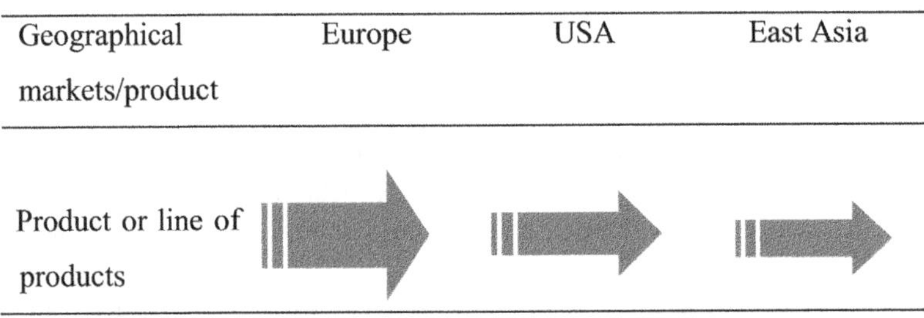

Figure 3.2 Horizontal strategy: expansion in international markets

Indirect export

We call exports indirect when a firm sells its product to import–export firms or trading companies which place the product on the foreign markets. Selling abroad through intermediaries, a firm can exploit their know-how and their network, so avoiding creating a specific organization for the sale which can demand high investments. This solution is often used by small and medium firms and in cases when the sale concerns products requiring post-sales assistance. The disadvantage of this solution is that a firm does not create a direct relation with the final users of its product and it cannot control the sales activity of its intermediaries.

Indirect selling is a form of international expansion particularly suitable for firms that want to explore the opportunities offered by the foreign markets but at the same time limiting the costs and reducing the investments and risks. The investment required principally regards the production and the logistic system.

Direct export

Through direct exports a firm enters into a foreign market creating its own sales structure. In this way a firm establishes a direct and durable relation with its customers, generally adapting its marketing and selling activities to customers' needs. This is the solution normally adopted for selling instrumental goods or consumption goods in high potential markets.

In these cases, the most frequent solutions are represented by networks of agents or franchise stores or of subordinate vendors, sometimes operating in direct stores and office branches. Generally, this last solution is adopted when the potential sales in the target area are high, as are the margins. Obviously, the optimal solution will depend on the product characteristics, firm size and customers' behaviour.

An expansion strategy which is characterized by direct export changes the firm's structure in depth, affecting both the operating and the supporting activities.

Production in foreign countries

The decision to locate new production capacity in a foreign country requires considering three principal factors (Grant, 1998):

- national resources;
- specificity of competitive advantage;
- difficulty in exporting products.

With regard to the first factor, a firm will locate its production capacity in a foreign country where the country's disposable resources have a relevant effect on the competitive advantage of the firm. For example, many firms locate facilities in other countries to have easier access to lower cost labour, energy and raw materials. Other firms locate activities to have access to critical suppliers or to customers. Secondly, a firm will locate its production in a country where its internal resources can be better exploited. Finally, the location of production capacity in a foreign country can be favoured by the high costs of transporting products, the customers' preference for local firms and products and the high barriers set by the local public authorities (import duty, customs duty, tax, etc.).

Investment abroad can involve the entire production cycle or only one or a few phases, depending on the comparative convenience. It is well known that the recent tendency in international trade is for the specialization of production in various countries, not only with reference to entire products, but also to working phases of the same product.

International alliances

The most common method for making expansion investments, especially in international markets, is through strategic alliances, in particular joint ventures and contract manufacturing.

A joint venture with a local firm may be preferred to wholly foreign owned subsidiaries. Setting up joint ventures with local firms can represent the most convenient solution for entering into a foreign market (Harrigan,

1986; Pisano et al., 1988). In fact, these solutions allow a firm to overcome the existing barriers to entry into an industry or a country and to reduce both the cost of the necessary investment and the risk. This solution also allows the firm to exploit its knowledge of and relationships with local firms already operating in the target market. This is, for example, the mode used by international car companies for entering the Chinese automobile market in the last decade. The disadvantages of this solution are the difficulties for the entrant firm in managing the business with local producers or distributors who over time can develop divergent objectives, and also become competitors.

Among the other different solutions concerning international alliances in a foreign country, the following are of particular interest: contract manufacturing and licensing. Contract manufacturing consists of outsourcing the production to local firms. Besides the advantages of avoiding import duties and taxes, there is the advantage of a smaller investment from the entrant firm. Licensing is an intermediate form of producing abroad. It is characterized by a firm which transfers the know-how necessary for producing to a local producer, so avoiding the direct investment in plant, machinery and a sales network. The licenser is normally paid a royalty on each unit produced and sold. The licensee firm makes the investment for manufacturing, marketing and distributing the goods or services and takes the risks. This solution also allows the entrant firm to benefit from the advantages of a local firm: especially relationships and market knowledge. Licensing is the least costly and the least risky mode of international expansion, but it has its disadvantages. It provides the entrant firm with very little control over the manufacturing and marketing of its products in foreign countries and offers the least potential return on products. Finally, the disadvantages come from the transferring of the know-how to firms which could become dangerous competitors in the future after the license has expired.

In summary, entry into a foreign market requires a correct valuation of the sources of the competitive advantage.[1] Generally, if the competitive advantage of a firm depends on factors linked to the country where the firm is already operating, exporting products is the best way for exploiting the opportunities of internationalization. Conversely, if the competitive advantage is firm-specific, a firm can either realise direct investment abroad through a foreign branch or subsidiary, or export its additional production. When products are not transferable, because of high transport costs or import barriers, a firm will enter into a foreign market through a direct investment.

Finally, the type of entry will depend on the required resources for obtaining a competitive advantage in a foreign market; if the entrant firm does not have the necessary resources, setting up a joint venture with a local firm will be the best solutions.

Phases in international expansion

When analyzing the history of large corporations, it emerges that overseas development over time generally follows a model characterized by three typical phases (Table 3.1).

The first phase is characterized by the indirect export of products, mainly using local distributors; the second phase by the consolidation of a presence abroad through the substitution of local import firms with a direct distribution network and sales force; the third phase by the investment in production capacity, in order to better adapt the product to the local customers' needs and to exploit local production advantages.

On this subject see, in particular, Hitt et al., (1997).

Table 3.1 Phases of international expansion strategy

Phases	Phase 1	Phase 2	Phase 3
Model of entry	Indirect export	Direct export	Direct investment
Investment	Low	Medium–High	High
Risk	Low	High	High

MODE OF HORIZONTAL EXPANSION

The expansion of a firm's production capacity can be obtained:

- through internal development (organic development), that is increasing its production capacity with direct investments;
- through acquisition and mergers, that is increasing its production capacity by acquiring firms already operating in the industry and thus exploiting their existing capacity.

The expansion through internal development (organic expansion) is carried out by making direct investments in new production capacity. These investments can take the form of new production lines or departments, as well as expansion of the existing plant or even the building of a new plant. The internal development can also require investments in new stores, commercial branches and offices and marketing activities.

Generally, organic expansion requires a long period of time from the date when the decision is taken to the date when the investments are completed. The disadvantages of an expansion realised through internal development are the risks of delaying the increase of production with respect to a faster growth of demand and a faster growth of competitors. The advantages of organic expansion are the possibilities of exploiting all the know-how the firm has accumulated in different business areas and of being able to monitor directly the entire expansion process. In addition, in realizing an internal development a firm can apply those technologies and organizational solutions which better fit the existing firm structure.

Conversely, the growth through M&A provides the advantage of a faster increase in production capacity and market share. In addition, the acquiring firm can rapidly increase the number of customers and sales and also exploit the technical and organizational know-how of the purchased firm. However, a horizontal expansion through M&A often involves high costs for integrating the different production processes and different firm culture and management systems. Furthermore, a growth through M&A also requires evaluating assets and resources in a condition of limited information, with the risk of overvaluing the target firm.

RATIONALES FOR INTERNAL HORIZONTAL EXPANSION: GROWTH OF DEMAND AND ECONOMIES OF SCALE

The main external conditions that favour horizontal expansion are the following:

- the growth of a firm's specific demand and of the aggregate demand in the industry;
- the opportunities emerging in geographically different markets;
- the possibility of exploiting economies of scale.

First, a horizontal expansion strategy can be favoured by the growth of a firm's specific demand, due to the success of new products launched on the market by the firm (Dringoli, 2009).

Second, a horizontal expansion strategy is favoured by the growth of the aggregate demand in the industry. In this case it is a matter of a dynamic firm taking the opportunity to increase its production capacity, sales and profits. The growth of aggregate demand can be driven by macroeconomic factors, such as population growth and per capita income, the diffusion among customers of new behavioural models and needs, etc. In other cases the growth of demand can be driven by the process of diffusion of new products into different or new market segments. That is what has happened recently in the PC, mobile phone, LCD video markets and in many others.

In the face of an increase in aggregate demand, a firm already operating in the industry can adopt either a strategy directed at maintaining its market share or a strategy directed at increasing its market share. In this latter case the firm will plan a rate of production expansion greater than the rate of increase of aggregate demand, so threatening the market shares of rivals firms.

Third, a horizontal expansion strategy can be favoured by emerging opportunities in geographically different markets, for example foreign markets, from those where the firm is already operating. In this case, it is a matter of extending firm's sales network and production capacity to the foreign country, while the production capacity can be realised either in the domestic country or abroad through direct investments in plant and machinery (international horizontal expansion strategy).

Finally, a horizontal expansion strategy can also be carried out in the presence of stable aggregate demand, for exploiting economies of scale made possible by technological progress (see Appendix A3.1). In this situation a dynamic firm can decide to expand its activity scale by investing in a larger scale plant or other operating structure, in order to obtain a competitive advantage in cost with respect to its rivals.

This cost advantage can also make it convenient to reduce the price of the product, thereby damaging the rival firms to the extent of provoking the exit of the weakest competitors from the market. That will happened if the economies of scale can give a substantial advantage in costs to the firm expanding its scale of production. Since the attack on the market share of the competing firms will cause reactions, this strategy must be undertaken only after correctly evaluating the advantages that can be obtained in comparison to the costs deriving from the possible reactions of the rival firms.

Examples of aggressive expansion strategies can be found in the oil-refining industry, as well in the chemical and pharmaceutical industries.

RATIONALES FOR INTERNAL HORIZONTAL EXPANSION: ECONOMIES OF EXPERIENCE

High economies of experience or learning economies can be a relevant factor favouring horizontal expansion strategy. Just on the basis of strong economies of experience, Ford realised an accelerated expansion strategy up until the mid 1920s, obtaining a relevant success over competitors.

Economies of experience represent the lower costs deriving from an increase in the cumulative production of a firm. These economies derive from learning processes in operations, developing as long as the production cycles are repeated with the increase of cumulative production (Abell and Hammond, 1979; Spence, 1981; Baden Fuller, 1983; Liebermann, 1984; Adler and Clark, 1991; Besanko et al., 1996).

The learning processes, especially in product manufacturing, determine a reduction in the quantities of factors necessary for operations, thereby reducing the unit cost of the product. These economies mainly depend on greater labour efficiency due to labour specialization, and the improvement in operations activities, working techniques and methods, by virtue of the increase in cumulative production. In fact, this phenomenon occurs as the effect of repeating the same operation or the same sequence of operations, that is as the effect of the number of times one operation or a sequence of operations is repeated. It is really this repetition of activities which produces learning, favouring organizational solutions that reduce the time of operations and thus the unit cost per product.

To clearly understand this phenomenon, let us consider the case of a manufacturing firm making an item. To produce the first unit one hour is needed but, if the same firm produced 100 items of the same type, it would make all the product cycle operations in a shorter time, because it would learn to find more and more efficient solutions in terms of resources employed. In other words, the increase in cumulative production will favour a learning process, determining a reduction in production time required for the last product. The hundredth product will require, for example, only 15 minutes labour instead of the one hour required for making the first product; consequently the unit cost per product will decrease with the increase of cumulative production. These are the so-called learning economies.

It must be emphasized that the reduction in unit cost depends on the cumulative production, given the production structure, not only on the amount of time involved. More precisely, the reduction in the time for making the required operations depends on the number of times the sequence of operations is repeated for the product to be obtained; hence, it is the repetition of operations that produces the learning and the innovation in the working method. Thus, the explanatory variable of the learning process is cumulative production. Consequently, if our firm makes a cumulative production of 100 units of the same item in ten days rather than in 100 days, to meet the demand of clients, it will obtain the same reduction in unit cost, because it will accumulate the same experience.

However, if the same cumulative production of 100 units is realised in one day, with a larger production structure, for example with 100 workers, no learning effect will be registered, because each labour unit will follow the same production cycle only once, thus having no opportunity for learning. Therefore, the relevant variable of learning economies is cumulative production, because it is the repetition in using of the same production factors that determines the learning effect. In other words, as workers gain more experience with the requirements of a particular process, or as a process is improved over time, the number of hours required to produce an additional unit declines.

High learning economies (or economies of experience) can favour a horizontal expansion strategy. In fact, if a firm anticipates the increase of its cumulative production, thus expanding its capacity, it would also anticipate the learning effect, so reducing the unit cost of a product and gaining a competitive advantage over its rivals (Saloner et al., 2001). In other words, because learning economies are a result of cumulative production and not simply of the period of time the firm has made a product, a firm growing more rapidly than the others can benefit from the experience effect earlier. Therefore, the presence of high learning economies drives a firm to accelerate its growth, in order to obtain a cost advantage over the competing firms (Ghemawat, 1985).

The intensity of learning economies differs from one industry to another, according to the complexity of operations. In fact, the learning economies are especially present in labour-intensive production.

According to the Boston Consulting Group (1972), in a large number of industries the learning economies are expressed by a rate of reduction of costs from 20% to 30% each time cumulative production is doubled. For example, in the aeronautical sector, where these studies were first developed, the learning process was considerably relevant, with a reduction in costs of approximately 30% at each doubling of production. That was due to the high specialization of the labour-intensive activities and the introduction of process standardization for many components, made possible by the increase of cumulative production.

In the microprocessors industry these economies have been higher than the mean for industries, with a rate of cost reduction from 40% to 50% at each doubling of cumulative production, while in the automobile industry this rate has been estimated as being approximately equal to 12%.

RATIONALES FOR INTERNAL HORIZONTAL EXPANSION STRATEGIES: COST REDUCTION FROM EXPLOITING RESOURCES AND INTERRELATIONSHIPS AMONG ACTIVITIES

Horizontal expansion can be also favoured by the interrelationships between existing and new activities and resources. This is especially true in cases of expansion into new market segments through the introduction of new models and types of a basic product and in cases of expansion into new geographical markets with the same product or line of products.

In the first case, a firm will be able to exploit the existing resources or activities such as sales force, the know-how in manufacturing and the expertise gained in managing marketing activities, etc. Relevant tangible interdependencies can derive from joint production, sharing logistics, machinery, quality control activities, etc.

In the second case, a firm expanding in new geographic markets will be able to use its know-how about product management, its expertise in operations and distribution, its brands, etc. Tangible interdependencies can derive from joint production, marketing activities (shared promotion, advertising, distribution channels and after-sales network), procurement activities (raw materials and financial resources) and infrastructure activities (planning and control system, finance, etc.). Intangible interdependencies can derive from know-how on products, brands, etc. (Figure 3.3).

By sharing sales channels, technologies and other assets and resources a firm will obtain lower costs or higher product differentiation, because of the interrelationships among similar activities and resources.

In conclusion, horizontal expansion is a matter of expanding the existing activities of the value chain and exploiting the excess resources leveraging on the existing stock of tangible and intangible assets. Generally, a horizontal expansion is favoured by:

- product interrelationships: the interrelationships among types and models of a basic product can allow a reduction in product costs by sharing technical and marketing activities and resources;
- geographical market interrelationships: expanding operations in different geographic markets allows the exploitation of existing production plants, sharing marketing expertise, brand image, etc.

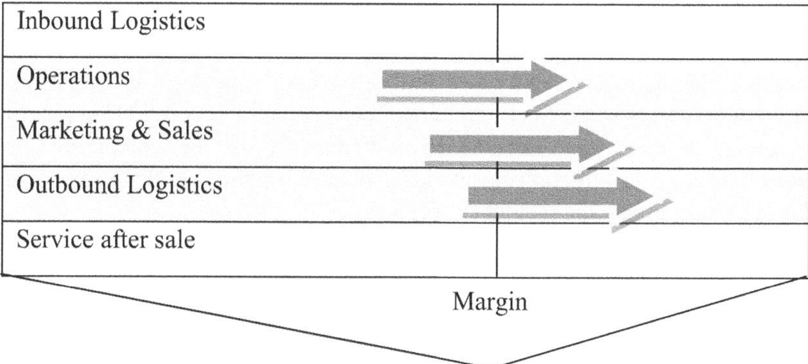

Figure 3.3 Horizontal expansion strategies: interdependencies among products and geographical markets

RISKS IN INTERNAL HORIZONTAL EXPANSION STRATEGIES

Generally, the failure of a horizontal expansion strategy realised through internal development is caused by a change in the external scenario and particularly by:

- the reduction in growth rate of aggregate demand;
- the unexpected evolution of technological progress and the accelerated obsolescence of plants and machinery;
- the reactions of rival firms and the consequent price war.

In particular, a reduction in the growth of aggregate demand can cause a structural imbalance between demand and supply with a consequent reduction in prices and in the profits of the firms operating in the industry. This situation can go on for a long time, especially when there are high exit barriers in the industry, which make it convenient for even the less efficient firms to remain in the industry.

It is well known that the risk of overcapacity and structural imbalance between demand and supply is particularly high in commodity industries, as all products are homogeneous. Also a rapid evolution in technologies following expansion can cause failure of this strategy because of the reductions in margins for all firms operating with old technologies and the consequent necessity for renewing the existing plant before the planned date.

Finally, a critical variable for the success of an expansion strategy is represented by the competitors' behaviour. If they too adopt an expansion strategy, the aggregate supply will further increase with negative effects on the product prices of all firms. As economic literature has proved, the risk of triggering a price war with negative effects for all the competitors is especially high in oligopolistic markets, because of the interdependence of the decisions among the incumbent firms.

Even if the conditions examined are the main causes of failure of a horizontal expansion strategy, sometimes the failure is due to insufficient internal firm resources. It is a fact that especially the inadequacy of managerial resources and organizational capabilities result in being the cause of failure of growth strategies, even when the external scenario has been correctly forecast. This is due to the increasing complexity of managing a larger-sized firm, adapting marketing and distribution processes to different markets and sometimes monitoring functions and activities developed in foreign countries.

In the case of a failure of a horizontal expansion strategy it will be necessary to adopt a downsizing strategy that is a strategy of reducing production by a decrease in the number of operating units and in the number of employees in order to meet the new conditions of aggregate and specific demand.[2] This strategy will allow the firm to concentrate its resources on the most profitable market segments and geographical areas.

A MODEL FOR EVALUATING INTERNAL HORIZONTAL EXPANSION STRATEGIES

For evaluating a horizontal expansion strategy, realised through internal (organic) development, it is first of all necessary to estimate the investments in plant and machinery needed for increasing production capacity. Then it is necessary to determine the investments needed for increasing sales: investments in sales network, brand equity, etc. Finally, the effects of investments in terms of incremental revenues and costs must be estimated for an appropriate period of time.

If a firm can exploit economies of scale, it is also necessary to consider the saving in costs due to the expansion of the firm's scale of activities. Generally this happens because a larger firm benefits from a better division of labour, higher mechanization and automation in production, distribution and administration processes. Further benefits can also derive from the economies of buying material and services on a greater scale.

Summarizing, a horizontal strategy can create value by:

- increasing product sales (ΔQ);
- reducing unit product cost by virtue of economies of scale and by exploiting interrelationships among activities and resources (ΔCu);
- increasing product price as the effect of a higher bargaining power towards the customers (ΔP).

Precisely, the *EBITDA* increment produced by a horizontal expansion strategy will be:

$$\Delta EBITDA = [Q(0) + \Delta Q] \{ [P(0) + \Delta P] - [Cu(0) - \Delta Cu] \} + \\ - Q(0)[P(0) - Cu(0)]$$

that is:

$$\Delta EBITDA = \Delta P[Q(0) + \Delta Q] + \Delta Q[P(0) - Cu(0)] + \\ + \Delta Cu\ [Q(0) + \Delta Q] \qquad (3.1)$$

In particular, the first term in (3.1) represents the increase in *EBITDA* due to the increase in product price ΔP for the larger bargaining power of the firm towards the customers and the increase in quantities sold ΔQ; the second term represents the increase in *EBITDA* due to the growth of quantities produced and sold, the price and the unit cost $Cu(0)$ remaining constant; the third term expresses the saving in cost ΔC due to the economies of scale, made possible by production expansion, and to the higher rate of utilization of common assets and resources. The expression (3.1) is equivalent to the operating cash flow, as discussed in Chapter 2.

If we suppose that the capital expenditure needed to maintain the assets' cash flows for an unlimited period of time is equal to ΔI, the average additional free cash flow from operations, $\Delta FCFO^*$, will be:

$$\Delta FCFO^* = \Delta EBITDA\ (1 - \tau^*) - \Delta I \qquad (3.2)$$

Using the model developed in Chapter 2, the analytical conditions for a horizontal strategy creating value are defined by the following expression:

$$V_{SH}(0) = \frac{\Delta EBITDA\,(1-\tau^*) - \Delta I}{\rho} - I_E(0) \geq 0 \qquad (3.3)$$

where: $V_{SH}(0)$ is the net value of the expansion strategy; $I_E(0)$ is the total investment in product capacity, marketing and logistic systems; τ^* is the tax rate; ρ the cost of capital; ΔI the periodical capital expenditure.

The critical variables for the value of a horizontal expansion strategy are:

- the expansion investment $I_E(0)$;
- the incremental *EBITDA*, that principally depends on the dynamics of aggregate demand, the competitors' behaviour, the economies of scale and the increasing bargaining power of the firm;
- the capital expenditure ΔI that is necessary to maintain a constant operating cash flow for an unlimited period of time; it will depend on the expansion investment and its obsolescence rate and therefore on technical progress in the industry;
- the cost of capital (ρ).

For correctly determining the incremental *EBITDA* it is necessary to estimate:

- incremental sales deriving from the strategy (ΔQ);
- the increase in product price (ΔP);
- the reduction in unit cost per product (ΔCu).

In particular, in cases where the uncertainty about the dynamics of demand and about the evolution of technical progress is high, the cost of capital will be higher and the value of a strategy will be smaller than that resulting in situations characterized by a low level of uncertainty.

Conversely, where the uncertainty is low, the expansion of capacity becomes a game of preemption; in this case it is a matter of anticipating the investment for discouraging the rivals to invest.

DETERMINING THE VALUE OF AN INTERNAL HORIZONTAL STRATEGY: A SIMULATION

The value of an internal horizontal expansion strategy can be determined by applying the model discussed in the previous paragraph.

We assume that a firm A presents, at the initial time $t = 0$, the following data:

- sales: $Q(0) = 100{,}000$ tons;
- product price: $P(0) = €60$;
- cost per unit product: $Cu(0) = €40$.

The estimated values of the relevant variables of the expansion strategy are the following (see Table 3.2):

- expansion investment $I(0) = €10{,}000{,}000$, with an obsolescence rate equal to 0.10 and thus an annual capital expenditure (ΔI) equal to €1,000,000;
- expected increment in sales per year: $\Delta Q = 100{,}000$ tons;
- expected increment in price due to a greater bargaining power: +10% ($\Delta P = 6$);
- expected reduction in variable costs per unit product, due to economies of scale: 10% ($\Delta Cu = 4$);
- tax rate on profits equal to 25% and cost of capital $\rho = 0.10$.

Applying the analytical model (3.1), we have:

$$\Delta EBITDA = \Delta P[Q(0) + \Delta Q] + \Delta Q[P(0) - Cu(0)] + \Delta Cu[Q(0) + \Delta Q] =$$

$$= 6\,[100{,}000 + 100{,}000] + 100{,}000[60 - 40] + 4[100{,}000 + 100{,}000] =$$

$$= 1{,}200{,}000 + 2{,}000{,}000 + 800{,}000 = 4{,}000{,}000$$

Therefore, the net value of the horizontal strategy will be:

$$V_{SH} = \frac{\Delta EBITDA\,(1 - \tau^*) - \Delta I}{\rho} - I_E(0) =$$

$$= \frac{4{,}000{,}000(1 - 0.25) - 1{,}000{,}000}{0.10} - 10{,}000{,}000 = €10{,}000{,}000 \qquad (3.4)$$

All expected conditions being verified, the expansion strategy creates a value for shareholders equal to €10.0 million.

If there are neither economies of scale or improvements in bargaining power and the increase in sales is equal to the new production capacity (100,000 tons), the strategy value will be negative and equal to –€5.0 million;

whereas with production and sales equal to 90,000 and 80,000 units the value of the expansion strategy will be respectively equal to −€6.5 and −€8.0 million.

The simulation highlights that economies of scale and increase in bargaining power can have a great influence on the strategy value (Table 3.2).

Table 3.2 The value of a horizontal expansion strategy: a simulation

Sales ΔQ	Price (€) ΔP	% change	Unit cost (€) ΔCu	% change	Strategy value (€mill.) V_{SE}
100,000	+6	+10	4	−10	10.0
100,000	0		0		−5.0
90,000	0		0		−6.5
80,000	0		0		−8.0
100,000	+6	+10	0		4.0
100,000	+12	+20	0		13.0
100,000	0		4	−10	1.0
100,000	0		8	−20	7.0

Since the product price and the cost per unit have relevant effects on the value of a horizontal expansion strategy, it is necessary to carefully evaluate not only the expected growth of sales in quantities, but also the competitive position of the firm in the industry, especially with regard to rival firms, and the economies of scale that can be exploited through a horizontal expansion strategy.

Considering the different values of the strategy under various hypotheses on the main effects of implementing the strategy, it will be possible to better evaluate the profit of shareholders and the risk of investment.

RATIONALES FOR HORIZONTAL ACQUISITION STRATEGIES: SYNERGY FROM M & A

In order for a horizontal acquisition strategy to create value for the shareholders of the acquiring firm it is necessary for the acquisition to produce synergies. This happens when the *EBITDA* of the combined firm (merger) will result larger than the sum of *EBITDA* of firms standing alone.

Synergy gains come from:

- increased market power which increases the product price;
- a reduction in the unit cost of the product to enable exploiting interrelationships among assets and resources (higher efficiency) and for exploiting some form of economies of scale.

First, a larger size and market share create greater market power thus favouring an increase in product price. Second, horizontal acquisitions present good opportunities for improving scale efficiency, because the merger concerns firms that exhibit similar strategic characteristics, such as common customers, common markets, directly competing products, etc., so favouring a higher utilization of resources. This happens, for example, when one company has slack resources that an increased scale would absorb.

In addition, after acquisition the acquiring firm can use resources from the target firm to change its resource profile, modifying competences and redeploying resources, thereby gaining revenue synergies (Karim and Mitchell, 2000). A balance sheet of the benefits and costs of horizontal acquisition is shown in Table 3.3.

Table 3.3 A balance sheet for evaluating horizontal acquisition

Potential benefits	Potential costs
Reduction in operating costs by exploiting interrelationships among assets and resources.	Cost of resource redeployment and assets divestiture
Reduction in operating costs by exploiting economies of scale.	Cost of coordinating and integrating new activities
Revenues synergies by increased market power and the consequent increase in product price	

If some assets become redundant, post acquisition asset divestiture can be necessary. In this case, to obtain a reduction in costs, the acquiring firm has to develop a dynamic process of resource redeployment and asset divestiture, after the acquisition. In other words, the acquiring firm has to reconfigure the structure of its resources and asset divestiture can be a way to realise the process of activities reconfiguration. More precisely it is a matter of selling a part of a firm's physical and organizational assets, reducing labour forces, shutting facilities and factories, etc. This asset divestiture can apply to both target and acquirer business units (Porter, 1987; Rovenscraft and Scherer, 1987; Weston, 1994; Capron et al., 2001). In this case, divestiture allows a firm to gain scale efficiency and reduce unit costs of product.

In any case, the costs of retaining and integrating the resources of the target firm, in redesigning the organization structure of the combined firm and the costs of asset divestitures have to be considered together with the positive effects expected by the acquisition.

A MODEL FOR EVALUATING HORIZONTAL ACQUISITION STRATEGIES

A horizontal expansion strategy, realised through the acquisition of firms already operating in the business, will create value for the shareholders when the value of acquisition is greater than the price paid for the acquired firm.

As we explained in chapter 2, the value of acquisition is given by:

$$V_{acq} = V_{AB} - V_A \tag{3.5}$$

where V_{AB} is the value of the combined firm AB after the acquisition and V_A and V_B respectively the value of the acquiring firm A and the target firm B before the acquisition.

Thus, the value of the acquisition strategy will be:

$$V_{SA} = (V_{AB} - V_A) - P_B \tag{3.6}$$

where P_B is the price for the target firm B.

For creating value for the shareholders of the A, it is necessary, first, that the value of the combined firm AB is greater than the sum of the values of firm A and firm B standing alone. Precisely:

$$V_{SY} = V_{AB} - (V_A + V_B) > 0 \tag{3.7}$$

This difference in value is the value of synergy, V_{SY}, that the merger will produce.

Second, it is necessary that a part of the value of synergy created through the merger remain with the shareholders of the acquiring firm and this will happen when the price for obtaining B is lower than the value of acquisition, that is:

$$P_B < (V_B + V_{SY}) \tag{3.8}$$

Conversely, there will not be a net increase in the value for shareholders of the acquiring firm A, because the entire value of synergies created by the merger will go to the shareholders of the acquired firm B.

Thus, synergy gains are the principal sources of value in expansion strategies implemented through M&A, but the price paid for the target firm is the means through which the shareholders of the acquiring firm can benefit or not from them. As we explained above, the synergy gains obtained by horizontal acquisition can derive, first, from savings in costs obtained by exploiting interrelationships among activities and by exploiting economies of scale by virtue of a reconfiguration of resources. Second, synergy gains can derive from the higher bargaining power of the acquiring firm over the competitive forces, due to the larger firm's size and the larger market share, which allow the firm to charge higher prices for its products. This occurs, in particular, when only a few firms remain operating in the industry, thereby making it easier to maintain collusive behaviour over time.

To summarize, the combined firm will obtain, as a consequence of the acquisition, an increase in its operating cash flows, with respect to the sum of operating cash flows of firms standing alone, by virtue of:

- a reduction in operating costs (ΔC);
- an increase in revenues (ΔR) due to an increase in price of product (ΔP);

Using the model already introduced in Chapter 2, the net value of a horizontal acquisition strategy V_{SA} can be determined, as follows:

$$V_{SA} = \frac{\Delta FCFO^*}{\rho} - P_B \tag{3.9}$$

where:

$$\Delta FCFO^* = \Delta EBITDA\,(1 - \tau^*) - \Delta I,$$

τ^* being the tax rate and ΔI the investment needed to maintain cash flows for an unlimited period of time.

Note that $\Delta EBITDA$ is the increment in $EBITDA$ of the combined firm AB due to the $EBITDA$ of the acquired firm B plus the synergy gains produced by the merger. Precisely, it will be:

$$\Delta EBITDA = EBITDA(B) + \Delta R + \Delta C$$

where ΔR are the revenue synergies and ΔC the reduction in costs produced by the merger.

The synergy gains can be directly estimated considering that:

$$\Delta R = \Delta P\,(Q_A + Q_B) = \text{revenue synergies;}$$

$$\Delta C = \Delta Cu\,(Q_A + Q_B) = \text{cost synergies.}$$

Q_A, Q_B are respectively the sales of firms A and B; ΔP and ΔCu^* are the increment in market price of product and the reduction in weighted average unit cost of firm A and firm B.[3]

The value of synergy gains created by the merger will be:

$$V_{SY} = V_{acq} - V_B = \frac{\Delta FCFO^*}{\rho} - V_B \tag{3.10}$$

where $V_B = FCFO_B/\rho$ is the value of the firm B standing alone. Therefore, it will be:

$$V_{SY} = \frac{\Delta FCFO^* - FCFO_B}{\rho} = \frac{(\Delta R + \Delta C)(1 - \tau^*)}{\rho} \tag{3.11}$$

DETERMINING THE VALUE OF A HORIZONTAL ACQUISITION: A SIMULATION

From a practical point of view, for determining the value of a horizontal expansion strategy, we have to first evaluate the firms involved in the merger standing alone, by discounting the expected free cash flows of each firm at the cost of capital (ρ), and then determine the value of the combined firm.

To this aim consider two firms A and B operating independently in the same industry and having the financial characteristics indicated in Table 3.2.

The values of these firms are respectively €10,000,000 and €3,000,000 and the total value of them standing alone is €13 million.

Let us assume that firm A evaluates the opportunity to buy firm B. As a first hypothesis the management of firm A estimates that the merger of the two firms allows firm A to reduce its total operating costs of products sold by 10% but it has no effect on the quantities sold and the price of product. The other relevant data of the two firms are shown in Table 3.3.

Therefore, we have synergy gains equal to €800,000, of which revenue synergy (ΔR) is equal to 0 and cost synergy (ΔC) is equal to €800,000. On the basis of these data and applying the expression (3.5), the value of acquisition of firm B is equal to €9,000,000.

In fact it is:

$$V_{acq}(B) = V_{AB} - V_A = €19{,}000{,}000 - €10{,}000{,}000 = €9{,}000{,}000.$$

According to expression (3.10), the value of synergies is equal to:

$$V_{SY} = €9{,}000{,}000 - €3{,}000{,}000 = €6{,}000{,}000.$$

The value created for the shareholders of the acquiring firm will depend on the price paid for the target firm. In fact, this price defines the sharing of synergies between the shareholders of the two firms.

In the case examined, the shareholders of firm A will find the merger convenient only if the price of firm B is lower than €9,000,000, that is the sum of the target firm's value standing alone (€3,000,000) and the value of total synergies (€6,000,000) (Table 3.4).

As a second hypothesis (case two), the management of firm A estimates that, as a consequence of the merger, the combined firm will increase its market power and product price by 5%, whereas the costs of goods sold will be reduced by 10%. In this case, again applying the analytical model shown above, the value of the combined firm will result in being equal to €23,050,000, the value of acquisition will be €13,050,000 and the total value of synergies will be €10,050,000 of which €4,050,000 is the value of revenues synergies, deriving from a higher market power, and €6,000,000 the value of cost synergies (Table 3.5). In fact it will be, according to (3.11):

$$V_{SY} = \frac{\Delta FCFO^* - FCFO_B}{\rho} = \frac{(\Delta R + \Delta C)\ (1-\tau^*)}{\rho} = \frac{(540{,}000 + 800{,}000)\ (1-0.25)}{0.10} =$$

$$= 4{,}050{,}000 + 6{,}000{,}000 = 10{,}050{,}000$$

Table 3.4 Value of acquisition and synergies: case one

Economic variables (€)	Firm A	Firm B	Firm AB combined	Firm AB – Firm A	Synergy
Total assets	5,000,000	3,000,000	8,000,000		
Price	60	60	60		
Sales (tons)	100,000	80,000	180,000	80,000	
Revenues	6,000,000	4,800,000	10,800,000	4,800,000	
Cost x unit	40	50	40		10
Total costs	4,000.000	4,000,000	7,200,000	3,200,000	800,000
EBITDA	2,000,000	800,000	3,600,000	1,600,000	800,000
Tax rate (%)	25	25	25	25	25
EBITDA (1 – *t**)	1,500,000	600,000	2,700,000	1,200,000	600,000
Capital expenditures	500,000	300,000	800,000	300,000	
FCFO*	1,000,000	300,000	1,900,000	900,000	600,000
Cost of capital (%)	10	10	10	10	
Value of firm	10,000,000	3,000,000	19,000,000		
Value of acquisition				9,000,000	
Value of synergies					6,000,000

Note: The firm value is calculated by using the following model: $V = FCFO^*/\rho$.

Table 3.5 Value of acquisition and synergies: case two

Economic variables (€)	Firm A	Firm B	Firm AB combined	Firm AB – Firm A	Synergy
Total assets	5,000,000	3,000,000	8,000,000		
Price	60	60	63		
Sales (tons)	100,000	80,000	180,000	80,000	
Revenues	6,000,000	4,800,000	11,340,000	5,340,000	540,000
Cost x unit	40	50	40		10
Total costs	4,000.000	4,000,000	7,200,000	3,200,000	800,000
EBITDA	2,000,000	800,000	4,140,000	2,140,000	1,340,000
Tax rate (%)	25	25	25	25	25
EBITDA (1 – *t**)	1,500,000	600,000	3,105,000	1,605,000	1,005,000
Capital expenditures	500,000	300,000	800,000	300,000	
FCFO*	1,000,000	300,000	2,305,000	1,305,000	1,005,000
Cost of capital (%)	10	10	10	10	
Value of firm	10,000,000	3,000,000	23,050,000		
Value of acquisition				13,050,000	
Value of synergies					10,050,000

APPENDIX A3.1: ECONOMIES OF SCALE

Economies of scale for a production unit occur when the unit cost of product decreases as the activity scale for that unit increases (Pratten, 1971; Scherer et al., 1975; Norman, 1979; Hay and Morris, 1979; Bellandi, 1995; Besanko et al., 1996). Generally, the scale of production units is measured by the rate of output per unit period.

More precisely, "economies of scale are said to exist with respect to a particular input, or to all total inputs, when the appropriate elasticity of the cost (production) function, evaluated at constant relative factor prices and incorporating a given technology, is less than the unity over some or all of the range of attainable scales" (Norman, 1979). This definition makes no presumption that the elasticity of the cost function will be constant with scale.

We can consider economies of scale with respect to a plant, an establishment (which may be made up of a group of contiguous plants) and a firm which can be reported as an organizational unit containing a number of establishments. In particular, there are technological economies of scale when the cost per unit of production decreases with the increasing scale of production.

When these economies of scale occur in other areas of a firm's activities, for example in distribution, marketing or R&D activities, we call them managing scale economies. In this case the economies of scale occur when the unit cost of distribution or R&D activities decreases with the increasing scale of the activity. In the pharmaceutical industry, for example, there are high economies of scale in R&D activity.

There are also economies of scale in capital funding and in raw material procurement. In this case, the lower unit cost comes from ordering and delivering larger quantities of raw materials and product components.

Technological economies of scale are present especially in industries where the technology allows the firms adopting the larger plants to carry out production processes in a more efficient way, with a production cost per unit decreasing with the scale of plant production. Figure A3.1 exemplifies that situation by representing the curves of unit production costs of five different plants, which are characterized by increasing scale of production. In particular, Figure 3.1 represents the descending lines of short-term cost curves regarding plants A, B, C, D and E, from which the long-term unit costs curve is derived. The increase of the scale of plant causes a decline in the unit cost of product from the highest value relative to the smallest plant A to the minimum level corresponding to the plant of optimal size E. Figure

A3.1 also highlights that plants larger than E do not present further reductions in costs, because there are no further economies of scale.

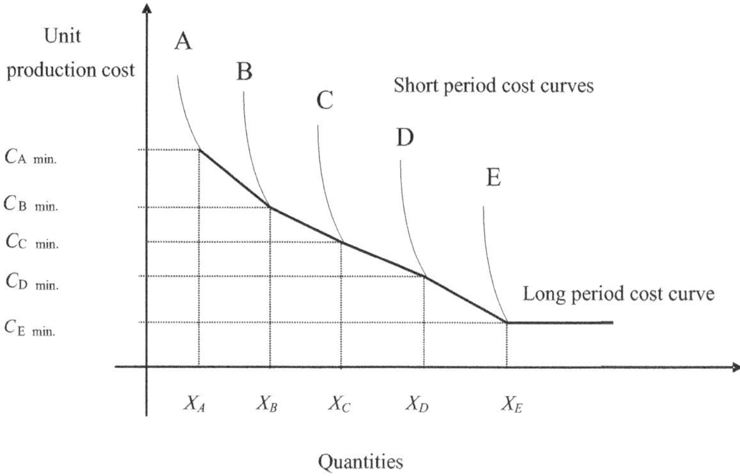

Figure A3.1 Economies of scale in production: the long period cost curve

When there are high scale economies, it is clear that a firm can gain a substantial cost advantage over its rivals by implementing a horizontal expansion strategy directed at using a large-scale plant.

What are the main factors that determine the economies of scale? According to economic literature, one of the principal factors is represented by the technical relationship between the input and the output of a product. Precisely, there are some inputs where an increase determines a more proportional increase of output, thus causing higher productivity. For example, the increase in the surface area of a store makes the cost of the store increase proportionally to the area, while the output, that is the capacity of storing, increases more than proportionally to the surface area of the store, because it is a function of the store volume not of the area. So the cost of storing per unit of product decreases with the increase of the store's area.

Another important factor of economies of scale is the indivisibility of some inputs. To be more precise, some inputs are not disposable in small quantities or, in any case, in quantities which are continuously variable and thus the indivisibility of these inputs favours a larger size, because it offers the possibility of dividing the cost of input, which remains substantially constant, on a larger quantity of products. Let us consider, for example, inputs such as plants or machinery, which cannot be reproduced in units having a production which is smaller than a certain capacity (for example presses, furnaces, etc.).

Similar situations also occur in R&D activity. In fact, in many cases, it is not possible to successfully carry out these activities under a certain structural or organizational dimension. A threshold of specialized persons is necessary, as is a minimum amount of laboratory machinery and a support structure, all of which constitute the minimum dimension in order for this activity to be successful. This is an extreme example of indivisibility factors, because smaller R&D structures determine insignificant output.

The third factor of economies of scale is specialization. In many cases, the use of a larger quantity of inputs makes it possible to develop more effective specialization processes, which conversely would not be possible when the size of the activity is small. These scale economies, linked to specialization, are typical of mass production processes, characterized by the continuous production of the same product or the same combination of products over time.

The higher scale of activity also allows specialized use of labour to be obtained. In fact, large production units offer the possibility of realizing a more effective labour division and a more advanced specialization in the different functions. More advanced labour specialization favours an increase in employees' abilities and a reduction in the amount of time lost by passing from one job to another.

In Table A3.1 some data on economies of scale in different industries are shown. In the first column the minimum efficient size of a plant is shown, in relation to the total production of the industry. For example, in the turbo-generators and in the diesel motors industries, it is seen that an efficient plant represents approximately 20% of the industry production (that means that five plants cover all the production of the entire industry). In the automobile industry the minimum efficient plant is equal to the production of one million cars.

From these data it is clear that the economies of scale are also barriers to entry for new competitors; in fact, in order to be competitive, they must enter with a large production scale, that will increase the industry supply with a consequent reduction in product prices and profits.

Obviously, there are also industries in which the economies of scale are negligible, so that the size of each plant or firm is small with respect to the total production in the industry.

Table A3.1 Economies of scale and rate of concentration in some USA industries

Industry	(MES)Plant size as a percentage of US consumption	Percentage elevation of unit costs at 1/3 MES	Number of plants needed to have not more than a "slight" overall handicap
Beer brewing	3.4	5.0	3–4
Cigarettes	6.6	2.2	1–2
Refrigerators	14.1	6.5	4–8
Paints	1.4	4.4	1
Oil refining	1.9	4.8	2–3
Glass bottles	1.5	11.0	3–4
Cement	1.7	26.0	1
Steel	2.6	11.0	1

Source: Adapted from Collis and Montgomery (2005, p. 69) on the original study of Scherer et al. (1975).

However, there are limits to the economies of scale (Pratten, 1971; Scherer and Ross, 1980). First there are limits due to the production technologies that do not produce further reduction in costs as long as the size increases; second there are limits due to the increasing organizational costs for managing and controlling an activity which is more complex.

The concept of economies of scale can be further clarified in analytical terms. In this context, we can definitely say that economies of scale are present where the total cost of producing a given quantity nq_1 with one plant having a production scale equal to nq_1 is lower than the total cost of producing the same quantity nq_1 with n plant, each of scale equal to q_1 . That is:

$$C(nq_1) < nC(q_1) \tag{A3.1}$$

where: $nC(q_1)$ is the total cost of producing the quantities nq_1 with n plants, each of scale or capacity q_1, and $C(nq_1)$ is the total production cost for producing nq_1 quantities with one plant with a scale (capacity) equal to nq_1.

The expression (A3.1) indicates that increasing n times the scale of production of a plant (nq_1), the firm obtains a unit cost lower than the cost the firm will bear realizing the same total production, but with n plants each having a scale of production equal to q_1.

Economies of scale can include labour input (the relationship between plant scale and labour costs), the capital cost for plants (the relationship between plant scale and capital cost) and materials and energy inputs.

A function of total long period production cost that exhibits economies of scale is offered, for example, by the following:

$$C = k\,q^a \qquad \text{(A3.2)}$$

where: C is the total production costs, k is a parameter; q is the production scale, the exponent a is a constant (with $a < 1$).

For example, assuming k = \$10,500 and a = 0.6 we obtain the following unit production cost function:

$$C/q = 10{,}500\,q^{0.6} \qquad \text{(A3.3)}$$

Over the range of plants from 10,000 tons of scale to 40,000 tons, the unit cost of production decreases from about \$264 to \$151 (Figure A3.2).

As we said before, economies of scale are not only present in production activity, but also in other activities of the firm, such as logistics, marketing and R&D activities. The increasing relevance of economies of scale has changed the competitive balance in many industries, to the advantage of those firms which carried out horizontal expansion processes more rapidly. Among these are the automobile, chemical, steel and cement sectors.

Finally, note that economies of scale are often confused with the reduction in unit production cost when production increases up to the maximum of the existing capacity of a given production unit (for example of a plant). This effect is simply caused by the distribution of total fixed costs over a larger quantity of production and thus by the reduction of the fixed cost per unit product as production increases up to the maximum of a given plant capacity.

For example, consider a firm with a given production capacity (that is a given production scale) equal to q_1 and the following linear function of total production costs $C(q)$ with respect to increasing values of quantities produced q:

$$C(q) = 500{,}000 + 80\ q \qquad \text{(A3.4)}$$

where: $q \leq q_1$; €500,000 are the fixed costs and €80 is the unit variable cost.

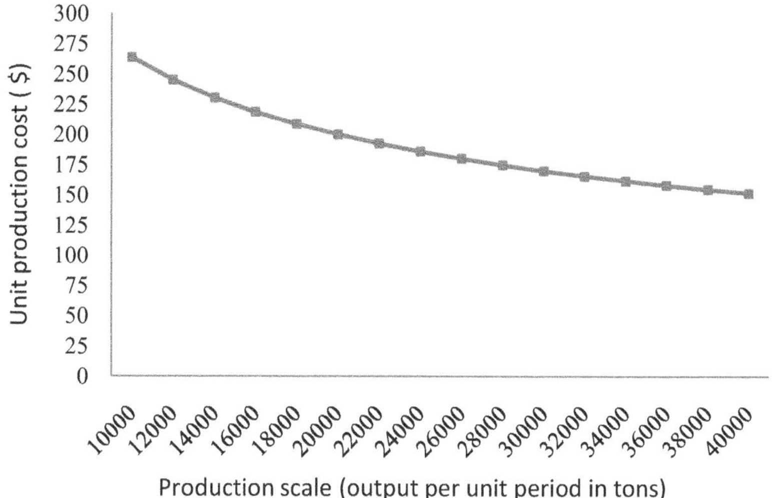

Figure A3.2 Economies of scale: an example

From expression (A3.4) we can obtain the following function of unit production costs, varying q:

$$C(q)/q = 500{,}000/q + 80 \qquad \text{(A3.5)}$$

Therefore, we have a decreasing unit cost of production as far as the production increases up to the maximum capacity q_1 (Figure A3.3).

If q_1 = 10,000 tons is the maximum capacity of the existing plant, the minimum unit production cost will be equal to €130:

$$C(q)/q = 500{,}000/10{,}000 + 80 = 130 \qquad \text{(A3.6)}$$

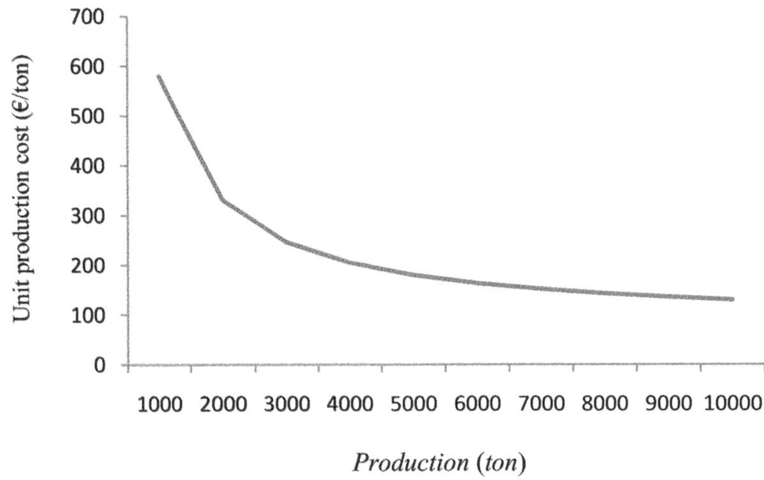

Figure A3.3 Rate of production and unit production cost for a given plant

APPENDIX A3.2: ECONOMIES OF EXPERIENCE AND LEARNING CURVES

Economies of experience are analytically described by the learning curves, which model the relationship between the quantities of factors necessary for operations (mainly labour) and the cumulative quantity of product.

Empirical evidence has shown that the learning curves are accurately represented by an exponential relationship. If we consider the labour as the main factor which is influenced by the experience, the learning economies can be expressed, in analytical terms, by a function of the following type:[4]

$$H(Q) = a\, Q^{-b} \tag{A3.7}$$

where: $H(Q)$ is the number of labour hours required for producing the Qth unit of product; a is the number of labour hours required to produce the first unit of product; Q the cumulative units produced and b the rate at which the marginal production hours decline as the cumulative number of units produced increases (rate of learning).

So, for example, if $a = 10$ labour hours and $b = 0.32$, the number of hours required for producing the 100th unit will result as being equal to 2.3 with a total reduction of 7.7 hours (77%) with respect to the hours required to produce the first unit.

Traditionally, learning curves are described by the percentage decline of the labour hours required to produce item $2Q$ compared to the labour hours required to produce item Q and it is assumed that this percentage is independent of Q. That is, an L per cent learning curve (for example 70% learning curve) means that the time required to produce unit 2Q is L per cent of the time required to produce unit Q.

This means that, at the first doubling of the cumulative production, the number of hours required is equal to 70% of the previous hours, and doubling the production again, the new hours required will be equal to 70% of the previous and so on. Thus, the number of labour hours required per unit product will reduce by 30% at each doubling in cumulative production and at the same rate also the labour cost per unit product will reduce, given the labour price per hour.

In analytical terms it is:

$$\frac{H(2Q)}{H(Q)} = \frac{a(2Q)^{-b}}{aQ^{-b}} = 2^{-b} = L \tag{A3.8}$$

where, in addition to already known symbols, $100L$ *is the per cent learning curve.*

Thus, if our learning curve is a 70% learning curve, it will be:

$$2^{b} = 0.7 \tag{A3.9}$$

and being:

$$-b\ log(2) = log(0.7) \tag{A3.10}$$

it will be:

$$b = -\ log(0.7)/log(2) = -\ 0.514 \tag{A3.11}$$

It is clear that the greater parameter b, the more rapidly the unit labour cost will decrease. In Figure A3.4 an example of unit cost dynamics is represented when the cumulative production becomes two, four, eight and sixteen times the initial production, in case $b = 0.514$.

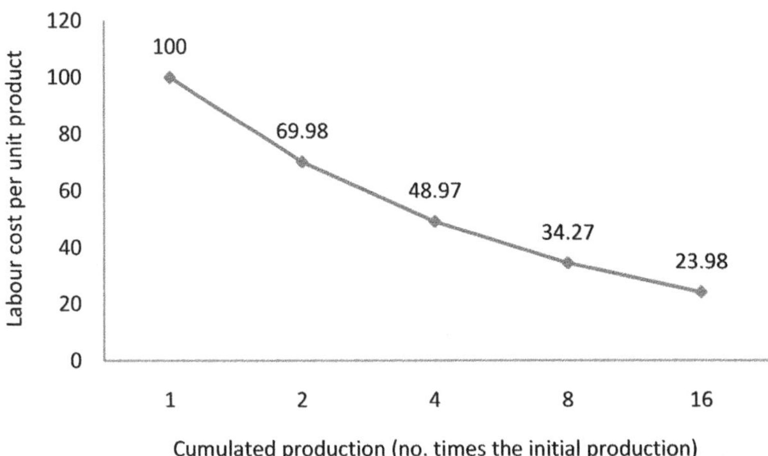

Note: $Cp = 100(n2)^{-0.514}$.

Figure A3.4 A typical learning economies function

In particular, passing from production 1 to production 2, the labour cost per unit product decreases from \$100 to \$70, and so on for each doubling in cumulative production.

Note that the function (A3.7) becomes a straight line if it is expressed in double logarithmic scale. Precisely, it will be:

$$log\ H(Q) = log\ (a) - b\ log\ (Q) \tag{A3.12}$$

A straight line relationship between the logarithm of the cumulative number of units produced and the logarithm of the hours required for the last unit of production can be very useful for the analysis. In fact, having empirical data about different cumulative production levels and labour hours required for producing a given item, it is possible to calculate the relative learning curve (Figure A3.5).

To this aim, a linear regression can be used to fit the values of a and b to actual data after the logarithm transformation of data has been make. Through the least squares method it is possible to estimate the slope term (the constant $-b$) and the intercept a. Since the intercept is log(a) the value of a will be equal to exp (log a).

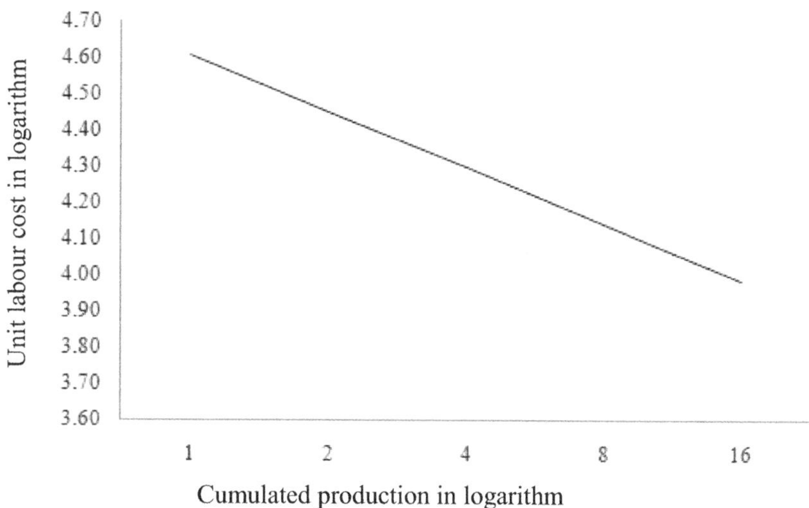

Figure A3.5 The learning curve expressed in logarithm

When the value of b is known, the value of L can be calculated by applying the expression (A3.8); precisely it will be:

$$L = 2^{-b} \tag{A3.13}$$

Hence, using empirical data it is possible to calculate the learning effect for the production of the considered item by an L per cent learning curve. This expression can be used to predict the number of labour hours that will be required for continued production of these items.

Obviously, a learning curve relationship is not valid indefinitely, because of the nature of the manufacturing process. With this limit in mind learning curves, when used properly, can be a valuable tool for decisions.

If the economies of experience apply to all factors of production, the effect of learning will be a reduction in direct product costs and thus in the production cost per unit of product. Therefore, a firm expanding its production more rapidly than its rivals will obtain an increasing advantage in costs.

In Figure A3.6 the unit labour cost of two firms A and B is shown. Firm B expands its production at double the rate of that of firm A, so obtaining an increasing advantage in costs over time.

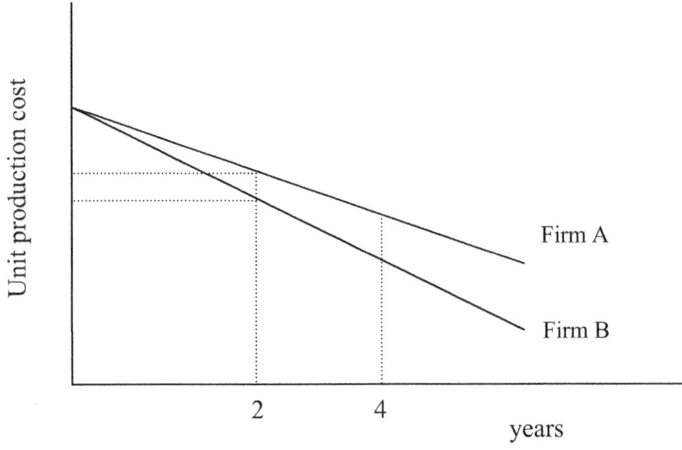

Figure A3.6 Comparison between unit production costs of two competing firms

NOTES

1. The analysis of decisions for entering into a foreign market can be also developed by using the theory of transaction costs. As it will be clarified in Chapter 4, barriers to entry can be considered as transaction costs, as well as the cost regarding the business deal and the monitoring of the agreement in licensing contracts and in joint ventures with local firms. Therefore, according to this theory, the direct investment is preferable when there are high transaction costs, because of the inefficiency of foreign markets and the high specificity of the relevant resources.
2. On the restructuring strategies see: Baden-Fuller and Stopford (1992); Gouillart and Kelly (1995); Hitt et al. (1997); Collis and Montgomery (2005).
3 In fact the variations in revenues and in operating costs of the combining firm with respect to the values of firm standing alone are the following:
$\Delta R = (P(0) + \Delta P)(Q_A + Q_B) - P(0)\,(Q_A + Q_B) = \Delta P\,(Q_A + Q_B)$
$\Delta C = Cu^*(0)\,(Q_A + Q_B) - Cu^*(1)\,(Q_A + Q_B) = \Delta Cu\,(Q_A + Q_B)$
Therefore, the synergy gains expressed in increment of EBITDA are:
$\Delta P\,(Q_A + Q_B) + \Delta Cu\,(Q_A + Q_B)$.
Note that P(0) is the market price of product and Cu*(0) is the weighted average unit cost of firms A and B standing alone, while $P(1) = P(0) + \Delta P$ and $Cu^*(1) = Cu^*(0) - \Delta Cu$ are respectively the price and the average unit cost after the merger.
4. Learning by doing has been documented in many studies concerning air-frames industry (Wright, 1936; Alchian, 1963), automobiles assembly (Baloff, 1971), chemicals (Pisano, 1994 and 1994), semiconductors (Bohn, 1995; Gruber, 1992; Hatch and Mowery, 1998 and Hatch and Dyer, 2004) industries.

4. Product diversification strategies

INTRODUCTION AND OBJECTIVES

In this chapter we analyse the different types of product diversification strategies and the modes for which they can be realised.

As diversification strategies imply the entry of a company into different industries, we discuss those structural characteristics of the industry which determine opportunities and risks and consider the possible reaction of existing competitive forces. The then analysis focuses on the conditions under which diversification strategies can ensure competitive advantage and create value for shareholders. In this context, we present some quantitative models for estimating the value of diversification strategies implemented both through internal development and M&A.

In the appendix a numerical application of economies of scope is presented.

TYPES OF PRODUCT DIVERSIFICATION STRATEGIES

A product diversification strategy consists of expanding the activity of the firm to industries that are different from those in which the firm is already operating, introducing different products in addition to the existing ones.

The objective of a product diversification strategy may be summarized in creating value for shareholders, mainly through the expansion of sales, the reduction in the unit cost of products and a decrease in the operating risk and thus in the cost of capital.

A product diversification strategy represents a fundamental strategy for the growth of a firm (Penrose, 1959; Gort, 1962; Berry, 1975; Chandler, 1990; Dringoli, 1995). This is confirmed by empirical studies that point out the positive relationships between product diversification and firm size (Gort, 1962; Rumelt, 1982; Utton, 1979; Berry, 1975).

The multiple forms of product diversification may be classified according to two fundamental types (Figure 4.1):

- related diversification;
- unrelated or conglomeral diversification.

Related diversification is characterized by the introduction of a firm into businesses having relationships with its existing business, with regard to activities along the value chain concerning production, marketing or the logistic network (Porter, 1985).

An example of related diversification is offered by Fiat with its diversified products in the automobile, truck, agricultural machinery and bus industries; all products are strongly related to each other by technological affinity. In other diversified companies products share a common sales force and sales service desk or supply logistics network, etc.

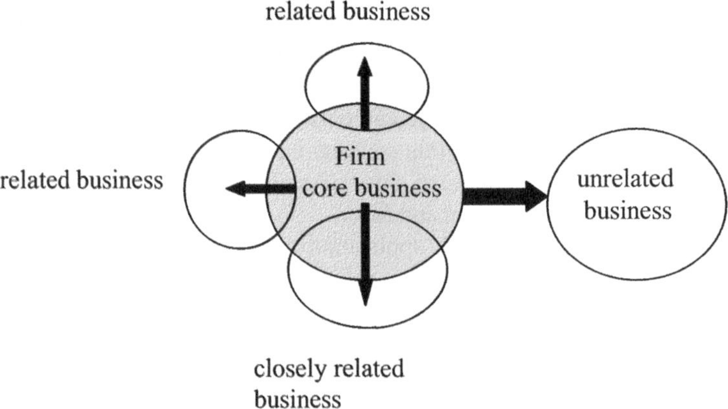

Figure 4.1 Patterns of product diversification

Conversely, an unrelated or conglomerate diversification is characterized by the introduction of products or services that have characteristics that are radically different from the technological, commercial, organizational and managerial specialization of the company. Examples are companies such as General Electric which operates in a number of unrelated businesses with different products and services: electronic instruments, aircraft engines, medical instruments, finance, etc.

These are quite different activities, grouped according to pure financial logic, aimed at exploiting the benefits deriving from the reduction of risk of the business portfolio.

MODES OF DIVERSIFICATION STRATEGIES: ORGANIC DEVELOPMENT AND M&A

A product diversification strategy can be implemented in two main modes:

- organic or internal development;
- acquisition and merger of other companies (external development).

An organic or internal diversification strategy consists of building a new business unit through direct investments aimed at manufacturing a different product and organizing a new sales and distribution structure. This solution allows the firm to adapt its investments to real, specific needs, choosing the most appropriate technology and the most effective marketing and distribution structure. Furthermore, internal development can be more easily sustainable financially, since it can be realised step by step. Conversely, internal diversification implies a production capacity increase at the industry level. The consequent supply increase can determine a significant sale price reduction if the increase of aggregate supply is larger than the increase of product demand. In these circumstances, the reaction of incumbent competitors can cause a price war, with negative effects on the outcome of all firms operating in the market.

On the other hand, external diversification is implemented through the acquisition of existing companies or production plants. The main advantages of this option are provided by the greater speed of strategy implementation and its neutrality related to the industry supply capacity, that remains the same. Further benefits can be derived from the possibility to increase capabilities and competences through resources available at the acquired companies. However, external growth exposes the firm to some risks. The most important ones concern the comprehensive costs related to the acquisition and the time periods needed for the complete organizational integration of the firms involved.

EVALUATING OPPORTUNITIES AND RISKS IN ENTERING A DIFFERENT INDUSTRY

In evaluating a diversification strategy it is necessary, first of all, to consider the opportunities and risks involved when entering a different industry. Careful industry analysis can help to understand whether a particular industry is attractive in terms of real opportunities for long-run profitability (Abell and Hammond, 1979; Day, 1990; Saloner et al., 2001).

More precisely, industry analysis illuminates the competitive landscape and the basic conditions that influence profit potential. In this context it is necessary to consider that the entry of a company will modify the existing competitive situation in the industry and will trigger a reaction of existing competitive forces influencing the level of sales prices and operating margins.

More precisely, the most relevant competitive forces a firm has to consider entering a different industry are the following (Figure 4.2):

- industry competitors;
- suppliers;
- clients;
- substitute products;
- potential entrants.

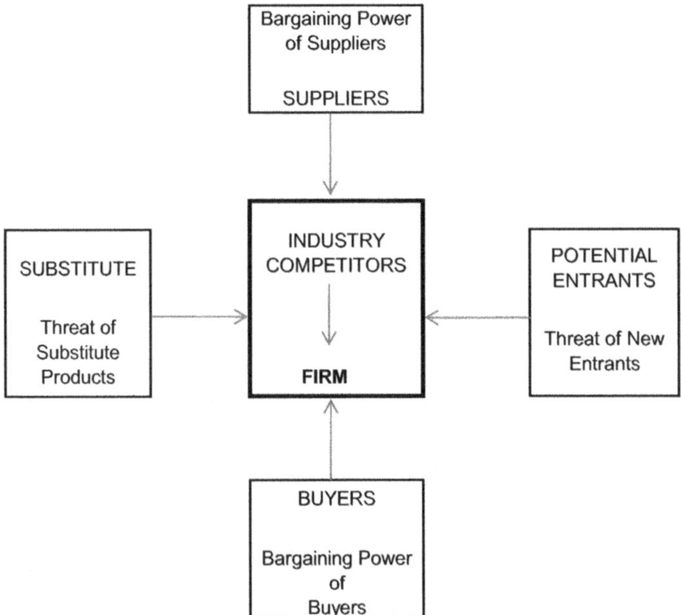

Source: Porter (1980).

Figure 4.2 Analysis of industry structure: the competitive forces

The industry competitors

The number of competitors and the concentration rate deeply affect the level of sales prices and therefore the profits in the industry. On this subject, remember that the continuum of competitive situations can be divided into four wide categories: perfect competition, imperfect or monopolistic competition, oligopoly and monopoly. To each of these a different intensity of price competition is related. Table 4.1 shows that each category of competitive state is related to a range of the industry concentration index (HH Index).[1]

Table 4.1 The effect of four categories of market structure on price competition

Type of competition	HH Index	Intensity of price competition
Perfect competition	Usually lower than 0.2	Fierce
Monopolistic competition	Usually lower than 0.2	May be fierce or weak depending on product differentiation
Oligopoly	From 0.2 to 0.6	May be fierce or weak depending on rivalry among different firms
Monopoly	From 0.6 and higher	Generally weak, unless there is the threat of new entrants

Source: adapted from Besanko et al. (1996).

Obviously, these frameworks provide only some schemes of reference, which are not to be generalized. For example, sometimes there are cases of high competition in the presence of only two competitors or cases of low competition in markets characterized by multiple firms with differentiated products or by firms with a strong dissuasive power of the possible reaction to price competition of other incumbent firms. This will depend on the amount of financial resources available and the capability of retaliating with relevant effects in the markets of possible competitors (Ferrucci, 2000).

However, in general, rivalry increases among competitors and price levels shrink when:

- the number of competitors increases and they become more similar in terms of size and capability;
- the industry conditions (for example the unemployed capacity) spur competitors to decrease prices or to use other competitive weapons in order to increase sale volumes;
- the switching from one brand to another is easy and not expensive.

The suppliers and their bargaining power

Suppliers may be considered a competitive force, since their bargaining power may increase the costs of raw materials, components and services, and reduce the margins and earnings of the buyer firm. In other words, suppliers, using their dealing power, may require changes in some elements of the supply relationship that are favourable to them: price increases, standardization of the products provided, reduction of product variables, lengthening of delivery time, increase of the minimum order, reduction of assistance or design support, etc. Conditions favouring an increase in the bargaining power of suppliers and in the price of factors are (Hax and Majluf, 1984; Grant, 1998):

- supply markets containing few firms and which are more concentrated than the industries of the buyer firms;
- a limited availability of substitute products for those of the suppliers;
- buyer firms are small compared with their suppliers;
- the significant contribution of the supplier's products to the quality of products of the buyer firm or to the efficiency of the production process;
- the high differentiation of the supplier's products and/or high re-conversion costs;
- the capability of suppliers to integrate downstream.

The clients and their bargaining power

Clients may be another important competitive force in the industry, since through their bargaining power they are able to compel the firm to lower prices, in this way gaining a part of the value created by it. Very often, small and medium-sized manufacturers operating with a large client suffer from the bargaining power of the client and accept lower prices.

In general, conditions increasing the bargaining power of clients are the following (Grant, 1998):

- the market is concentrated;
- re-conversion costs for clients are low;
- products are not significant for the quality of the client's product;
- clients can integrate upstream.

The threat of substitute products

Manufacturers of substitute products may represent a further important competitive force, capable of affecting the prices and profits in the industry. Beyond certain price levels, in fact, the demand will move towards substitute products, causing a reduction of the firm's profit in the medium term. So, the existence of substitute products increases the price elasticity of the demand, since clients may move their demand towards substitute products each time the product price exceeds what they are likely to pay.

For example, producers of artificial sweeteners threaten sugar manufacturers; producers of glass bottles compete against manufacturers of plastic, paper, cardboard and aluminium containers; producers of artificial fibres for the textile industry compete against producers of natural fibres, and so on.

Obviously, if substitute products are not perfect, thanks to the product differentiation, the firm will have greater running control in prices and will be able to stably maintain higher profits.

The threat of potential entrants

The level of profits in an industry also depends on the threat of potential entrants and therefore on the barriers to entry, that is structural entry obstacles.

It is common knowledge (Bain, 1956; Modigliani, 1958 and Sylos Labini, 1964) that entry barriers are mainly represented by:

- scale economies;
- product differentiation;
- cost advantages independent of scale.

Scale economies are entry barriers because they compel the new competitor to enter the business with a high level of production, and therefore with a significant supply, such as to determine a considerable post-entry price decrease (demand given). The entry of new firms, by adding production capacity, would trigger a price reduction and therefore decrease the profits of all firms over a long period. Post-entry price conditions can therefore diverge significantly from pre-entries and cause the annulment of extra profits before the entrance. So, scale economies tend to discourage the potential rivals, creating a condition favourable to the incumbent firms and thus a higher level of price and profits in industry (Besanko et al., 1996).

Product differentiation is another entry barrier because it is not sufficient for the entrant to build the production capacity and offer the product. It is necessary to differentiate the product significantly, in order to move already consolidated preferences. However, product differentiation is not easy to be realised: it requires investments, sometimes extremely high ones, the results of which are very uncertain by nature.

Cost advantages not depending on scale are the advantages the incumbents firms have independently of their size. They are related to different factors, among which are control over scarce resources in the procurement (natural resources, raw materials) or sales markets (long-term or exclusive relationships with suppliers or customers), the availability of patents or owned technologies, non-replicable production and distribution locations, the experience and availability of a qualified labour force, any other market imperfection, or the amount and the cost of capital of new entrants compared to firms already operating in the industry.

High entry barriers favour the sustainability of high prices and consequently of profits in the industry.

Further relevant characteristics of the industry structure influencing the level of prices and profits

Finally, a firm evaluating a diversification strategy will have to consider the following structural characteristics of the industry into which it intends to enter; because they are relevant for its performance in the long term:

- the balance between aggregate demand and supply;
- the ratio between the aggregate demand and the minimal efficient scale of production;
- the rate of growth of aggregate demand;
- the presence of barriers to exit.

The relationship between the aggregate demand and the production capacity in the sector is of particular importance. Unused production capacity is one of the critical factors forcing existing firms to compete on product prices. In particular, the higher the amount of fixed costs, compared with variable costs, the higher the propensity of firms to compete on prices. An aggressive strategy of price reduction for increasing sales volumes, and therefore reducing the excess capacity, can cause significant reductions of margins and operating earnings. Excess capacity can be the result of a decreasing rate of market growth and an excess of investments on the part of the existing firms.

The duration of the negative effects arising from an excess production capacity principally depends on exit barriers, that is on the possibility of firms exiting the business and mobilizing their resources to different businesses. When costs or barriers to the mobility of resources are high, it is difficult to exit the sector. So, the condition of having excess capacity, with its negative effects on prices and incomes, may last for a long time. Conversely, when the aggregate demand exceeds the production capacity of the industry, prices and incomes will be higher, as the result of weaker competition.

A further relevant characteristic of the industry structure, influencing prices and firm earnings, is the ratio between the aggregate demand and the minimal efficient scale of production. This influences the number of competitors able to operate conveniently in the market and significantly affects the conditions to entry in the industry, as highlighted before.

Finally, the performance of an entrant firm will be significantly affected by the growth rate of the aggregate demand of products and services. Businesses characterized by a low growth rate usually show a greater rivalry among competitors and lower profitability in the long run. The opposite considerations count in sectors that are characterized by high growth rates (Thompson and Strickland, 1998). In fact, these dynamics can have a determining affect on product prices and sales, determining the success of a diversified strategy. In particular, a rapid growth in aggregate demand can favour the reaching of planned sales and the increase in product price; conversely, a small growth with a large increase in product supply can produce in-excess product capacity, thereby causing a fall in product price and destructive retaliation from rival firms.

Also the presence of barriers to exit, determined by specialist investments, can be a negative factor for the entrant firm, because less efficient firms will be able to continue operating in the market, even bearing a loss for a long time, and consequently preventing the market from returning to balance.

Summarizing, the earnings and cash flows that a firm can gain through a diversification strategy will be strongly affected by the structure of the industry into which the firm decides to enter. In particular, the most relevant variables that a firm has to evaluate when deciding to entry the new business are the following:

- the entry barriers, that are the relevant obstacles to entering the business, and the exit barriers;
- the number of competitors, their production capacities and the concentration rate of supply;
- the number of buyers, their purchase capacity and the concentration of demand;
- the number of substitute products;
- the relationship between the aggregate demand for the product and the whole production capacity;
- the growth rate of aggregate demand.

CREATING A COMPETITIVE ADVANTAGE OVER THE INCUMBENT COMPETITORS

To create value entering in a different business a firm has to adequately position itself with respect to the competitive forces, so as to achieve high margins and high cash flows. In particular, to compete successfully in a different business and create a sustainable value, a firm must be configured so as to emphasize its differential elements compared with its competitors, achieving a strong and certain competitive advantage. As the existing competitors play a major role among forces affecting the performance of the firm entering a new business, it is particularly relevant for this firm to create an adequate positioning in relation to existing rivals, in order to gain a competitive advantage (Day, 1990).

On this subject, we recall that the competitive advantage may be of three different forms:

- cost advantage;
- differentiation advantage;
- cost–differentiation advantage.

The cost advantage arises when the firm succeeds in organizing more efficiently the activities for manufacturing and selling the product, so that the product costs less, even if it is basically equal to competitors' products. The cost advantage may result from different factors: input costs, operating efficiency, scale economies, employment capabilities and competencies, outsourcing of some production activities, etc. The cost advantage enables the firm to create value by selling at lower prices a product which is more or less equal to those of its competitors, thereby obtaining higher sales volumes.

The differentiation advantage depends on the greater benefits provided by the product, compared with those offered by competitors. The differentiation advantage may derive from different factors: the innovation of products or services, distribution and logistic activities and brand policies, so as to qualify the supply of the firm in comparison with that of its competitors. The differentiation advantage allows value leveraging to be created on the product, in terms of quality or image, so that customers are willing to pay a premium price or to buy higher quantities (Porter 1980 and 1985; Day, 1990; Grant 1998).[2]

The cost–differentiation advantage arises when a firm is capable of gaining competitive advantage by offering two types of value to customers, some differentiated features (but fewer than those provided by the product-differentiated firm) and at a relatively low cost, but not as low as the products of the low-cost leader (Hitt et al., 1997; Dess et al., 1995).

Having said that, for creating value the firm adopting a diversification strategy will have to offer real advantages, in terms of costs or differentiation or a combination of them, in comparison with its competitors.

In the first case, the firm will create value through lower costs and higher volumes of production and sales. In the second case, leveraging on product differentiation, the firm will be able to establish a higher price for the product, with higher unit margins. In the third case the firm will benefit from combined forms of premium price and low cost and higher volumes (Table 4.2).

Table 4.2 Competitive business strategies and competitive advantage

Main competitive business strategies	Competitive advantage
Cost Leadership	• Lower cost • Higher sales volume
Differentiation	• Higher margin; • Higher brand loyalty

RATIONALES FOR INTERNAL DIVERSIFIED STRATEGIES: COST ADVANTAGES FROM SHARING ACTIVITIES AND RESOURCES (ECONOMIES OF SCOPE)

A firm entering a different industry can achieve a competitive advantage over the existing firms when it possesses resources excess the needs deriving from the original activity, which can be shared and transferred to new businesses and which have a great potential in value creation.[3] In particular these polyvalent or sharing resources can be: plants, commercial network, logistic structures, brands, firm reputation, patents, technological know-how, etc.

A firm will use the versatility of its excess resources in activities which are different from the present, when there are limits to implementing a horizontal expansion, due to fierce competition from rival firms or to a steady demand for mature products or technologies. In these cases, through a diversification strategy a firm will be able to realise a "lateral transfer" of its excess resources, that is a move towards business areas where these resources can be used and where connections and shared inputs may arise.

Sharing activities and resources a firm can benefit from cost savings or from an increase in product differentiation, so achieving a cost or a differentiation advantage over the rival firms. On this subject, the economic literature (Panzar and Willig, 1979; Besanko et al., 1996) has emphasized the importance of economies of scope in the explanation of successful diversifications.

To be precise, the notion of economies of scope refers to the cost savings that the firm can realise combining the production of two or more products at a single location or using the same multipurpose equipment. In more general terms, economies of scope are the economies of jointly producing, selling and distributing different products, coming from the use within a single operating unit of processes enabling the production and distribution of different products.

In analytical terms, we can say that these economies arise when the cost of jointly producing and selling products X, Y is lower than the cost of separately producing and selling each product X and Y. That is, where the following condition is true (Besanko et al., 1996):

$$C(Q_X, Q_Y) < C(Q_X, 0) + C(0, Q_Y) \tag{4.1}$$

In this case, the cost advantage for the firm adding the product Y to its line X, over the firm producing only the product Y, is given by:

$$C(Q_X, Q_Y) - C(Q_X, 0) < C(0, Q_Y) \tag{4.2}$$

This formula expresses the idea that it is cheaper for a single firm to produce both goods X and Y than for one firm to produce X and another to produce Y.

All that considered, it is clear that the presence of economies of scope favours product diversification, because the joint production of two or three products by the same firm reduces its costs. In particular, the excess resources that might be shared and transferred in other businesses are (Figure 4.3):

- tangible assets, such as the technical structure and therefore plant, production facilities, the sales network, the outbound logistic system, the R&D laboratories, etc.;
- intangible assets, such as the brand image and notoriety, firm reputation, patents, etc.;
- capabilities and competences, such as the marketing and administrative expertise, R&D know-how, technological know-how, managerial skills and experience in problem solving, etc.

Such a resource is, for example, the distribution network which, once set up, can be used for selling the new products or services with negligible additional costs or even negative costs if the new products or services complete the assortment, so facilitating the sale of other products and improving the service to the client.

Among the resources with a great potential in value creation there are technological know-how and organizational capabilities. A firm which is particularly endowed with these resources will be able to use them profitably in businesses where they constitute an important source of competitive advantage. That is they are distinctive resources capable of constituting a key successful factor in the portfolio of businesses (Hamel and Prahalad, 1994). In particular, Porter (1985) identifies the fundamental key for successful diversification in process skills, when these skills can be shared across businesses or transferred, thereby producing a competitive advantage. In particular, general managing capabilities have a great relevance in the diversification processes: they are competences that enable a more effective management of the business system.

Empirical studies, showing a positive and statistically significant relationship between product diversification and intensity of R&D (Gort, 1962), as well as between diversification and technological capabilities of the firm (Chandler, 1969 and 1990), widely confirm the relevance of these resources for diversification.

Therefore, it is a matter of evaluating interdependences across businesses and the available resources that are crucial to a successful diversification strategy, by identifying the benefits and costs associated with their use (Prahalad and Doz, 1998). To this aim a comparison of value chains of businesses can offer fundamental information (Figure 4.3).

Sharing activities and resources, mainly among closely related businesses, can give a competitive cost advantage to a diversified firm through:

- a more intense exploitation of a firm's production structure and in general of technical resources;
- a larger scale in buying raw materials, components and services, etc.;
- the sharing of distribution channels, outbound logistic structure, promotional and advertising investments;.
- the sharing of an R&D department and technical and production know-how;
- the sharing and transferring of managerial resources, knowledge and experiences in problem solving.

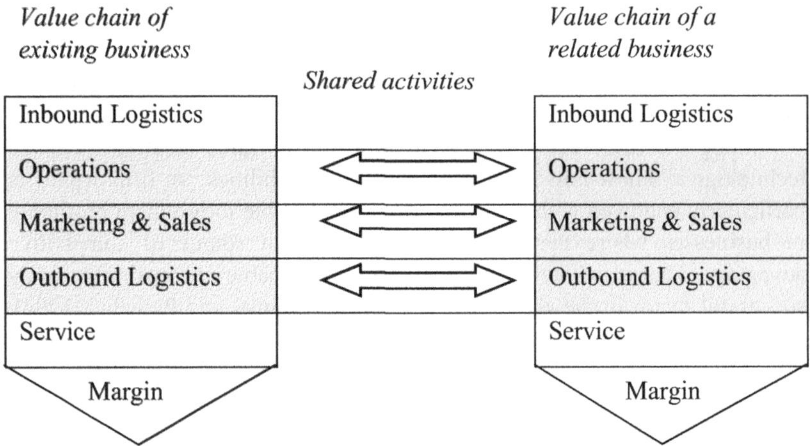

Figure 4.3 Illustrative interrelationships between activities of value chain concerning two related businesses

The importance of scope economies in favouring product diversification strategies is also confirmed by the history of many large enterprises. A clear example is offered by oil companies which diversified their activity by entering the business of alternative energies, mainly leveraging on scope economies generated by the sharing of technological know-how among different energy activities (Teece, 1980).

Summarizing, a firm can have benefits in terms of higher efficiency by diversifying its products when there are tangible and intangible resources that can be used in a number of different activities, without sustaining relevant supplementary costs.

Obviously, the economies of scope are less relevant in conglomerate diversification, which is characterized by the aggregation of quite different activities managed according to a pure financial approach aimed at diversifying risk. This type of diversification that entails a great capability for selecting and controlling businesses allows only the general managing capabilities and synergies of an exclusively financial nature to be exploited.

ADDITIONAL COST OF DIVERSIFICATION: COSTS FOR INTEGRATING DIFFERENT BUSINESSES

In all cases, when evaluating a diversification strategy, it is also necessary to consider the additional costs deriving from internally organizing and managing the new production and distribution activities (Porter, 1985; Collis and Montgomery, 2005). In fact, often a diversification strategy fails because the additional costs sustained for organizing and coordinating a firm's activities are larger than the economies of scope. The integration costs result from these components: coordination, compromise and inflexibility costs.

Coordination costs derive from the need to coordinate different businesses in order to create value by transferring competences and exploiting economies of scope. They arise because managing a shared activity often requires high-cost managers with competence and experience in identifying opportunities and threats in different businesses. High coordination costs come from the number of business units that the firm has in its portfolio: the higher the number of business units, the more complex the coordination among them. Top management has to collect and interpret a large amount of information and that requires extra time to coordinate (i.e. meetings, call conferences, etc.) and a specific experience in order to identify the inefficiencies and the potentialities of the different businesses. The complexity of coordinating a number of business units in a portfolio also requires people dedicated to coordination activities and a specific organization structure to support the general manager in interpreting a lot of different information, taking decisions and controlling the outcome of division managers.

Compromise costs result from suboptimal decisions since two different businesses are sharing some activities or resources. Inflexibility costs are associated with the impossibility for one division to modify its process because of the needs of the other divisions (for example difficulty in reacting to competitors' actions).

In addition to the limits due to resource saturation, a loss of control may also occur as happens in any large organizations in which people opt for a decentralized structure (Chandler, 1969). The greater the organizational costs, the higher the risk that a diversification strategy will incur possible value disruption.

Therefore, the sole existence of scope economies does not justify, per se, entrance into a new business. It is necessary that the business considered singularly is profitable and that the possible economies of scope compensate for the greater integration costs.

A MODEL FOR EVALUATING INTERNAL DIVERSIFICATION STRATEGIES

As we said before, a diversification strategy implies extending the range of products and entry into new businesses. Generally, the changes caused by this decision in the firm structure are relevant. It is a matter of making investments in the production and marketing system, as well as in the logistic and administrative ones. The amount of these investments principally depends on the correlation between the new business and the existing one.

In the case of a related diversification, the investments will be smaller than in the case of a conglomerate diversification, because a part of the existing firm system can be shared with the new businesses.

For evaluating a diversification strategy it is necessary to compare the investment required with the present value of the expected incremental cash flows the firm will be able to obtain over a long period. To rightly estimate the incremental cash flows expected from a diversification strategy, it will be necessary to consider the incremental sales and the margin the firm will obtain from the new business, considering both the competitors' reactions and the dynamics of demand.

Precisely, the *EBITDA* increment produced by a diversified strategy will be:

$$\Delta EBITDA(t) = Q_i\,[P_i(t) - Cu_{,i}]$$

where Q_i, $P_i(t)$ and $Cu_{,i}$ are respectively the sales, the price and the operating unit cost of the new product *i*, also considering the integration costs. If we suppose that the capital expenditure needed to maintain the asset's cash flow for an unlimited period of time is equal to ΔI, the free cash flow from operations, $\Delta FCFO^*$, will be:

$$\Delta FCFO^* = \Delta EBITDA\,(1 - \tau^*) - \Delta I$$

With reference to the required investment $I_{SD}(0)$, it will include the specific plants and machinery necessary for the new product and the interventions on the marketing structure, the sales network and the distribution channels.

Therefore, the value created by a related diversification strategy can be expressed as follows:

$$V_{SD}(0) = \frac{\Delta FCFO^*}{\rho} - I_{SD}(0) \qquad (4.6)$$

with:

$$I_{SD}(0) = I_{PS}(0) + I_{MS}(0) + I_O(0) \qquad (4.7)$$

where, in addition to the known symbols, $V_{SD}(0)$ is the value of diversification strategy; $I_{PS}(0)$ is the investment in the production structure for the new product *i*, $I_{MS}(0)$ the investment in the marketing structure; $I_O(0)$ the investment in organizational structure for coordinating new activities; ρ the cost of capital and ΔI the capital expenditures that are necessary for maintaining the firm's efficiency over time and the assets' cash flows for an unlimited period of time.

Note that the greater the relationship among the businesses, the lower the additional investments and the unit cost of the new product will be. This is due to the economies of scope.

Thus, the net value of a diversification strategy will depend on:

- the additional investment required for entering the new business and managing the more complex organization $I_{SD}(0)$;
- the unit margin (price minus unit cost of product) and the cash flows produced by the investment in the new product;
- the risk of investment and thus the cost of capital (ρ);

In the case of a related diversification, the unit cost of product is mainly affected by the economies of scope; they will have to be relevant and durable over time for a diversification strategy to give the diversified firm a competitive advantage over the competitors already operating in the business into which the firm decides to enter.

Under the above defined conditions a diversification strategy will ensure an increase in firm value, if:

$$V_{SD}(0) > 0 \tag{4.8}$$

In a more general perspective, it is also necessary to consider the opportunity of selling the excess resources on the market, instead of using them through diversification. In effect, it could be more advantageous to sell the excess resources to other firms, obtaining capital or a flow of income for a determined period of time. Let us think about the value of royalties obtained by some fashion companies from the use of their trademark. In other words, the use of the market may provide shareholders with better results than diversification.

Obviously, for this solution to be feasible these resources must be transferable on the market and this must be efficient, so that fair value may be assigned to them. Therefore, high transaction costs will favour diversification processes. On transaction costs and the conditions favouring high transaction costs see the appendix in Chapter 5.

In conclusion, it is a matter of comparing the net value that can be obtained from the diversification with the value obtainable from selling the excess resources on the market, after the relative transaction costs. More precisely, if $V_{EM}(0)$ is the value of the excess resources sold on the market, a diversification strategy will be more convenient than releasing excess resources on the market when

$$V_{SD}(0) > V_{EM}(0) \tag{4.9}$$

Instead, in the case of unrelated diversification (conglomerate) there are no relevant excess resources and thus economies of scope to be exploited when entering different businesses.

Therefore, the conditions for a value-creating strategy will depend on the total new investment required for setting up the new business unit and the opportunities offered by the dynamics of the industry.

RATIONALES FOR DIVERSIFIED ACQUISITION STRATEGIES

A diversification strategy can also be realised through the acquisition of firms already operating in the business into which the firm is interested in entering. This solution presents the advantage of avoiding most of the problems examined before, arising from the entry into a new sector through internal development.

In a related diversification, the creation of value for shareholders will depend on the synergies that can arise from the acquisition and the merger of firms. As we said in Chapter 2, the equity value for shareholders of the acquiring firm will increase when the value created by the acquisition (V_{acq}) is greater than the investment made, which corresponds to the price paid for the target firm (P_B). That is true when:

$$V_{acq} - P_B > 0 \tag{4.10}$$

As we know, the value of acquisition is the difference between the value of the combined firm AB and the value of firm A before the acquisition:

$$V_{acq} = V_{AB} - V_A \tag{4.11}$$

This value is given by the present value of incremental free cash flows from operations obtained by the combined firm ($\Delta FCFO$). More precisely, the combined firm will obtain, as a consequence of the acquisition, an increase of its gross margin ($\Delta EBITDA$). If this incremental margin is larger than the margin produced by the target firm B standing alone, the merger will produce synergies and therefore the value of acquisition will be larger than the value of the target firm standing alone (V_B).

In particular, the synergy gains that can be obtained through a diversified acquisition are the following:

- revenue synergies (ΔR), that is the incremental revenues derived from exploiting new resources;
- costs reduction (ΔC), that is the lower operating cost of products derived from exploiting the interrelationships between the businesses of the merged firms and the divestiture of redundant assets.

As far as revenue synergies are concerned, they arise from the availability of new resources, for example advanced technologies or innovative patents, as well as information or knowledge of markets or well-known brands.

Among these resources the immaterial assets are very important, since they have the characteristic of being useful in other contexts. The firm image and reputation, once they have been developed, also become intangible assets which are useful for promoting all of the firm's products.

For these reasons, the acquisition of a firm can be the best solution for successfully diversifying, first because of the position occupied in the industry by the target firm; second, the quality of its management and the already specialized personnel; and finally, the existing relationships with customers and suppliers.

Regarding cost synergies, we can distinguish among operating, financial and managerial synergies. The operating synergies arise mainly from reducing the redundant resources in activities with strong technological and market relationships. It is a matter of eliminating double structures and assets in all activities of the value chain of products. Financial synergies, expressed by lower financial costs, are mainly due to more convenient contractual conditions generally obtained by a larger firm. That is true both for raising equity and debts. Finally, managerial synergies are represented by lower costs due to the reduction of excess managerial resources as a consequence of the merger.

A MODEL FOR EVALUATING DIVERSIFIED ACQUISITIONS

In analytical terms, for an acquisition strategy to create value for the shareholders of the acquiring firm it is necessary that the value of the acquisition is larger than the price of the target firm. Precisely:

$$V_{SA} = V_{acq} - P_B > 0$$

Applying the general model exposed in Chapter 2, the value of acquisition can be determined as follows:

$$V_{acq.} = \frac{\Delta FCFO^*}{\rho}$$

with:

$$\Delta FCFO^* = \Delta EBITDA\ (1 - \tau^*) - \Delta I$$

and:

$$\Delta EBITDA = EBITDA(B) + \Delta R + \Delta C$$

where, in addition to the known symbols, *EBITDA*(*B*) is the gross margin of firm B standing alone and ΔR and ΔC are respectively the revenue synergies and the cost synergies produced by the merger. Precisely, revenue synergies will depend on the increase in sales and eventually the increase in the price of products as a consequence of the merger (for example of the higher image and reputation of the firm).

Cost synergies will depend on exploiting the interrelationships among activities and the divestiture of redundant assets and the resource redeployments, and eventually on scale economies.

In the more general case where the merger generates synergy gains both for the business unit B and the business unit A, we will have:[4]

$$\Delta R_B = [P_B(0) + \Delta P_B]\,\Delta Q_B + \Delta P_B\,Q_B(0)$$

$$\Delta R_A = [P_A(0) + \Delta P_A]\,\Delta Q_A + \Delta P_A\,Q_A(0)$$

$$\Delta C_B = [Q_B(0) + \Delta Q_B]\,\Delta Cu_B$$

$$\Delta C_A = [Q_A(0) + \Delta Q_A]\,\Delta Cu_A$$

Therefore, the total revenue synergy for the merger will be:

$$\Delta R = \Delta R_A + \Delta R_B$$

and the total cost synergy will be:

$$\Delta C = \Delta C_A + \Delta C_B$$

In conclusion, the incremental margin, $\Delta EBITDA$ that the combined firm will obtain as a consequence of the acquisition of firm B will include the margin of the target firm stand alone plus the synergy gains ($\Delta R + \Delta C$) produced by the merger.

The net value of the diversified acquisition strategy will be as follows:

$$V_{SA} = \frac{\Delta FCFO^*}{\rho} - P_B \qquad (4.12)$$

where P_B is the price of the target firm B.

DETERMINING THE VALUE OF A DIVERSIFIED ACQUISITION: A SIMULATION

For further clarification, let us consider two firms A (acquiring) and B (target) independently operating in different industries and having the financial characteristics indicated in Table 5.3. To simplify the analysis let us assume that the merger of the two firms will produce:

- cost synergies (ΔC) equal to a 8% reduction in the total costs of products sold;
- revenue synergies (ΔR) equal to a 5% increase in total revenues.

Let us also assume that the combined firm has a lower cost of capital (12%) than the target firm standing alone, because of the reduction in risk.

Applying the model shown above, on the basis of our assumptions the value of the combined firm results in being equal to €16,908,333 and the total synergies from the merger result in being equal to €6,575,000, of which €2,875,000 is revenue synergies and €3,200,000 is cost synergies. The increase in value due to the reduction in cost of capital results equal to €500,000.

In fact, the value of acquisition is:

$$V_{acq.} = \frac{\Delta FCFO^*}{\rho} = \frac{1{,}029{,}000}{0.12} = 8{,}575{,}000$$

and the value of synergy gains is:

$$V_{SY} = V_{AB} - (V_A + V_B) = 16{,}908{,}333 - (9{,}333{,}333 + 2{,}000{,}000) =$$

$$= 6{,}575{,}000.$$

If the price of the firm B is equal to €4,000,000, the value created by the acquisition for the shareholders of firm A will be equal to €4,575,000 and the value of synergies transferred to the shareholders of firm B will be equal to €2,000,000 (€ 4,000,000 – €2,000,000). Under our assumptions the shareholders of firm A will find the merger convenient only if the price of firm B is lower than €8,575,000. In fact, this is the value of the target firm standing alone (€2,000,000) plus the value of total synergies produced by the merger (€6,575,000) (Table 4.3).

Table 4.3 Financial data of firms A and B

Variables (€)	Firm A	Firm B	Firm AB combined	Firm AB – Firm A	Synergies
Product price	60	40			
Sales (tons)	100,000	80,000	180,000		
Revenues	6,000,000	3,200,000	9,660,000	3,660,000	460,000
Cost per unit	40	30	40		
Total costs	4,000,000	2,400,000	5,888,000	1,888,000	512,000
EBITDA	2,000,000	800,000	3,772,000	1,772,000	972,000
Tax rate	25%	25%	25%	25%	25%
EBITDA (1 – t*)	1,500,000	600,000	2,829,000	1,329,000	729,000
Capital exp.	500,000	300,000	800,000	300,000	0
FCFO*	1,000,000	300,000	2,029,000	1,029,000	729,000
Cost of capital	12%	15%	12%	12%	
Firm value (1)	8,333,333	2,000,000	16,908,333		
Value of acquisition				8,575,000	
Value of synergies (2)				6,575,000	
Cost synergies					3,200,000
Revenue synergies					2,875,000
Cost of capital synergies					500,000

Note: (1) The value of firm A, B and AB is calculated considering *FCFO* constant for an unlimited period of time. (2) Value of synergies: cost synergies = 512,000 (1 – 0.25)/0.12 = 3,200,000; revenue synergies = 460,000 (1 – 0.25)/0.12 = 2,875,000; cost of capital synergies = (300/0.12) – (300/0.15) = 500,000.

It is easy to demonstrate, using the model above, that if the merger produces a 10% reduction in the total costs of products and a 15% increase in the total revenues, the value of synergies will increase to €13,625,000. Conversely, if cost synergies are equal to an 8% reduction in the total costs of products whereas revenue synergies are equal to zero, the value of total synergies will reduce to €3,700,000 (of which €3,200,000 is cost synergies and €500,000 is the cost of capital synergies).

EVALUATING UNRELATED DIVERSIFIED ACQUISITIONS

An unrelated (conglomerate) diversification can be realised through the acquisition of firms operating in industries which are not related to the original one. In this case, the increase in value of the acquiring firm does not come from cost synergies (eventually only managerial synergies) but mainly arises from the higher operating flows obtained by restructuring firm processes and substituting managers, rather than from cost synergies.

Situations favouring these operations are the following:

- a target firm with a managerial group pursuing objectives which are not coherent with the creation of value for shareholders;
- a target firm with a top management endowed with inadequate competences to run the actual business and the availability of superior managerial competences in the acquiring firm, able to improve the performance level of target firms.

Indeed, managerial capabilities are the determinant resource for the success of conglomerate acquisitions, mainly in industries where the complexity of the competitive environment and the dynamics of evolution processes require high managerial competences and know-how. In this case, the transfer of managerial resources between companies, both purchased and purchaser, can contribute to increasing the economic value of entities involved in the operations of extraordinary management.

Other operations of a conglomerate type can be justified by speculative reasons, market imperfections and asymmetric information. In some cases the possibility of creating economic value depends on the capability of exploiting advantageous prices in the negotiations. In this case a takeover (change of shareholders) is launched by raider investors, when market prices do not mirror the real business value or the value that can be obtained by different managers.

Finally, a conglomerate acquisition can also be realised for reducing variance of cash flows and creating firm value through the reduction of the firm's cost of capital, as an effect of the decrease in comprehensive risk following the diversification in business portfolio. As the capital asset price model shows, diversification lowers unsystematic risk not systematic risk. However, shareholders can also reduce their risk through a diversified portfolio of securities.

THE CONDITIONS FOR SUCCESSFUL DIVERSIFICATION STRATEGIES

The analysis presented above suggests that success in diversification is difficult to obtain, especially in unrelated diversification. As our quantitative models clearly show, a complex interaction among multiple variables is necessary for a diversification strategy to create value for shareholders. Many of these variables are internal to the firm but many are external and their estimate is highly uncertain.

Furthermore, it is necessary to highlight that potential synergy benefits are not sufficient to ensure the success of a strategy; they must be larger than the additional costs of integration of the new activities. Therefore, the success of a diversification strategy also depends on the implementation processes and particularly on how effectively linkages between business units are designed and managed.[5]

With this belief, in the next chapter we will examine the changes required in the organizational structures of firms in order to solve the complex organizational problems that diversification produces, making possible a full deployment of potential synergies.

EMPIRICAL EVIDENCE AND THE THEORY OF DIVERSIFICATION

Many empirical studies have found no significant relation between diversified strategies and firm performance.[6] Some studies have documented that diversified firms have a mean return on invested capital or a market value significantly below that of the portfolios of matched single-business firms (Rumelt, 1982; Berger and Ofek, 1995; Lins and Servaes, 1999; Rajan et al., 2000).

These results do not mean that a diversification strategy itself destroys value, thereby denying that a diversification strategy can create value by exploiting economies of scope and other favourable environment conditions. The phenomenon of over-diversification and other factors may explain a low performance (Markides, 1995; Miller, 2004).

First, the existence of extra profits in oligopolistic markets acts as an incentive for companies to enter markets that are technologically related, even if this is inefficient in terms of costs. High rents can lead to an over-diversification, in the sense that companies end up being more diversified than they would be based on pure cost efficiency. In particular, when the capital market is imperfect, the investment opportunity could arise not for the most efficient producer but for the producer that possesses the funds to finance it. A company endowed with enough funds could diversify in such an industry even though a multi-product production is more expensive than specialization. This motivation arises especially in large companies endowed with relevant capital, and mostly in those industries in which start-up costs are very high.

Second, the interests of managers may spur them towards over-diversification; in fact, they can act in order to favour the dimensional development of the firm through diversification, even reducing the equity value for shareholders. Also in the presence of cash constraints, a manager can be induced to diversify for reducing his/her own employment risk (that cannot be assured) and for increasing the power and prestige more strictly linked to the size of a firm rather than to its profits (Marris, 1964; Marris and Wood, 1972). Agency theory clearly explains why managers would over-diversify (Jensen, 1986; Jensen and Murphy, 1990; Tosi et al., 2000). Assuming that managers act to maximize their utility, not shareholders' wealth, they tend to over-diversify because this strategy is the way to build the size of the firm on which compensation and perquisites are more important than performance. So over-diversification can be explained as a bad governance problem.

Third, managers can overestimate their ability to achieve synergies or at least the fact that synergies take time to be achieved (Miller, 2004). Diversifying can be an easy way to grow rapidly, but is not an easy way to create value as we have already demonstrated.

Finally, diversification can be an attractive option for firms operating in declining or mature industries or with low innovation resources before the diversification, so the lower level ex ante of performance is part of the reason why a diversification discount is observed ex post (Rumelt, 1974; Miller, 2004). Thus, in statistical studies, which do not properly control these effects, a diversified firm may appear to have lower performance even though managers made optimal investment decisions creating value for shareholders.

However, in the last analysis, the key question for us is not whether diversified firms create more value than single business firms, but whether a firm can create more value diversifying than if it does not diversify, and under which conditions.

APPENDIX A4: ECONOMIES OF SCOPE: AN EXAMPLE

As we said above, the economies of scope arise when the cost of jointly producing and selling products X and Y is lower than the cost of separately producing and selling each product X and Y, that is, where the following condition is true:

$$C(Q_X, Q_Y) < C(Q_X, 0) + C(0, Q_Y) \tag{A4.1}$$

When this happens it is cheaper for a single firm to produce both goods X and Y than for one firm to produce X and another to produce Y. Therefore, the diversified firm gains a competitive advantage over the other specialized firms.

To illustrate the economic logic of exploiting the economies of scope, let us suppose the following cost functions of a hypothetical manufacturer of a product X and of a manufacturer of a product Y:

$$C(Q_X,0) = 200 + 0.30\ Q_X \tag{A4.2}$$

$$C(Q_Y,0) = 50 + 0.10\ Q_Y \tag{A4.3}$$

To produce the good X the first manufacturer must sustain a fixed cost of \$200 million and a unit variable cost of \$0.30 for each product. Producing a quantity equal to 500 million units this firm will have a total cost of \$350 million. The second manufacturer must sustain a fixed cost of \$50 million and a unit variable cost of \$0.10 for each product Y. Producing a quantity of 200 million units it will have a total cost of \$70 million.

Now, let us suppose that the first firm X decides to exploit its know-how and its plant capacity adding the good Y, with an increase in fixed cost equal to \$20 million and a unit variable cost of good Y equal to 0.09.

The function of total cost of this firm will be:

$$C(X,Y) = 220 + 0.30\ Q_X + 0.09\ Q_Y \tag{A4.4}$$

If this firm produces a quantity of 500 million units of product X and 200 million units of product Y jointly, it will sustain a total cost of \$388 million. Thus the additional cost for adding product Y to its line is only \$38 million (\$388 million – \$350 million). This will give a competitive cost advantage of \$32 million over the firm Y.

In other words, economies of scope occur when a single firm producing a specific combination of different products is more efficient than specialized firms separately producing one single good.

NOTES

1. This is the Herfindahl – Hirshman index; it equals the sum of the squared market shares of all firms in the market. For its mathematical structure the HH index represents a more informative measure than the N-firm concentration ratio.
2. Porter (1980) considers cost leadership and differentiation strategies mutually excludible: 'firms trying to pursue both, risk ending up "stuck in the middle". For these firms the almost certain result is low profitability. Either they lose clients which ensure high volumes, or they assist in the volatilization of the greatest part of profits in the attempt to compete with firms with lower costs. At the same time, they will lose also those clients that ensure higher margins – the cream of the market – leaving them to firms that have focused on higher margin segments or that have succeeded in a substantial differentiation. The firm that stops in the middle of the ford has probably a less defined business culture, and operates in a conflicting organizational and motivational structure' (p. 42).
3 According to Porter (1985), the interrelationships among the relevant activities of the value chain of business units are the basis of diversification. In particular, sharing activities can lead to a sustainable competitive advantage for a diversified firm, by lowering costs and enhancing differentiation. However, sharing does not necessarily lowers costs unless it favourably affects the other cost drivers of an activity. According to Porter, sharing has the potential of reducing costs if the cost of an activity is driven by economies of scale, learning or the pattern of capacity utilization. Focusing on the firm's activities rather than on firm resources, Porter distinguishes among tangible, intangible and competitors' interrelationships and proposes to analyse the interrelationships between the value chains of different business units.
4. In fact, for the business unit B the revenue synergies will be:
   $\Delta R_B = [P_B(0) + \Delta P_B]\,[Q_B(0) + \Delta Q_B] - P_B(0)\,Q_B(0) =$
   $[P_B(0) + \Delta P_B]\,\Delta Q_B + \Delta P_B\,Q_B(0)$
   And the cost synergies will be:
   $\Delta C_B = [Q_B(0) + \Delta Q_B]\,\Delta Cu_B(0)$.
   It will be similarly for the business unit A.
5. Among the numerous empirical studies on the performance consequences of diversification strategies see: Christensen and Montgomery (1981); Montgomery (1985); Grant et al., (1988); Hill et al. (1992).
6. On this position see Larsson and Finkelstein (1999); Haspeslagh and Jemison (1987); Gary (2005).

5. Vertical integration strategies

INTRODUCTION AND OBJECTIVES

In this chapter we examine the different types of vertical integration strategies and the conditions favouring these strategies.

As vertical integration strategies imply the entry of a company into a different industry, they can be viewed as a particular form of product diversification. Therefore the analysis follows the lines already discussed in the previous chapter with a particular focus on transaction costs as a relevant and specific factor of vertical integration.

After the analysis of advantages and drawbacks in vertical integration with respect to market use, different forms of coordination among firms are considered as effective alternatives to vertical integration. Finally, the conditions for a vertical integration strategy which creates value are defined through an analytical model.

Some fundamental elements of transaction costs theory are presented in the appendix.

TYPES OF VERTICAL INTEGRATION STRATEGIES

Through vertical integration a firm decides to produce raw materials, components or services for its product directly, instead of buying from other firms. Thus, it is a matter of directly carrying out operations or phases in the production cycle which before were carried out by external firms. In this way a firm uses its internal organization rather than the market, moving its activities top stream or bottom stream in the product cycle.

In particular, with upstream integration (backward integration) a firm directly carries out the early phases of the product cycle, thereby obtaining unfinished products or components of its product. On the other hand, with downstream integration (forward integration) a firm integrates the terminal phases of the product cycle or those regarding the selling and the distribution of its product.

In any case, the growth of the firm is realised by adding new production lines, new plants or new commercial structures, so increasing the invested capital and the number of employees.

In economic terms vertical integration causes the increase of the firm's added value, not necessarily the increase of revenues which can remain constant if the total final output does not increase. The extent of vertical integration is generally indicated by the ratio of a firm's value added to its sales revenues.

The potential scope of a vertical integration strategy is shown in Figure 5.1.

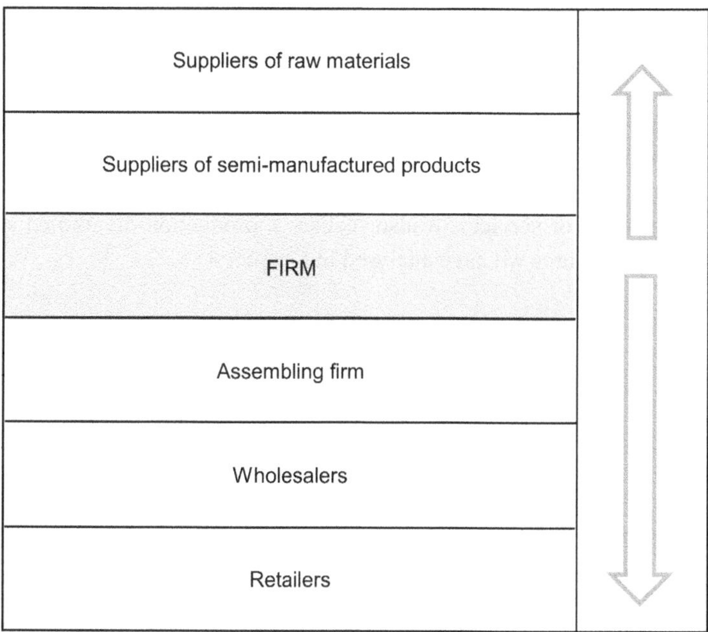

Figure 5.1 The potential scope of a vertical integration strategy

Highly integrated companies are, for example, the major oil companies that own and control their value chain from exploration to the retailing of gasoline (Exxon, BP, Sheel, Eni, etc.) and the major steel companies with their integrated plants (Nippon Steel, Arcelor-Mittal, Thyssen-Krupp, Posco, etc.).

According to the output obtained from the integrated activities with respect to that required from the final output of the firm, the vertical integration can be balanced, partial or exceeding (Grant, 1998; Rispoli, 1998).[1]

A balanced vertical integration occurs when a firm produces internally the quantities of inputs necessary for satisfying its entire planned production flow or all the services necessary for selling the entire production (Figure 5.2). A partial integration occurs when the quantities of inputs produced are smaller than quantities required from the planned production. Finally, an exceeding integration occurs when the quantities of inputs produced are larger than what is required from the final planned production, or when the services realised after the final production exceed the firm's needs and it is necessary to sell them on the market. An exceeding vertical integration can be favoured by profit opportunities in upstream or downstream sectors, or forced by minimum efficient dimensions (MES) of up stream or downstream activities[2] which are larger than those characterizing the firm's activities which are already developed.

In any case, when a firm enters the market with an exceeding production of components or services, it also realises a production-diversified strategy, with all the features we have analysed in Chapter 4.

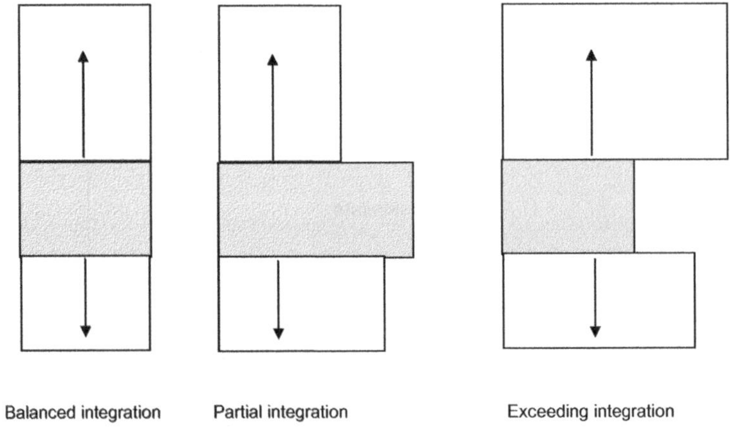

Figure 5.2 Types of vertical integration: partial, balanced or exceeding

RATIONALES FOR INTERNAL VERTICAL INTEGRATION STRATEGIES: COST ADVANTAGES FROM EXPLOITING INTERRELATIONSHIPS AND MARKET POWER

The first condition favouring a vertical integration strategy carried out through internal development is the cost advantage from directly making, instead of acquiring, semi-manufactured items, products and services.

These cost advantages are relevant especially when technological interdependences are present in different phases of the operating cycle of a product, as happens for example in the steel, paper and chemical industries. They mainly reflect differences in technical efficiency when producing items internally and externally. This especially happens with goods requiring high asset specificity, so implying specialized uses for inputs, determining fewer outlets for the outside supplier.

The cost advantage of vertical integration can also be derived from existing excess resources that can be exploited in upstream or downstream activities with respect to those already carried out by a firm. In particular, they can be physical resources, such as plants and logistic structures, as well as intangible resources such as know-how, organization and management capabilities, etc. In addition, the incremental investment required to enter a business may be significantly reduced by sharing some basic assets. As we know, the resource-based view suggests that a firm that owns these or similar valuable and difficult-to-imitate resources can have significant benefits from a vertical integration of activities that allows the exploitation of slack strategic resources.

To these benefits, associated with sharing activities and resources, we must add the advantage that a greater degree of vertical integration gives to capturing the high margins that suppliers or middlemen gain in their businesses. See, for example, the case of Luxottica examined in Chapter 10.

A degree of self-sufficiency can also give significant bargaining advantages with suppliers with a consequent reduction in prices. Not only does it allow the firm to know the cost structure of an item, a component or service, but it makes the firm a competitor of its suppliers or clients, threatening their businesses (Porter, 1984; Prahalad and Doz, 1986 and 1998).

Furthermore, an increased control of the value added chain can provide an opportunity for active price management: a more integrated firm can enlarge, for example, the margin it has at its disposal to fight competitive battles.[3] In particular, the control of critical raw materials and components or of distribution channels can allow the vertically integrated firm to gain a larger market power against its competitors and customers.[4]

RATIONALES FOR INTERNAL VERTICAL INTEGRATION STRATEGIES: ECONOMIZING TRANSACTION COSTS

Above all, vertical integration can be motivated by the high transaction costs that a firm sustains acquiring raw materials, components and services on the market, because of the inefficiency of the supply market and of the opportunistic behaviour of suppliers.

As it is known, transaction costs are the costs a firm has to sustain for stipulating contracts with third parties: costs for defining an agreement, securing its observance and for adjusting and correcting the contract, as well as solving disputes (on transaction costs theory see Appendix A5).

Opportunistic behaviour is favoured by the asymmetry in information between the buyer and seller of materials, semi-manufactured products, components and services. In particular, the information asymmetry means a lack of fair information about the quality of the product and the guarantee of the seller's correct behaviour. All this means that a buying firm has to sustain an additional cost for obtaining the necessary information and that can reduce the advantage of buying raw materials, components or services.

Thus, vertical integration is convenient where a firm has to sustain high transaction costs when using the market, for reducing the asymmetry in information and the opportunistic behaviour of suppliers that exists when there are few operators. According to Williamson (1975 and 1981), failures of intermediate product markets are the most important factors underlying the vertical integration of firms. In fact, if the market works well with low transaction costs, and prices are not distorted by the monopolistic position, market intermediation is to be preferred to internal organization of activities by virtue of specialization advantages.

Conversely, vertical integration is preferable to market use when the variability of external conditions requires a continuous adaptation both of the design of a product and of production programmes.

In these cases long-term contracting does not solve the problem either. In fact, there is the risk that all parties can interpret the contractual ambiguities to their own advantage, so as to require expensive forms for the contract to be respected, including appealing to justice. To avoid disputes, all possible implications deriving from a contract should be specified before, but this even if were possible it may be quite expensive.

Also a sequential and adaptive decisional process, realised through a series of short-term contracts, presents high risks if the investments are firm specific, since its interruption would cause high costs and regaining the investment would be impossible. In addition, this situation can offer one of the negotiators a position advantage, due to the specificity of resources, when the contract has to be renewed, especially when the post contract situation is characterized by a small number of competing firms.

In these situations, a vertical integration strategy can reduce costs and risks, allowing a process of sequential adaptive decisions to be taken through internal adjustments made by the different organs of the firm and coordinated in order to reach a common objective. Hierarchical structures can allow better results to be obtained, overcoming the problem of limited information and making the rise of opportunistic behaviour easier to combat.

Uncertainty and asymmetry in information between buyer and seller also increase the transaction costs. The information market represents an example of market failure, because frequently in this market one party knows relevant facts for deciding a transaction, while the other can acquire information only by bearing high costs. These are situations which are characterized by considerable uncertainty as well as a high risk of opportunistic behaviour by the more informed party. The malfunction of the information market can also derive from incomplete information. In other words, even if all parties had the same information, a different interpretation of that information would be possible, due to the difficulties in deducting all possible implications. That makes it difficult to find an agreement in a context of limited rationality, contractual opportunism and specificity of resources.

As is known, high transaction costs are mainly related to two types of fundamental resources: know-how and specialized and indivisible physical goods.

As far as know-how is concerned, high transaction costs derive from problems related to the identification, diffusion and organization of information. In the market of owned know-how there is an objective difficulty in identifying an exchange opportunity reciprocally advantageous for the two parties, because of the situation of imperfect information. Furthermore, a market exchange may not work, due to problems regarding the diffusion of the value of the information to the buyer. In some cases there is a problem of information block related to the protection of technological know-how ownership. This happens because the value of know-how is unknown to the buyer while he does not possess the information, but, when he possesses it, he has already obtained it without cost (Arrow, 1974). Finally, a third transaction problem arises because know-how shows strong characteristics of learning by doing, which makes necessary for human capital its transfer.

As far as specialized and indivisible goods are concerned, high transaction costs derive from the limits and the difficulties in using them on the part of other companies. In these cases the advantages of diversification are clear. Any time an indivisible good is the common input for two or more production processes, joint production will provide scope economies. The extensive use of an item in more than one field of activities is the source of possible scope economies; for example, a machine already used to shape the bodyworks of cars can be used for shaping the bodywork of trucks.

In conclusion, these conditions increase the transaction costs of market contracts and make it convenient to integrate vertical activities:

- a small number of suppliers or clients (typically bilateral monopoly);
- specificity of investments and resources;
- imperfect information and high risk of opportunistic behaviour.

Empirical evidence also confirms that vertical integration strategies are strongly influenced by both transaction costs and firm-specific resource (Monteverde and Teece, 1982; Leiblein and Miller, 2003).[5]

A classic example of high transaction costs leading to market failure and vertical integration is represented by the relationship between General Motors and Fisher Body for the supply of car bodies (Klein et al., 1978; Williamson, 1986a). General Motors used to buy all its car bodies from Fisher Body, according to a contract which established the prices on the basis of costs and a margin and required all disputes to be solved by a binding referee. Through this agreement the two parties intended to avoid opportunistic behaviour. As a matter of fact, this relationship worked well until the demand for car bodies largely exceeded the forecast. When this happened, GM evaluated the price agreement as no longer being satisfying and asked Fisher Body to reduce prices and to build a new plant adjacent to a GM car assembly factory, for reducing transport costs and stocks.

Fisher Body refused, fearing that, once the factory was built, it would have had no real choice other than to supply GM, because of the high costs involved in finding and switching to a new customer. Thus the risk of opportunistic behaviour from GM, once Fisher Body had made the investment, led to a market failure. To reach the objective of reducing production costs by having the production plant built next door, GM bought Fisher Body and merged its activity, thereby realizing a vertical integration expansion (Collis and Montgomery, 2005).

Another classic case of vertical integration led by high transaction costs is offered by Alcoa (Perry, 1980; Williamson, 1986). This firm succeeded in expanding into the aluminium market by virtue of exploiting a big plant close to Niagara Falls. In order to ensure a constant supply of raw materials, this firm also invested in bauxite mines in Arkansas, only maintaining a few external suppliers. Later, thanks to the introduction of new refining processes, the internal raw material production became insufficient to satisfy the entire need of the firm. So the firm found it worthwhile to eliminate all external suppliers through a further upstream vertical integration (Chandler, 1990). The acquisition of bauxite mines was motivated by the particular nature of the raw material that differs from one deposit to another and therefore requires a specialized refining plant, so determining a tight bond between the supplier and the user. Another reason was the dispersion of bauxite mines in a vast territory. In conclusion, the specificity of assets and the specificity of location led Alcoa to integrate upstream activities, so avoiding the high transaction costs for using the market.

ADDITIONAL COSTS OF VERTICAL INTEGRATION STRATEGIES

When deciding to grow through vertical integration, it is also necessary to consider the costs of integrating new activities. In fact, the costs of integrating activities can reduce the advantages obtained through the internal production of semi-manufactured products, components and services. In particular, the major sources of vertical integration costs are the following:

- differences in the optimal scale of operations between different stages of production;
- strategic dissimilarities between businesses requiring different technological processes and product development capabilities;
- activities with different organization capabilities in vertical adjacent activities, for example in marketing and production;
- rigidity of firm structure and a disadvantage in responding quickly to new product development opportunities that require a new combination of technical capabilities;
- need for coordinating and controlling internal activities.

These costs are relevant especially when the efficient dimension of activities in the different stages of the production cycle are very different, due to technical and market reasons. When this situation occurs, a firm has to increase its production capacity in the different phases of the cycle in order to balance the flow of output, sustaining the investments needed.

The high costs for coordinating activities can derive from the consequent modifications of firm structure: the new functions can require an internal restructuring of the organization, with the assignment of new positions of responsibility, the need to develop new knowledge and to motivate subordinates, etc. A balance sheet of benefits and costs of vertical integration is shown in Table 5.1.

According some authors (Stigler, 1951), vertical integration strategies are more frequently adopted by firms operating in the introductory or declining phases of an industry, while outsourcing processes normally prevail in the development and maturity phases. This happens because in the introductory phase of an industry, firms have problems in adjusting products both on technological or organizational terms; firms do not have the necessary experience for defining the relationships needed with suppliers, managing the procurement channels and organizing their production processes. So in this phase of the industry's development cycle vertical integration is the most convenient solution, because it avoids the high transaction costs for widespread difficulties in defining reliable market relations, these markets not being large enough to allow specialized firms to be present.

Conversely, in the development and maturity phases of an industry there is a widespread tendency towards vertical disintegration. The increase in market size and the diffusion of technological knowledge frequently makes it convenient to outsource a part of the production operations or phases to external specialized firms, capable of making them more efficiently. The expansion of the market tends to favour the increase in the number of these firms, reducing the risk of monopoly and of an excessive market power of suppliers. Finally, in the declining phase of an industry, the fall in demand makes the vertical integration convenient again.

Table 5.1 A balance sheet of effects from vertical integration

Potential benefits	Potential costs
Cost reduction for higher technical efficiency	Cost of coordinating and integrating new activities
Control over value added and margins capture	Loss of focus on a business
Reduction of transaction costs	Loss of flexibility

ALTERNATIVES TO VERTICAL INTEGRATION: FORMS OF COORDINATION AMONG FIRMS

Instead of realizing a formal vertical integration, a firm can establish various forms of coordination with its suppliers and clients, for assuring stability in procuring semi-manufactured products, components and services (Harrigan, 1986; Rispoli, 1998).

These relations take the form of a permanent and organic collaboration with some suppliers for the delivery of semi-manufactured products, components or services, which are of relevant importance for the firm. Close relationships can be made also with clients like wholesalers and retailers. Consider, for example, the relations among the large production companies in the automobile, clothing and furniture industries and the network of their retailers. All these relations can be regulated by sale with exclusive or franchising contracts or others forms (quasi-vertical integration).

In other cases, the relationship between the production firm and its suppliers or clients can take the form of a contractual integration, through long-term agreement for the delivery of raw materials, semi-manufactured product components or for the distribution of non-exclusive products. These situations are very frequent in some sectors of the chemical, oil and steel industries where, given the specificity of production plants, it is of fundamental importance that a firm can secure the necessary raw materials, components and services.

Finally, a firm can establish systematic and durable exchange relations with suppliers of products or services, which are autonomous but linked together by a substantial and continuous convergence of interests (a network of firms). In this case, a firm frequently assumes the role of "central or leader firm" of the net (Vaccà,1986; Lorenzoni, 1990 and 1992). The external units of the network are essential partners for the central firm that can operate effectively because they are in charge of a consistent part of the planned work. The network structure allows the leader or central firm to lighten the business system, so obtaining greater flexibility.

Obviously, for these relations to work effectively, it is necessary for the leader firm to be capable of managing the complex relationships among firms, carefully defining the different roles of suppliers. In this context, the leader needs to choose with great attention the firms participating in the network, considering their capability of securing a stable relationship over a long period, rather than just satisfying its short-term requirements. With this purpose in mind, the leader has to select suppliers capable of developing the existing technical know-how, fitting the new requirements of being leader, due to the dynamics of technological progress and the changes in consumer behaviour (Lorenzoni, 1990).

By building a network of firms, a leader firm can realise a real integration among firms remaining autonomous but being linked together for exchanging information, promoting innovation and developing common and related businesses. When building this structure, a leading or guide firm must pursue on one hand a strong differentiation among the different suppliers and on the other realise a high level of integration and stability of relations, justly defining the requirements, autonomy and role of each participant.

In conclusion, it is a matter of realizing a system of agreements among firms that makes it possible to exploit all possible economies of specialization, at the same time limiting the transaction costs, through stable relationships and a concurrence of interests between suppliers and a leading firm. The economic factors that make it more convenient to adopt this solution, rather than a formal vertical integration, are lower integration costs and cost advantages deriving from supplier specialization, as well as lower transaction costs by virtue of stable relationships and the concurrence of interests among the firms within the network.

A MODEL FOR EVALUATING INTERNAL VERTICAL INTEGRATION STRATEGIES

The decision to produce, rather than buy, semi-manufactured, components or services requires a careful evaluation of the investments needed and the results expected in terms of lower operating costs.

Summarizing, a vertical integration strategy can create value by:

- reducing the unit cost of the product by virtue of suppliers' margin capture and sharing assets and excess resources, ΔCu;
- saving in transaction costs, ΔC_T.

Conversely, a vertical integration strategy will produce additional costs for coordinating a larger number of internal activities.

To be precise, the *EBITDA* increment produced by a vertical integration expansion will be:

$$\Delta EBITDA = \Delta Cu\, Q(0) + \Delta C_T - \Delta C_O$$

where, in addition to the known symbols, ΔC_O are the additional costs of internal coordinating activities, and $Q(0)$ the production, assuming a balanced integration.

If we suppose that the capital expenditure needed to maintain the asset's flow for an unlimited period of time is equal to ΔI, the additional free cash flow from operations, $\Delta FCFO^*$, will be:

$$\Delta FCFO^* = \Delta\ EBITDA(1 - \tau^*) - \Delta I$$

Therefore, in analytical terms, the net value of a vertical integration strategy V_{SV} will be:

$$V_{SV}(0) = \frac{\Delta FCFO^*}{\rho} - I_{SV}(0) \qquad (5.1)$$

where, in addition to the known symbols: $I_{SV}(0)$ is the total investment that is necessary for vertical integration and ρ the cost of capital.

Usually, transaction costs are high when the specificity of resources is high and the variability of external conditions requires continuous production adaptation. As far as the investment is concerned, the implementation of a vertical integration strategy can require not only investments in the production system, but also in the marketing and administrative structures because of the greater size and complexity of new activities within the firm.

For a vertical integration strategy can create value for shareholders, it must be:

$$V_{SV}(0) > 0 \qquad (5.2)$$

In general, a vertical integration is favoured by the imperfections of markets and the absence of commercial rules that ensure correct behaviour from the operators, as well as the absence of parties with a high reputation to defend and who are thus less subject to opportunistic behaviour. Where the costs of using the market are high, due to the high specificity of resources and the small number of suppliers, vertical integration, that is the organizational hierarchy, offers a comparative advantage in costs.

Conversely, market is preferred where the specificity of resources is low and the incidence of bureaucracy costs for the internal governance is relevant.

DETERMINING THE VALUE OF AN INTERNAL VERTICAL INTEGRATION STRATEGY: A SIMULATION

In order to determine the value of a vertical integration strategy, we present a simulation of the model illustrated above. We assume that a firm A presents the following data at the initial time $t = 0$:

- sales: $Q(0) = 100{,}000$ tons;
- product price: $P(0) =$ €60;
- unit cost of product: $Cu =$ €40

As a first hypothesis the management estimates the following effects of a vertical integration strategy carried out through internal development:

- investment required: $I_{SV}(0)$ = €4,000,000;
- annual capital expenditure: ΔI = €400,000;
- expected reduction in unit cost of product: $\Delta Cu = 25\%$;
- saving in transaction costs: $\Delta C_T = 15\%$ of operating costs;
- additional costs of coordinating internal activities: $\Delta C_O = 10\%$ of operating cost.

Under these assumptions, the *EBITDA* increment produced by the strategy will be:

$$\Delta EBITDA = 0.25(100{,}000 * 40) + 0.15\ (100{,}000 * 40) - 0.10\ (100{,}000 * 40) =$$

$$= 0.30\ (4{,}000{,}000) = 1{,}200{,}000 \qquad (5.3)$$

Therefore, the value of the vertical integration strategy will be:

$$V_{SV}(0) = \frac{\Delta EBITDA(1-\tau^*) - \Delta I}{\rho} - I_V(0)$$

$$V_{SV}(0) = \frac{1{,}200{,}000\,(1-0.25) - 400{,}000}{0.10} - 4{,}000{,}000 = 1{,}000{,}000$$

Simulation proves that the value of the strategy is highly sensitive to the reduction in total product costs. For example, with a 20% reduction in costs from a higher productivity from the integrated process, with the other effects remaining constant (15% saving in transaction costs and 10% additional cost of coordinating internal activities), the value created by the strategy is equal to €–500,000 (hypothesis two).

Finally (hypothesis three), with a 30% reduction in costs from higher productivity (15% saving in transaction costs and 10% additional costs of coordinating internal activities), the value created by the integration strategy will be equal to €2,500,000.

Therefore, using the model, it is possible to evaluate the effectiveness of the strategy under different hypotheses about the effects on costs, as is shown in Table 5.2.

Table 5.2 The value of a vertical integration strategy: a simulation

	Hypothesis 1	Hypothesis 2	Hypothesis 3
Sales: $Q(0)$	100,000	100,000	100,000
Unit product cost: Cu	40	40	40
Operating costs	4,000,000	4,000,000	4,000,000
Investment required for strategy	4,000,000	4,000,000	4,000,000
Reduction in product cost	25%	20%	30%
Saving in transaction costs	15%	15%	15%
Additional cost for coordination	10%	10%	10%
$\Delta EBITDA$	1,200,000	1,000,000	1,400,000
Tax rate %	25	25	25
Cap. exp: ΔI	400,000	400,000	400,000
FCFO	500,000	350,000	650,000
Cost of capital	0.10	0.10	0.10
Value of strategy	1,000,000	–500,000	2,500,000

RATIONALES FOR VERTICAL ACQUISITION STRATEGIES

A vertical integration strategy can be realised also through the acquisition of firms producing raw materials, components or services utilized by the acquiring firm. This solution allows the acquiring firm to avoid most of the problems arising from the entry into a new sector through internal development. The creation of value for shareholders will mainly depend on the synergies that will arise from the acquisition and the merger of firms.

In particular, the synergies that can be obtained through a vertical integration strategy come from costs reduction, that is:

- the lower operating cost of products, which derive from exploiting the interrelationships between the businesses of the merged firms and from the divestiture of redundant assets and resources;
- the saving in transaction costs.

Obviously, it is necessary also to consider the negative effect of the additional costs that the merger has to sustain for coordinating new activities.

Since vertical integration strategies are a particular form of related diversification strategies, the analysis developed in Chapter 4 largely applies to this subject.

A MODEL FOR EVALUATING DIVERSIFIED ACQUISITIONS

In analytical terms, for a vertical acquisition strategy to create value for the shareholders of the acquiring firm it is necessary that the value of acquisition is larger than the price of the target firm B. Precisely:

$$V_{SA} = V_{acq} - P_B > 0 \tag{5.4}$$

Applying the model shown in Chapter 4, the value of acquisition can be determined as follows:

$$V_{acq.} = \frac{\Delta FCFO^*}{\rho} \tag{5.5}$$

where $\Delta FCFO^*$ is the incremental free cash flow from operations obtained by the combined firm

More precisely,

$$\Delta FCFO^* = \Delta EBITDA\ (1 - \tau^*) - \Delta I \tag{5.6}$$

In its turn, the incremental free cash flow will depend on the increase in the gross margin ($\Delta EBITDA$) which is equal to the gross margin produced by the target firm B standing alone plus the synergies generated by the merger.

If ΔC is the cost synergy, ΔC_T the saving in transaction costs and ΔC_O the additional coordination costs, the increase in the gross margin will be:

$$\Delta EBITDA = EBITDA(\mathrm{B}) + \Delta C + \Delta C_T - \Delta C_O \tag{5.7}$$

Therefore, the net value of the vertical acquisition strategy will be as follows:

$$V_{SA} = \frac{\Delta FCFO^*}{\rho} - P_B \tag{5.8}$$

where P_B is the price of the target firm B. In particular, the value of synergies created by the merger will be:

$$V_{SY} = \frac{\Delta C + \Delta C_T}{\rho} \tag{5.9}$$

The larger the reduction in the operating costs of products, which derive from exploiting the interrelationships between the businesses of the merged firms, and the larger the transaction costs, the larger the value of synergy will be.

APPENDIX A5: THE THEORY OF TRANSACTION COSTS: FUNDAMENTAL CONCEPTS

The theory of transaction costs (Williamson, 1975) concerns the costs of markets and hierarchies, which are considered the two extreme forms for organizing economic activities. This theory has as its central focus of analysis the transaction that occurs when a good or a service is transferred through a technologically separable interface: a phase of activity ends and another phase starts (Williamson, 1981).

Whereas market transactions involve an exchange between autonomous entities, hierarchical transactions are ones for which a single administrative entity spans both sides of the transaction. In this case, some form of subordination prevails and typically consolidated ownership is obtained (Williamson, 1975).

Transactions have to be organized and that implies, in any case, costs. According to the transaction costs theory, the prevailing of one or another form of economic organization (hierarchical organization or market) principally depends on the level of transaction costs that each of them implies, not just on the level of production costs.

Transaction costs can be divided into two categories: ex ante and ex post transaction costs. The first, referring to the phase of contract stipulation, have to be sustained for defining an agreement and securing its observance; the second, concerning the phase of its execution, have to be sustained for adjusting and correcting the contract and solving disputes. If there were an effective and inexpensive juridical system, ex post costs would not be relevant, but this situation is considered non real and therefore refused.

Transactions in markets are different from transactions in hierarchical organizations (that is firms), so it is necessary to analyse their different characteristics and the consequent costs, in order to choose the most efficient organization.

The main factors affecting transaction costs can be divided into two groups:

- human factors;
- environmental factors.

Human nature strongly affects the behaviour of people when making economic transactions, on the basis of two fundamental characteristics: bounded rationality and opportunistic behaviour.

Bounded rationality means that economic agents are rational in intention, but not entirely rational in their decisions, because of their limited knowledge and limited capacity for elaborating information. That implies that they have an inherent difficulty in managing complex problems and in realizing totally comprehensive contracts. When the costs of overcoming this limitation are very high, a hierarchical organization can represent the best choice, because it allows the transaction costs to be economized.

Opportunistic behaviour means that economic agents tend to pursue self-centred interests in order to cheat or defraud the counterpart. It is a matter of actions directed at twisting and hiding information from the other party, taking advantage of asymmetric information (Williamson, 1981). This behaviour determines an increase of uncertainty on the results of a contract, which are influenced not only by incomplete definition of covenants but also by the opportunistic behaviour of one counterpart.

In this context, a hierarchical organization (like a firm) presents a clear advantage with respect to the market, since the possibility for opportunistic behaviour is considerably reduced, being transactions realised internally with more efficient means for controlling and quickly solving possible controversies among agents of the same firm.

Among the environmental factors, the following characteristics of a transaction have a relevant influence on the choice between market and hierarchical organizations: the asset specificity, the frequency of transactions and the uncertainty.

Asset specificity means that an asset can have only a specific use, that is that it is dedicated to a particular application. In such cases, the party that has made the investment is vulnerable to exploitation, because the asset would be worthless in another application. The specificity of an asset, on one hand, offers the firm the advantage of a higher specialization, and on the other hand it reduces the possibility of alternative uses of the asset. Since an asset is not easily transferable to other activities, the cost sustained for its acquisition can be recovered only by using it for a long time. That creates a strong bind to suppliers of raw materials, increasing the negative effects of contractual opportunism and so determining high transaction costs.

Specificity of assets also modifies the conditions of markets after the transaction from competition to a bilateral relation. Consider a firm that has customized its production facility to use a particular grade of raw material supplied by a producer. The firm considered has no alternatives other than using raw materials and thus it is bound to the supplier and to its price and delivery policy. It can look for a different supplier, but that implies reconfiguring its production facility for the new grade of material, which would be very expensive.

Types of asset specificity include: location, physical and human capital (Collis and Montgomery, 2005).

- Location specificity occurs when buyers and sellers locate the fixed asset in close proximity to minimize transport and inventory costs.
- Physical asset specificity occurs when one party or both parties in a transaction invest in equipment that has a particular, limited use.
- Human capital specificity occurs when employees develop skills that are specialized to a particular relationship or a given organization.

Specific investments create a small number bargaining problem. After making such an investment, the purchasing firm is unable to negotiate freely and equally with other potential suppliers; it is locked into buying from only a few suppliers and often only one. This gives the supplier the bargaining power that allows it to act opportunistically and so leads to the market failure.

Uncertainty about all possible future eventualities makes it impossible or prohibitively expensive to write a contract for the duration of the asset to simply prevent opportunistic behaviour. This contract would have to cover an enormous number of clauses and it would cover all possible contingencies that are impossible to evaluate, also for the bounded rationality, that is, the physical limits to which the mind can process information.

Finally, it should be noted that high transaction frequency increases the likelihood of market failure. Frequent transactions repeatedly expose a firm to holdup, so that haggling and negotiation occur more often. To eliminate these costs and remedy to the market failure, vertical integration is often necessary. In contrast, for only one or for occasional transactions, such as a public construction project, vertical integration is unlikely (Table A5.1).

In summary, transaction cost theory identifies durable relationships involving asset specificity, uncertainty and high frequency of transactions as conditions for market failure. Whenever market exchange for the sale (or purchase) of a good or a service fails, a firm will have to establish some form of hierarchical control over the transaction.

According to this approach, vertical integration and diversification strategies can be regarded as winning solutions to economize on transaction costs, by harmonizing interests and permitting more efficient incentives and control processes to be activated. Table A5.1 summarizes the main factors affecting transaction costs.

Table A5.1 The main factors affecting transactions costs

Group of factors	Factors affecting transaction costs
Human factors	Bounded rationality
	Opportunistic behaviour
Environmental factors	Asset specificity • Location specificity; • Physical asset specificity; • Human capital
	Frequency of transaction
	Uncertainty

NOTES

1. We have a balanced integration when Q(t) = Q(0), an exceeding integration when Q(1) = Q(0)(1 + β) and a partial integration when Q(1) = Q(0)α with $\alpha < 1$.
2. The minimum efficient scale (MES) of production is the smallest output at which average cost is minimized. If a firm A requires a number of units of an item 1 smaller than MES, to meet its own need, it cannot benefit from economies of scale. Instead, if a firm realises in-house production of the item through an exceeding vertical integration it can fully exploit minimum cost. However, to increase the production of this item profitably, beyond its own needs, this firm would need to find buyers to sell its excess items.
3. On the vertical integration strategies as an instrument to increase the market power in pharmaceutical industry see Pammolli (1996).
4. However, on this subject there is still a theoretical controversy; see in particular Moomaw (1974); Grant (1998).
5. On the choice between in-house production and external purchase see Monteverde and Teece (1982). In their empirical study on the automobile industry these authors show that transaction costs have an important consequence for the vertical integration, thereby supporting the transaction cost paradigm.

6. Designing the appropriate organizational structures for implementing growth strategies

INTRODUCTION AND OBJECTIVES

The focus of this chapter is on the organizational structures and the control systems used to manage large and diversified companies, as a result of growth strategies. In effect, given the increasing complexity in the management of a firm, especially for processing information and taking decisions, it is necessary that the expansion of activities is effectively accompanied by the appropriate changes in organizational structures, in order to obtain the desired outcomes.

The main organizational structures and control systems that are used to help executives in enhancing firm performance and creating value through growth will be described, as well the mechanisms used by companies for governing their operations and aligning various parties' interests, especially those of top-level executives and the firm's owners. In effect, governance mechanisms can influence a company's ability to successfully implement strategies and thereby facilitate reaching competitive advantage and creating value. As many cases suggest, the proper use of organizational structure and accompanying control systems improves firm value. So, it is a fundamental challenge for top level managers to select the appropriate organizational structure and controls for an effective implementation of chosen growth strategies. In the appendix some fundamental elements of organizational design are reiterated to make the analysis more effective.

DESIGNING AN ORGANIZATIONAL STRUCTURE FOR IMPLEMENTING HORIZONTAL EXPANSION STRATEGIES

In order for a firm to create value it is necessary for the organization structure to be coherent with the strategies to be implemented and contingent with the tasks a firm must perform where interacting with its environment (Abell et al., 1993: Hitt et al., 1997; Collis and Montgomery, 2005).

More precisely, in the case of horizontal expansion, top management has to design an organizational structure to effectively manage a larger amount of activities and to rule and control the greater complexity of relationships determined by a firm which is larger in size.

An effective solution can be obtained by adapting the functional organizational structure. As is known, this organizational structure is characterized by a firm system divided into units which specialize in the different activities carried out: production, human resources, logistics, marketing, R&D, etc. These functional units are assigned to line managers to which the entrepreneur or the general manager delegates decisional power regarding the operating management. Because the differences in orientation among organization functions can impede communications and coordination, the central task of a general manager is that of integrating the decisions of individual business functions for the benefit of the entire firm (Galbraith, 1977).

A typical functional structure is represented in Figure 6.1.

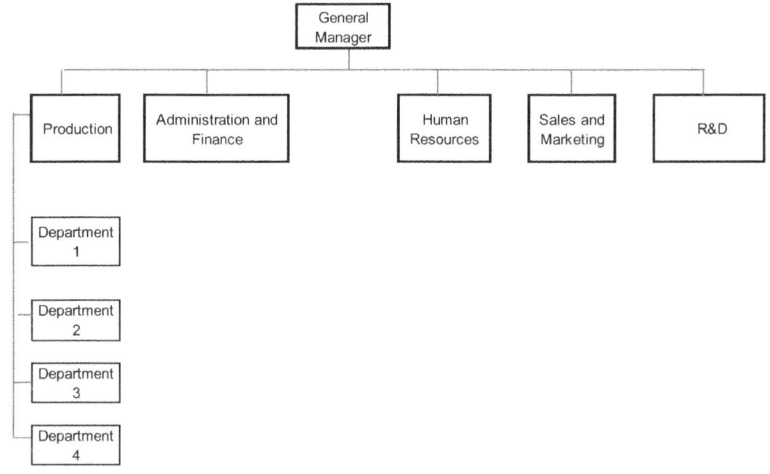

Notes:

(1) Most functions are decentralized but Administration and Finance may have centralized staff that works closely with the general manager;

(2) Production and Sales and Marketing are often the main functions.

Figure 6.1 A typical functional organization structure

Figure 6.1 shows a chart (or a graphic description) of the organizational model of a firm, providing essential information about the sub-units into which the firm is divided, the number of hierarchical levels, the coordination relationships among them and the top management, etc.

A horizontal expansion strategy can be implemented effectively by enlarging the functional departments, such as production, marketing or sales, to manage the additional activities: a new line of production, a new factory or a new sales network, etc. Obviously, horizontal expansion can also require adapting other functional departments, for example logistics, R&D and administration, requiring an increase in their operating capacities, plant, machinery and personnel.

Through a functional organization structure a firm can benefit from economies of scale at a single function level and from specialization, concentrating specialists in the same unit thereby creating a "critical mass" which is necessary for having up-to-date knowledge and competences in every functional activity. In particular, the concentration of resources that share homogenous specializations in the same organization unit means using these resources in the most efficient manner and avoiding their dispersion in many different structures.

An example of a functional organization structure adopted by a firm for implementing an international expansion strategy is represented in Figure 6.2. The expanding activity abroad required enlarging the production department with a new organizational unit and developing the marketing department to enable a more efficient sales policy. It was also necessary to increase coordination and control activities with a larger and more complex central structure, with new functions, such as finance, engineering, etc. and a larger staff office for the CEO.

To improve the level of horizontal coordination among functional managers, which is a classical limit of functional organizational structures, the use of joint committees, task forces or teams can be provided for conflict resolution, by increasing horizontal relationships and favouring a continuous flow of information.

More significant changes in the organization structure are necessary when the expansion of a firm takes place in geographic markets and countries having different characteristics with respect to the existing firm markets, to the point of requiring differentiated promotional and selling activities. In these cases a functional structure, such as that represented in Figure 6.2 can present important drawbacks for successfully dealing with additional local issues and for coordinating and monitoring day-to-day operations. For example, more complex organizational structures may be necessary for supporting an international expansion. They must be designed to effectively integrate the work of the manufacturing and marketing personnel operating in each country, thereby facilitating the tailoring of products and services to local markets.

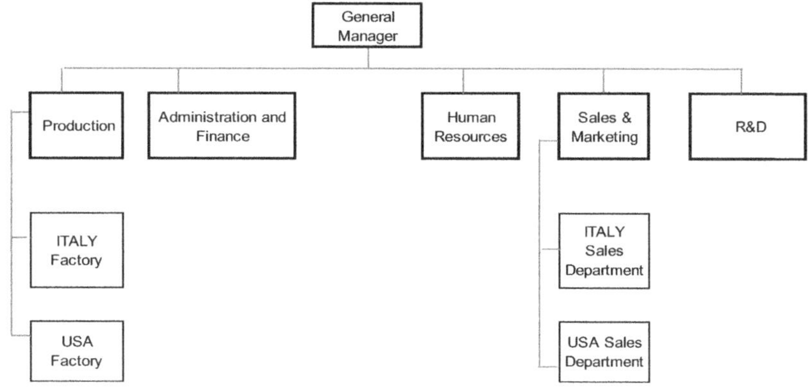

Figure 6.2 A functional organization structure for the implementation of horizontal expansion strategies

In these cases, a worldwide geographic area structure can be used successfully to implement a multi-domestic expansion strategy. This structure is an organizational form in which national interests prevail and the manager's efforts are facilitated to satisfy different local needs. To this aim, some local market areas are selected and organizational units are formed to satisfy customer sales and service needs. These market areas are assigned to area managers who are responsible to top level managers for their results. Company headquarters usually coordinates financial resources among different country area managers, defines the general investment policy and controls activities and results (Figure 6.3).

This is an organizational structure that can progressively evolve in a divisional structure, as differences in products become bigger and bigger.

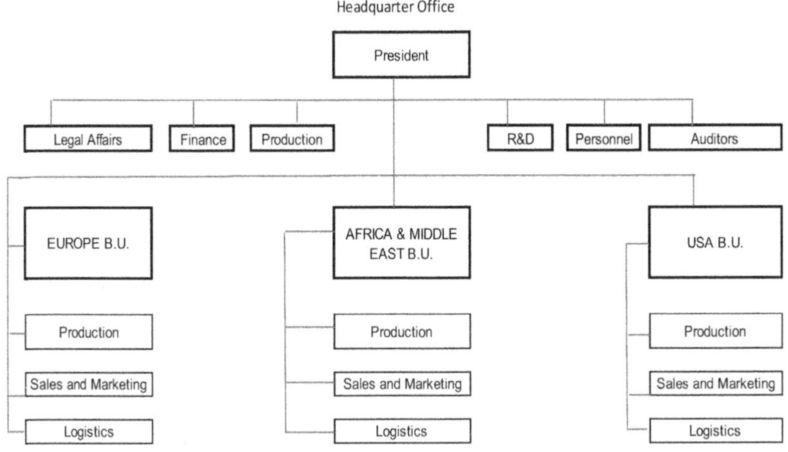

Figure 6.3 A worldwide geographic area structure for implementing horizontal expansion

DESIGNING A PRODUCT DIVISIONAL STRUCTURE TO IMPLEMENT DIVERSIFICATION STRATEGIES

The limits of a functional organization structure are clearly evident when a firm grows through product-diversifying strategies. In these cases, efficiently managing a number of products and markets is quite difficult, because of the complexity of knowledge required and the need for coordination and integration of different firm functions.

The most effective and efficient solution for ruling a diversified company is represented by a multidivisional organization structure (*M*-form).[1] It is a matter of dividing the firm system into sub-units which are relatively autonomous (divisions), each of them specialized in operating a determined business (a line of product).

To this purpose, in each sub-unit or division all the necessary resources have to be concentrated in order to produce, sell and distribute the assigned product or line. The decisional power for day-to-day operations regarding each business will be delegated by the chief executive manager (CEO) to a specialized organ, the divisional manager, both having the power to rule the division (business unit) as well as having the responsibility for its performance (Figure 6.4). The corporate CEO will maintain the decisional power concerning strategic resources, over all human and financial resources, assigning them to different divisions, according to their specific needs in order to reach the ultimate company objective. The corporate officer will also define the corporate strategy and carry out coordination and control activities on the various divisions. For this job, staff organs have to be provided comprised of personnel specialized in the various firm functions.

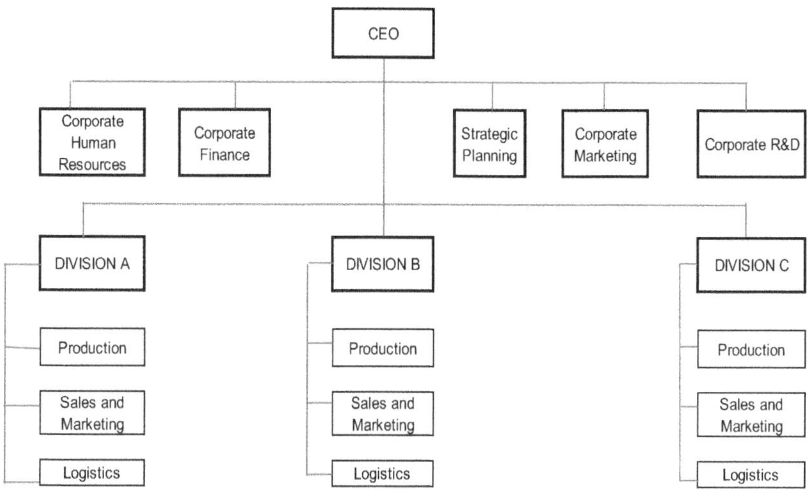

Figure 6.4 A typical multidivisional structure

This organization structure, designed around businesses rather than functions, will allow the firm to remove the disadvantages of a functional structure in highly product-diversified firms. In fact, under such conditions a functional structure is not capable of elaborating the amount of information the firm receives from the different markets, and of making forecasts and suitable evaluations, or of deciding the tasks each product line has to carry out. Conversely, a divisional structure is capable of quickly elaborating information and making decisions since each business is followed by a manager who has the authority to run the division and to use the assigned resources being responsible for the outcome. A divisional structure also allows competences and resources to be assigned more efficiently, according to the specific needs of each business. It offers high managerial and organizational flexibility, enabling an easier coordination of activities within each division and an easier focus of the activities on cost and time objectives.

In addition, the corporate office, being relieved of the operating problems of different products and markets, can concentrate its activity on strategic decisions involving the company in its totality, as well as on the coordination and control activities of different divisions.

In particular, the corporate office assumes a fundamental function for an efficient end effective management of a diversified corporation. It must correctly choose where to develop a resource, so as to exploit economies of scale and be of a sufficient size to support specialists. In this way it has also to avoid the duplication of effort when multiple divisions make investments in similar resources or skills. For example, basic R&D will be concentrated in a corporate organizational unit, while the amount of experimentation on new knowledge processes and practices will be assigned to product divisions.

The corporate office must be capable of taking advantage of opportunities for sharing resources among the different businesses. It is a matter of sharing resources and skills across businesses to create value and at the same time minimize the interference in the autonomy of divisions. For example, this could be obtained by using best demonstrated practices, such as supply chain management, sharing a sales force, or by using a common component manufacturing facility or a joint distribution system.

Besides centralization, a number of structural links have to be used to foster cooperation among divisions. Direct contact between division managers must be frequent in order to encourage and support cooperation and the sharing of strategic assets. Temporary teams or tasks forces may also be formed around projects to achieve the desired levels of coordination.

A particular organizational structure for managing a diversified company is the so-called strategic business unit form (SBU). This organizational structure consists of at least three hierarchical levels, with the top level being corporate headquarters, the next level SBU groups and with the final level being the divisions, grouped by product relationships within each SBU. Thus divisions within groups are related, but groups are largely unrelated each to other. Within the SBU structure, divisions with similar products or technologies are organized in order to achieve synergy. Each SBU is a profit centre that is controlled by the firm's headquarters office (Figure 6.5).

This organizational structure is principally appropriate for large diversified firms, where complexity is a reflection of the size and diversity of the firm's operations.

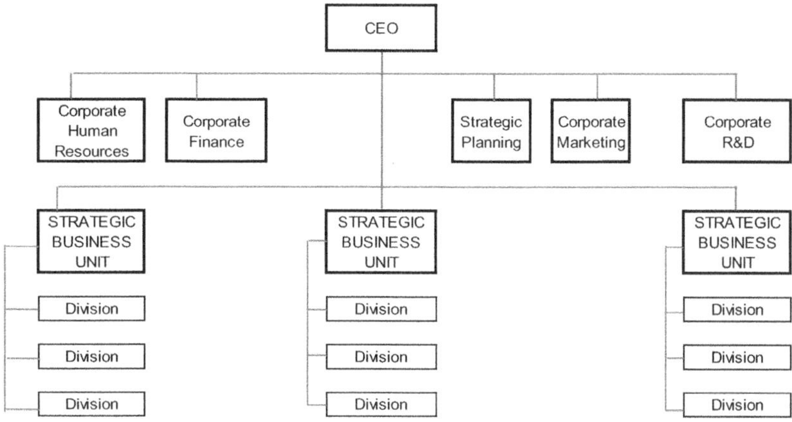

Notes:

(1) Structural integration among divisions within SBUs, but independence among SBUs;
(2) Strategic planning is the most prominent function of CEO corporate office;
(3) Corporate staff serve as consultants to SBUs and divisions.

Figure 6.5 SBU form of a multidivisional structure for implementing related diversification strategies

When defining the organizational structure of a diversified company, the choice of the mechanism by which coordination among divisions has to be achieved is of utmost importance.

There are no universal solutions for the process of introducing coordination into an organization. The common mechanism of coordination is given by the hierarchy in which a superior guides the direct subordinates and imposes the objectives to be reached. Other solutions are represented by joint committees of divisional managers and corporate office managers. Nonetheless, introducing coordination in autonomous businesses can be very difficult, because it requires the divisional managers to limit their power and to accept the choice of optimizing corporate not divisional performance, thereby changing attitude and behaviour. Transferring resources and skills across businesses can also be a powerful way to create value, for example moving highly skilled managers.

In effect, a multi-business corporation will not be able to justify its existence if it cannot be organized to leverage valuable corporate resources across the divisions. This may not only reduce costs, but also provide greater benefits to the customers, improving the level of differentiation in products.

In conclusion, a divisional structure generally makes it easier to cope with the organization complexity of a large diversified company operating in different businesses; it increases the flexibility of the business system and its capability of quickly adapting to the changes in the external environment. In fact, the divisions have a substantial authority for their own decisions, so these may be made by those who possess the relevant knowledge, while minimizing the amount of information transfer to the hierarchy. Moreover, each division or business unit can also be specialized in succeeding in its own competitive environment; in particular it can develop and tailor its resources and shape the details of its own organization to fit its unique tasks. Finally, the motivation of managers who are given control of an entire division will be high, particularly when they are rewarded directly for the performance of that unit.

The limits of this organizational model are given by the larger need for resources in divisions and the corporate office, due to the central organizational structure required for the corporate activity of leadership and coordination. Thus, a divisional structure may lead to inefficient functional activities, for example with multiple sales forces calling on the same customer. The advantages of functional specialization are reduced and the risks in managing the different divisions increase.

When more initiative, power and autonomy is necessary, the business divisions can be transformed into autonomous firms, controlled by a holding company but open to the market (holding organizational structure). In this case, the companies controlled by the holding remain autonomous from a legal point of view, so as to create a stronger incentive to innovation and a more competitive behaviour, with a less centralized bureaucratic structure (Figure 6.6). In this way each company becomes a source of ideas, resources and knowledge, can operate successfully in its business and be better exploited by the entire group structure (Boari et al., 1989).

This organizational structure is more flexible than a divisional structure, but at the same time maintains a control link with the peripheral firms. The central direction also gives these firms strategic and operating responsibility, delegating to them the management of the selected business area and the pursuing of innovative development lines.

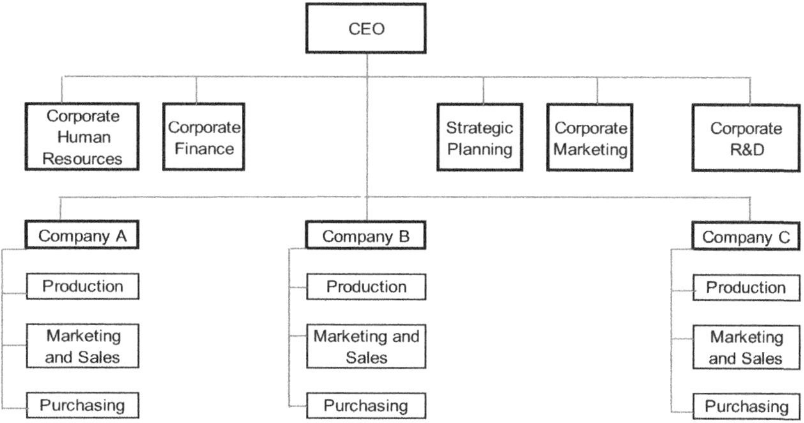

Notes:

(1) Structural integration among companies, but independence among them;
(2) Strategic planning and human resource assignation are prominent functions of CEO corporate office;
(3) Culture emphasizes cooperation between companies.

Figure 6.6 A multidivisional structure for the implementation of a related product diversification strategy: the holding structure

This organizational structure will be used especially when it is necessary to improve the development of the entrepreneurial capacity of unit business managers through a more direct rapport with the market, so stimulating capabilities of learning and innovating, in order to exploit all the opportunities offered by the business. The greater operating flexibility of this structure is also increased by the fact that the business units are juridical distinctive companies. Generally, this organization is set up through the breaking up of existing divisional units or through the acquisitions of companies which maintain their own autonomy as distinctive companies.

DESIGNING A MATRIX ORGANIZATIONAL STRUCTURE TO IMPLEMENT DIVERSIFICATION STRATEGIES

An alternative solution for the implementation of a related diversification strategy can be represented by the matrix organization structure.

As is known, a matrix organization is an organizational structure in which there is a dual structure combining both functional specialization and business product or project specialization. In other words, resources are stably organized in functional departments according to their field of competence, but they are temporarily assigned to a product or project operating unit. In this way, they offer their specialist knowledge under the supervision of a product or project manager, but at the same time keep their position inside the functional department to which they belong (Figure 6.7).

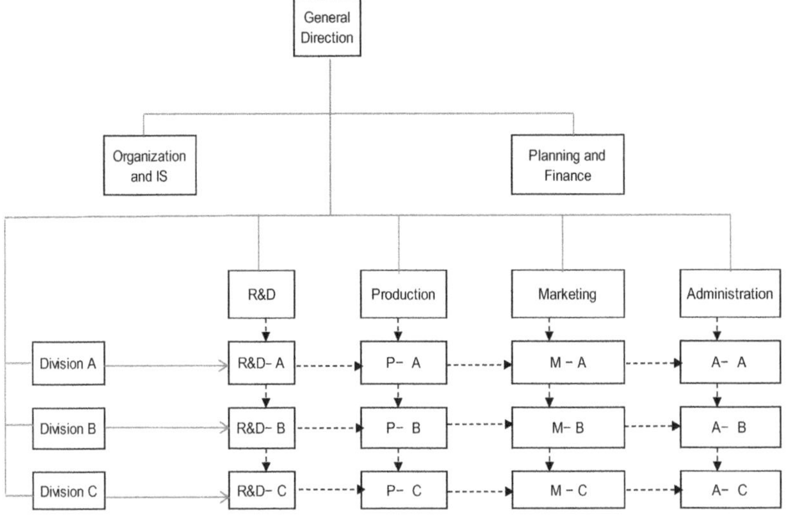

Figure 6.7 A matrix organization structure for the implementation of related product diversification strategies

Although complicated, effective matrix structures can lead to improved coordination among firm's various products or projects activities. To this aim it is necessary that functional managers recognize the authority of the project manager for decisions which have an impact on project–product results, costs and realization time. The product or project manager has to handle his group, address and coordinate the assigned resources and ensure the advancement and the final results. The functional directors, on the other hand, are responsible for planning, managing and developing their pool of specialists and the methodologies used.

Such a structure can be useful for implementing growth strategies especially in companies which temporarily need organization units for realizing different complex products or large works or projects over a period of time. It can also improve the chances of professional growth, creating more managerial positions and at the same time improving communication and decisional autonomy. The matrix structure allows the development of highly specialized resources and the coordination of the resources needed by new projects or products requiring rapid adjustments to environmental changes and quick elaboration of information.

In multinational firms the matrix structure is generally used for combining functional managers and country managers. This structure accommodates both viewpoints and also provides for the efficient utilization of resources while integrating their deployment across units (Figure 6.7). This structure gives good results if the three following conditions occur:

- the existence of products or projects contemporarily demanding specialist knowledge and a unitary vision of the development process;
- product or project activities requiring a system with a great capacity for elaborating information;
- the possibility of employing human resources with flexibility, so that each specialist can work on a particular task and at the same time be ready to move to another task.

However, matrix organization also produces ambiguity and complexity because individuals have to balance the demand of two superiors who do not often operate in a consistent way. To solve the difficulty of handling complex products or projects with a double command system, the matrix structure can be adapted in different shapes, according to the division of power between department and project managers.[2]

The so-called weak matrix or functional matrix is a form characterized by product–project managers not having the hierarchical power over the human and technical resources working on the product or project line; such authority remains within the power of the functional director. Conversely, in the so-called strong matrix, the balance of power is in the favour of product–project managers: departments supply human and technological resources to the project manager, only maintaining the role of specialist and technical support.

ORGANIZATIONAL STRUCTURES TO IMPLEMENT CONGLOMERATE STRATEGIES: THE HOLDING STRUCTURE

Generally, to implement an unrelated (conglomerate) diversification strategy the most appropriate solution is a holding organization structure. In this case different businesses are managed by separate and autonomous firms controlled from a legal point of view by a holding company and competing one against the other for corporate capital (Figure 6.8).

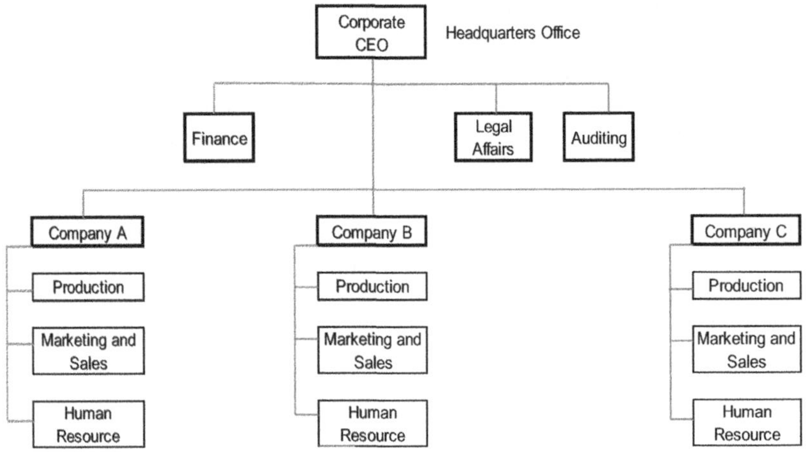

Notes:

(1) Corporate headquarters has a small staff;
(2) Finance and auditing are the most prominent functions of corporate headquarters;
(3) Companies are independent and separate for financial evaluation purposes;
(4) Companies retain strategic control but compete for corporate financial resources.

Figure 6.8 A holding organization structure for implementing unrelated product diversification strategies

To gain benefits from efficient resource allocations, companies must have separate identifiable profit performance; the headquarters office does not intervene in single firms affairs except to audit operations and to discipline managers whose firms perform poorly. The corporate office sets the rate of return targets and monitors the results of controlled companies. The entire organization emphasizes competition rather than cooperation between member companies of the group.

CONTROL SYSTEMS IN LARGE AND DIVERSIFIED COMPANIES

In large and diversified companies specific control systems are necessary for preventing the abuse of delegated decision-making authority by functional managers and by managers of autonomous divisions, as well as for providing coherence to the corporation activity by deploying resources across otherwise structurally differentiated units.

Even if these systems may add bureaucracy to functional activities and the entrepreneurial activities of divisions, and may therefore cause additional costs, such systems are a powerful discipline for managers and a necessary instrument to enable the interests of the whole company to be able to prevail over the interests of functional units or product divisions (Collis and Montgomery, 2005).

The most pervasive form of corporate control is the use of systems and processes that continually monitor and regulate the behaviour and performance of functional units or divisions. Typically these are the budgeting, strategic planning, capital budgeting and measurement and reward schemes installed by corporate managers.

First, it is a matter of setting the targets that the sub-unit managers have to reach and monitoring the progress towards those targets, rewarding and motivating the managers to meet the targets. Second, the system must also include mechanisms to intervene when performance deviates from acceptable bounds, assisting or also replacing the unit manager, rather than adjusting the goal. The value of the system lies in setting an appropriate incentive structure for managers and a control mechanism for intervening when performance is not reached. To this regard, control systems have to be differentiated on the basis of the characteristics of the organization unit and the emphasis on outcome or behaviour control.

A system based on outcome control means that managers are evaluated on the outcome of activities assigned. That requires structuring the organization into autonomous and self-contained organization units and aligning responsibility and managerial authority as closely as possible. Conversely, managers will be improperly incentivized and motivated if they are held accountable for events and actions beyond their control. That is of particular importance for divisional managers. To this aim it is necessary to select an appropriate performance measure for evaluating divisional executives. Most firms use one or very few financial measures of performance: some of them focus on measures of accounting profitability such as return on investment (ROI), while others have installed value-base measures. The approach used in this book reveals our clear preference for this last measure.

However, outcome control is the most appropriate control system when there are simple interdependencies among divisions and when there are few exogenous influences on the business outcome. Conversely, this system is less feasible when there are complex interdependencies among divisions. In these cases a behaviour control system is more effective. It consists of monitoring multiple operating and financial measures of performance, such as delivery lead times, reject rates, sales statistics, and cash flows as well as qualitative goals. Obviously, it does not allow the results of divisions to be evaluated, but it permits solving the agency problem, by directly evaluating the behaviour of divisional managers. In this control mode the role of corporate officers becomes more similar to a coach rather than a monitor; they offer constructive advice and criticize behaviour in a way that improves the decisions of divisional managers.

In practice, most firms use elements of both systems, placing a relative emphasis on one or the other according to the characteristics of their activities and markets.

CONTROL SYSTEMS AND INCENTIVES FOR AVOIDING MANAGERS' OPPORTUNISTIC BEHAVIOUR

In small and medium firms there is a combination of property and governance functions in the entrepreneur. Usually an entrepreneur defines strategies and directly runs a fundamental operational activity, such as production, sales or administration and finance, according to his competences. Managers, when they are present, have strictly operating functions, which are generally of a specialist nature.

A firm's growth produces a radical change in this governance system, because a progressive delegation of decisional power from property to managers is necessary for managing a larger sized firm and a more complex set of activities. But, when decision rights are delegated, self-interested managers may act in a way that maximizes their interests at the expense of shareholders' interests. As a consequence when property (principal) delegates decision making to managers (agent), adverse results of self-interested behaviour can occur (agency costs).

The extreme situation is where the property and governance of a firm are totally separate. The property, largely fractionated, delegates decision rights to managers, only maintaining the right of defining general objectives and controlling the outcomes. So, management concentrates not only on the operating decisions but also on the strategic decisions regarding the development of the firm (the so-called managerial company).

Because the property objectives may be different from the manager's objectives, management that favours growth only for satisfying personal objectives and destroys equity value needs to be avoided.

Given the conditions of information asymmetry in favour of managers and the objective difficulty in controlling manager activity, due to the shortage of information and the complexity of data, it is necessary to carefully discipline the internal relationship between property and management. For this reason, a system of behaviour rules and incentives must be defined in order to reduce or mitigate the intrinsic divergence of interests between property and management and the consequent agency costs, so that the objective of creating value for shareholders can be constantly pursued.[3]

In order to reach this objective, that is avoiding the opportunistic behaviour of managers, it is necessary to have certain mechanisms such as the setting up of a board of directors composed of expert members, in addition to proprietors, and powerful control organs, such as an internal control committee, audit company, etc. On a different plane, the definition of incentives for managers bound to firm performance can represent an important instrument for manager objectives to meet those of the proprietors.

Finally, we must remember that the efficiency of the financial market can play a fundamental role in reducing manager behaviour that conflicts with shareholders' interests, thereby reducing the equity value. This situation can cause a hostile takeover from new investors interested in restructuring the company and creating value, removing the current managers (Marris, 1964; Marris and Wood, 1972).

APPENDIX A6: THE FUNDAMENTAL ELEMENTS OF ORGANIZATION DESIGN

While referring to specialist texts in organization for a more complete and exhaustive analysis of these topics (Galbraith 1977; Mintzberg, 1983; Gerloff, 1985; Daft, 2001), we recall that the fundamental elements of organization design are the following:

- formal organizational structure;
- planning and control systems;
- human resource management.

Formal organizational structure is a firm's formal role configuration, procedures and authority and decision-making processes through which a firm is managed. Designing an organizational structure means defining the subsystems into which the firm system is divided, as well as the organs to which the decisional power for managing the subsystems is assigned. For this purpose, each organ can be conceived as a temporal system which receives, elaborates and communicates information to others organs, either subordinate or superior. Therefore a business system can be represented through a set of organs linked together by hierarchical and coordination relationships.

Through the organizational structure top management determines what a firm does and how it works. So a firm can create value only when the firm's selected structure is congruent with its formulated strategy (Hitt et al., 1997; Collis and Montgomery, 2005). Thus, as firms evolve and change their strategies, new structural arrangements are required.

As is known, the most frequently used organization structures can be delineated in three basic models:

- functional;
- divisional;
- matrix structures.

A functional structure is characterized by a firm system divided into operating units specializing in certain functional areas, generally phases of the business process. These functional units are assigned to line managers to which the general manager delegates decisional power regarding the operating management. The functional structure offers relevant advantages to a one-business firm:

- it promotes an effective organization of the main technical, marketing and administrative activities needed for carrying out the business process;
- it facilitates communication and interaction between specialists with the same background and professional interest;
- it favours in-depth analysis and fast solutions of relevant management problems creating an environment that motivates operators.

A divisional structure is characterized by a firm system divided into units linked to certain products or product lines. These sub-units are relatively autonomous in operating a determined business (a line of product); the decisional power for day-to-day operations regarding each business are delegated by the chief executive manager (CEO) to the divisional managers who have the power to rule the division and the responsibility for its performance. The CEO maintains the power over corporate strategy and the assigning of resources to divisions.

A matrix structure is characterized by a firm system divided into units specializing in functional areas and projects. To be more precise, the firm system is both divided into functional units specialized in various groups of activities, production, marketing, logistics and so on, and into different specialized product or project units, each with a temporarily assigned group of specialists of various business functions. This solution permits matching the advantages of the functional and product–project models, especially when temporary teams or task forces have to be formed around products or projects. However, it is necessary also to consider that the double authority system, typical of the matrix structure, has some drawbacks: it can cause ambiguities, stress and conflicts among the personnel.

A hybrid organization structure can be found in different sectors to adequately resolve managing problems connected to various innovative processes and different environment conditions. For all organs to work as a consistent system, so that their impact is interactive and mutually reinforcing, it is also necessary for the planning and control systems to be designed in such a way that objectives are clearly defined and assigned to different organs. In this way the behaviour of one reinforces the behaviour of others rather than creating conflict.

In addition, human resource management will have a significant importance in implementing strategies and creating value. In particular, the incentive system will have to reward the different organs on the basis of their performance, without hindering the necessary cooperation. In fact, managerial behaviour results from the complex interplay of all the organizational elements that affect individual motivations. Therefore they must be designed as a coherent system so that the impact is mutually reinforcing, making it possible to reach the various objectives while creating value for shareholders.

All that given, no single design is optimal for every corporation or strategy, but the characteristics of an effective organization must be coherent with the environment in which the company operates, as well as with the competitive forces and the strategies to be implemented (Chandler, 1969).

Therefore, in order to implement a successful growth strategy, it is necessary to define the appropriate change of the organizational structure to achieve an effective management of large and diversified companies. In other words, the organizational structure must evolve in its response to the new managerial and organizational needs caused by the implementation of growth strategies.

Principally, the existing organizational structure must be changed because it no longer provides effective coordination and control for successfully implementing growth strategies. In fact, a structure's ineffectiveness typically results from an increase in firm size and level of production diversification; in particular, strategies involving a greater level of diversification demand relevant structural changes in organization.

NOTES

1. Chandler's study of strategies and structures of large American firms documented the M-form development as an innovative response to coordination and control problems that large firms such as DuPont and General Motors had during the 1920s, using functional structures to implement diversification strategies. Chandler's studies showed that these firms found significant difficulties in coordinating the conflicting priorities of the firm's new and different products and markets, while using a functional structure. On this topic, see Chandler (1969) and Sloan (1963).
2. The matrix structure has been successfully used by many corporations such as IBM and Unilever which adapted it to their own objectives and characteristics.
3. On the importance of incentive contracts as a response to the moral hazard problem see Milgrom and Roberts (1992).

7. Limits to firm size

INTRODUCTION AND OBJECTIVES

As described in the previous chapters, a company can grow by expanding the scale and scope of its activities within an industry and entering into new businesses or industries. Now, the question is: is there a limit to the size of a firm?

A satisfactory answer to this question requires defining what the appropriate boundaries are for a firm in each direction of its possible expansion, horizontal, vertical and conglomerate, and which activities and businesses should be retained inside and which should be pursued by other means.

In this chapter we try to give a satisfactory answer following the general principle that a firm should perform an activity or compete in a business only if it possesses the resources that provide a competitive advantage, so as to generate value for shareholders. In this context, the determinants of the firm size are on one hand the opportunities offered by industries and on the other the availability of suitable resources and the capacity for improving them.

LIMITS IN EXPANDING FIRM SIZE WITHIN AN INDUSTRY: THE HORIZONTAL BOUNDARIES OF THE FIRM

Internal limits to horizontal expansion come from a shortage of resources for managing a larger sized firm and the increasing complexity of organizational structure, especially in the case of international expansion. External limits to the expansion derive from the dynamics of aggregate demand and from the force of competitors in the industry.

Finally, limits to horizontal expansion are imposed by the antitrust Authorities, in order to impede the emergence of a firm with a dominant position in the industry, capable of cancelling any competition in the market, and therefore seriously damaging its customers.

As shown in Chapter 3, the capability of creating value through horizontal expansion strategies principally depends on the economies of scale in the industry. Economies of scale are present whenever large-scale production, distribution or administrative processes have a cost advantage over small processes. In these cases, a firm exploiting economies of scale can drive out its smaller rivals and increase its supply, market share and margins.

Therefore, the presence of economies of scale in an industry affects the size of firms favouring internal development strategies and M&A operations. That explains why in some industries, such as aluminium production, cement, steel and chemical-based products, a few large firms account for an extremely large share of industry sales and there are virtually no viable small firms.

However, the possibility of achieving a long-term advantage in a market through horizontal expansion strategies generally reaches a limit due to the diseconomies of scale that is the increasing average cost as output increases beyond a certain scale of activity.[1]

Diseconomies of scale can arise for a number of reasons, the most relevant of which are the following (Besanko et al., 1996):

- rising labour costs;
- spreading of specialized resources;
- bureaucracy costs and agency costs.

First, larger firms generally pay higher wages compared to smaller firms, because they are more unionized than smaller firms. That progressively reduces the advantage of expanding the scale of activity.

Second, the expansion, spreading specialized resources to several activities, reduces the effectiveness of these resources, making costs rise as production runs up against capacity constraints. In other terms, if a specialized resource input is a source of advantage for a firm, the expansion of activity and operations without duplicating the input may overburden the specialized input with a consequent reduction in performance.

Finally, larger firms generally have increasing bureaucracy and agency costs. As the firm grows, difficulties in monitoring and communicating with workers increase too. So a firm has to adopt work rules to ensure that workers do not slack off. While these rules may lead workers to perform specific tasks as desired, they may also stifle creativity and lead workers to feel detached from the organization. Drawbacks are typically associated with the bureaucracy of large-scale organizations that impede efficient information processing.

However, probably the greatest costs of larger firms are what are called agency costs.[2] They are costs that arise where individuals act in their own self-interest rather than acting to maximize corporate performance. The increasing size of a firm generally favours a divergence of interests between shareholders and managers and between the general manager and functional executives.

The resulting behaviour may involve simply slacking on the job, but it will more likely involve actions to reach targets that trigger managers' bonuses even at the expense of corporate profits. Such behaviour incurs both additional production costs resulting, for example, from inappropriate decisions, as well as the governance costs of the monitoring and control systems, such as budgets, capital expenditure approvals and HR reviews set up to prevent such behaviour. To these costs we must add the expenses involved in the design and operation of any incentive scheme required to align the interests of division managers with those of the shareholders. This is necessary in order to minimize self-interested behaviour that cannot be prevented by direct monitoring.

Finally, limits to firm size within an industry are set by the antitrust laws.

LIMITS IN EXPANDING FIRM SIZE: THE VERTICAL AND SCOPE BOUNDARIES OF THE FIRM

Growing through vertical integration and diversification strategies meets limits due to the capabilities of creating competitive advantage positions and a sustainable value exploiting in-excess resources. As shown in Chapters 4 and 5, for vertical integration and diversification strategies to be able to create value it is necessary that the benefits are larger than the costs produced, also considering the cost of capital.

In the context of vertical integration strategies, benefits and costs must be analysed considering the activities to be performed inside the firm rather than accessed on a market. In this case, benefits will derive from economies of scope and from reducing transaction costs, while increasing costs will derive from a more complex corporate hierarchy.

In general terms, activities should be performed inside the firm if the corporate hierarchy is more efficient than conducting them through a market exchange. According to this view, a vertical integration strategy will create value when a company hierarchy is more efficient than the market, that is, when the organizational arrangement minimizes the sum of production and governance costs. Therefore, the vertical boundary of the firm will be principally determined by the economies of scope and the hierarchy costs associated with the activities concerning the production phases of the existing products.

The same principle of comparing the costs and benefits of various organizational arrangements applies equally to diversification strategies. In this case hierarchy costs increase in a significant way as the firm expands its scale by entering into new businesses.

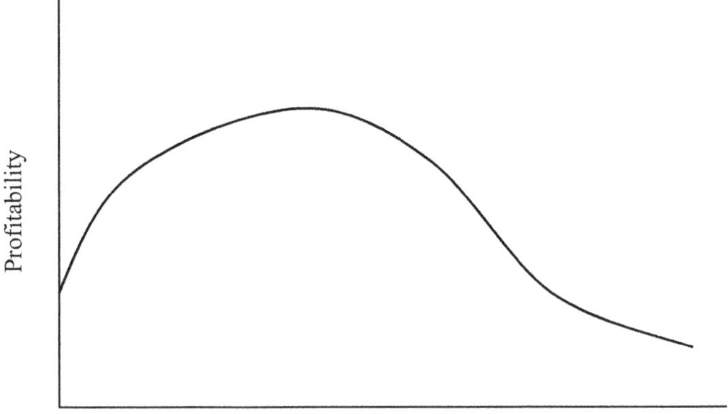

Figure 7.1 The relationship between diversification and performance

In particular, these costs derive from the bureaucracy necessary for providing efficient information processing to solve the difficulties that the corporate executive has in leading a corporation operating in a number of businesses and in controlling businesses that may have different dominant logics (Figure 7.1).

Frequently, in diversified firms the greatest costs of a corporate hierarchy are agency costs. As a firm increases the number of businesses, the expenses of minimizing self-interested behaviour by the direct monitoring of division managers progressively increase, as well as the expenses for aligning their interests with those of the corporate office, through appropriate incentive (variable compensation and stock options).

In conclusion, limits to firm size occur when the economies of scope become minimal or non-existent and the expenses of hierarchy become high. When this happens, a vertical integration or a diversification strategy is no longer consistent with the creation of value for the shareholder. Rather than incur the agency costs of operating a new division or department inside the corporate hierarchy, it will be more convenient to employ outside specialized firms. Therefore, the dimension of a firm is determined by the relative costs of administering business transactions within the firm and there is a limit to how much a firm can grow creating value.

Empirical studies support this theory. They present increasing evidence that firms often lose some of their efficiency and earn declining rents when they grow, diversifying away from their core business. In particular the scope of diversified firms is limited by the transferability of firm-specific resources and skills. As a consequence, they reduce their diversification by refocusing on their core business to improve profitability after over-diversification strategies (Ollinger, 1994; Markides, 1995).

THE ROLE OF CAPITAL MARKETS IN LIMITING THE GROWTH OF A FIRM (CAPITAL MARKETS DISCIPLINE)

In the previous points we discussed how managers should behave for maximizing the firm's equity value through growth strategies. In this context, the limit to firm size only depends on the ability to create value, given the environmental opportunities and threats.

For that really to happen, it is necessary for shareholders to check the behaviour of senior corporate executives through appropriate corporate governance systems capable of limiting the managers' freedom and aligning executive objectives with those of the shareholders.

Conversely, managers can be induced to implement growth strategies capable of quickly expanding a firm, thereby satisfying their personal motives or hubris, but destroying equity value. Similar behaviour is quite frequent. It is sufficient to consider the high number of acquisitions made in the 1970s and in the 1980s that rapidly increased the size of many companies but destroyed value for shareholders.

The efficiency of capital markets plays an important role in disciplining corporate executives' behaviour. In particular, takeovers can be an imminent threat for companies quoted on the stock markets and realizing poorly performing growth strategies. This threat can limit firm diversification when this strategy does not create value; in case of unrelated and unprofitable over-diversification, managers will be induced to sell off many of their unprofitable businesses, focusing on the firm's core business. Conversely, aggressive takeovers will happen followed by sell-offs of business units and substantial fractions of the target over-diversified firm.

By the end of the 1980s investment banks and LBO funds took over a number of conglomerates without any size restrictions and then obtained value by breaking them up and selling part of the existing divisions on the market (Ollinger, 1994; Shleifer and Vishny, 1994; Collis and Montgomery, 2005; Markides, 1995).

Today hostile takeovers[3] are becoming an accepted tool in the business arsenal. As a consequence, we can consider virtually no company to be free from the threat of takeover. In this way, we believe that one more lever, in an elaborate system of checks and balances, is currently in place for reducing the immunity of even the largest firms and conditioning managers to pursue growth strategies that are more consistent with the creation of value for shareholders.

NOTES

1. Some economists disagree about the severity of diseconomies of scale. When diseconomies of scale are minimal or non existent, that is when average costs are L-shaped instead of U-shaped, a firm that has reached the minimum efficient scale (MES) may continue to grow without experiencing increases in average costs. If it did a company could extend its scope indefinitely, but that does not correspond to the reality.
2. On the agency approach see: Jensen (1986); Jensen and Meckling (1976) and Milgrom and Roberts (1992).
3. On takeovers and defence tactics see Jensen (1988) and Weston et al. (1990).

PART II

GROWTH STRATEGIES IN PRACTICE: FOUR CASES OF SUCCESSFUL FIRMS

INTRODUCTION AND OBJECTIVES

In this part four cases of successful enterprises are presented: L'Oreal, Campari, Luxottica and Geox. These enterprises, even if operating in different industries, are all characterized by a decade of continuous growth, accompanied by a systematic creation of value for shareholders.

The growth strategies of these enterprises are deducted by analysing their annual reports for more than a decade. The strategies are described in their characteristics and in their economic and financial effects, as well as in their consequences on organizational structure.

Each company is characterized by specific growth strategies and reveals its own original pattern of growth, leveraging on different resources and exploiting different environment and industry conditions and dynamics.

The direct analysis of strategies carried out by the enterprises analysed confirms the top management view of growth as an instrument for increasing the competitive advantage and creating value for shareholders, as well as the constant attention to tune the firm's resources to environmental changes.

8. L'Oreal: product diversification and horizontal expansion

COMPANY PROFILE

L'Oreal is a France-based global cosmetics company, engaged in the production and marketing of a range of perfume, make-up, hair and skin care products. With 100 years of existence L'Oreal is today the top world's company in cosmetics. The company operates all over the world with a wide range of products covering almost all segments and all distribution channels.

The mission of the company is "to meet all beauty expectations at all prices for all lifestyles, in all regions of the world" (L'Oreal, Annual Report 2009).

The company's products are sold under well-known brands such as L'Oreal Paris, Garnier, Maybelline, Vichy, SoftSheen Carson, CCB Paris, L'Oreal Professional, Kerastase, Redken, Matrix and Mizani, Lancome, Biotherm, Helena Rubinstein, Kiehl's, Shu Uemura and Giorgio Armani.

In 2009 L'Oreal realised €17,473 million of consolidated sales and €2,608 million of operating profits.

The following data (2009) complete the firm profile of L'Oreal:

- 23 international brands with annual sales of more than €50 million euro each;
- 67,000 employees and 40 establishments all over the world;
- 30,000 total patents registered and 674 patents registered in 2009.

L'OREAL'S POSITION IN THE COSMETICS WORLD INDUSTRY

Worldwide cosmetics markets reached a total of €117,300 million in 2009. In this market L'Oreal has a leading position with a market share of 14.9% (L'Oreal, 2009). In the cosmetics industry, consumers' preferences depend on the season, on the social and cultural environment and on the effects of previous marketing communication for fashion items or substitute products. Responding in a timely way to these changing demands is thus vital for success. Customers demand products with innovative styles, realised with exclusive physical attributes and top level quality by scientists and designers that have built the reputation of powerful brands.

Nowadays the cosmetics market is driven by innovation including new colour palates, treatments targeted to specific skin types and unique formulas concentrating on different needs (Kumar et al., 2006; L'Oreal, 2009). The speed at which fashion markets change is very high, resulting in very short product life cycles. Most cosmetics products have a lifespan of less than five years and manufacturers reformulate 25% of their products every year. Cosmetic firms need to improve products constantly in order to stay ahead in a highly competitive market, where more choice and ever greater effectiveness are expected by the consumer (Table 8.1).

Table 8.1 Revenues of leading companies in cosmetics industry in 2008

Company	$ billion
Procter and Gamble	26.3
L'Oreal	25.8
Unilever	16.0
Avon Products	7.6
Beiersdorf	7.5
Estèe Lauder	7.3
Shiseido	6.9
Kao	5.9
Johnson & Johnson	5.6
Henkel	4.4
LVMH	3.7
Coty	3.5
Chanel	3.0

Note: Sales of Procter & Gamble and Unilever only regard the beauty care division.

Source: The Cosmetic Chemist's Resource Site, 2010.

Under a strategic profile, over time L'Oreal has concentrated all its resources on the cosmetics business, as sales in the dermatology sector represent only 2.8% of total sales. This focus has allowed the firm to exploit and improve its resources progressively covering the five major businesses and the different market segments worldwide with a wide range of products and brands.

L'Oreal's competitors present different strategic profiles. There are companies focused exclusively on perfumes and cosmetics businesses, such as Estée Lauder, Avon, Shiseido or Beierdorf, while other world leaders are diversified conglomerates, such as Johnson & Johnson, Colgate Palmolive, Unilever, Procter & Gamble which also operate in food, personal care goods and house consumer goods (Kumar et al., 2006). In Table 8.1 the revenues from perfumes and cosmetics of the most important companies are compared.

THE GROWTH OF L'OREAL IN THE LAST DECADE

Data shown in Tables 8.2 and 8.3 clearly highlight the growth of L'Oreal from 1999 to 2009. Sales increased from €10,751 million to approximately €17,473 million, with a growth rate of 62.5% in ten years (Figure 8.1) and invested capital grew from €12,137 million in 1999 to €23,291 million in 2009 (91.9%).

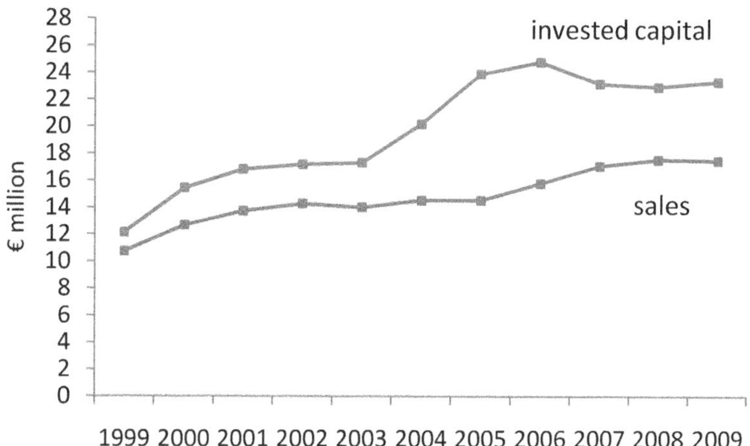

Source: Our elaboration on L'Oreal *Annual Reports* from 2004 to 2009.

Figure 8.1 L'Oreal sales and invested capital

Table 8.2 L'Oreal outcomes and assets from 1999 to 2004

(€ million)	1999	2000	2001	2002	2003	2004
Sales	10,751	12,671	13,740	14,288	14,029	14,534
Operating profit	833	1033	1,236	1,464	1,661	1,659
Net profit	827	1,028	1,229	1,456	1,653	1,656
Fixed assets	5,918	7,605	8,140	8,130	8,136	11,534
Current assets	5,139	6,256	6,724	6,843	6,876	6,645
Cash	1,080	1,588	1,954	2,216	2,303	1,981
Invested capital	12,137	15,449	16,818	17,189	17,315	20,160
Equity	5,470	6,179	7,210	7,434	8,136	10,564
Debts	1,914	3,424	2,939	2,646	1,941	2,175
Cash flows	n.a.	n.a.	1,418	1,579	1,763	1,923
Net profit share	1.22	1.52	1.82	2.15	2.45	2.46

Note: Data according to French accounting standard.

Source: Our elaboration on L'Oreal *Annual Reports* from 2004 to 2009.

In the period 1999–2009 the company sales grew on average by 6% a year compared with an average growth rate of 3.9% in the cosmetics industry. In this period the operating profit increased by 129.2% and shareholders' equity value increased from €5,470 million to €13,598 million, providing clear evidence of the effectiveness of growth strategies in creating equity value.

Over the last 20 years an initial capital of €100 invested in L'Oreal shares in 1989 has at 31 December 2009 a value of €1,493 with an average rate of return of 69.6% per year.

Table 8.3 L'Oreal outcomes and assets from 2004 to 2009

(€ million)	2004	2005	2006	2007	2008	2009
Sales	13,641	14,533	15,790	17,063	17,542	17,473
Operating profit	2,089	2,266	2,541	2,827	2,725	2,578
Net profit	3,970	1,972	2,061	2,656	1,948	1,792
Non-current assets	15,734	18,686	19,155	17,030	16,380	17,350
Current assets	4,075	4,537	4,847	5,015	5,450	4,768
Cash	576	663	781	1,087	1,077	1,173
Invested capital	20,385	23,886	24,783	23,132	22,907	23,291
Equity	11,825	14,657	14,624	13,622	11,563	13,598
Debts	1,568	2,217	3,329	2,373	3,700	1,958
Cash flows	1,923	2,130	2,410	2,720	2,746	2,758
Net profit per share	n.a.	2.60	2.98	3.36	3.49	3.42

Note: Data according to IFRS.

Source: Our elaboration on L'Oreal *Annual Reports* from 2004 to 2009.

THE GROWTH STRATEGIES: CLOSELY RELATED DIVERSIFICATION AND HORIZONTAL EXPANSION

Closely related diversification strategy

L'Oreal has developed over time a closely related diversification strategy, progressively entering and growing into three different industries, which are:

- cosmetics;
- dermatology;
- cosmetics retail distribution.

In the cosmetics industry L'Oreal covers the five major sectors: hair products, skin care, make-up, fragrance, and toilet products.

In the dermatology industry L'Oreal specializes in skin diseases such as rosacea, psoriasis, eczema and skin infections such as acne. L'Oreal also operates in the dermatology with the activity of the company Galderma Laboratories (dermatological company), a joint venture with Nestlé. Galderma boasts three of the top 25 best-selling drugs in dermatology in a highly competitive specialty market.

In the cosmetics retail industry L'Oreal operates through The Body Shop, a chain of cosmetic stores specializing exclusively in hair and skin care products based on natural ingredients; by the end of the financial year 2009 the company operated a total of 2,550 stores in 62 countries worldwide.

The most important industry in which L'Oreal operates is the cosmetics industry, with a weight of 93% of sales and 94.6% in operating profits (Table 8.4).

Table 8.4 L'Oreal outcomes breakdown by industries in 2009

	Consolidated sales (€mill.)	%	Operating profit (€mill.)	%	OP/sales (%)
Cosmetics	16,257	93.0	2,608	94.6	15.9
Cosmetics retail distribution	726	4.2	54	2.1	7.4
Dermatology	489	2.8	85	3.3	17.4
Total	17,473	100.0	2,747	100.0	15.7

Source: L'Oreal, *Annual Report 2009*.

In the cosmetics industry L'Oreal has developed over time a closely related diversification strategy, progressively entering into and growing in the five major cosmetics businesses:

- skin care;
- hair products;
- make-up;
- fragrances and
- toiletries.

The cosmetics sales, divided by businesses, are shown in Table 8.5.

Table 8.5 Breakdown of cosmetics sales by businesses, 2009

	Sales (€ million)	(%)
Skin care	4,381	27.0
Hair care	3,692	22.7
Make-up	3,421	21.0
Hair colourants	2,429	15.0
Perfumes	1,713	10.5
Other	620	3.8
Total cosmetics sales	16,257	100.0

Source: L'Oreal, *Annual Report 2009*.

In the cosmetics industry L'Oreal has distinguished four different market segments, thus offering different product lines through different market channels:

- professional products,
- consumer products,
- luxury products,
- active cosmetics.

The professional products are hair care products directed at professional hairdressers, who use or sell these products in their hair salons. Therefore the sector's key focus is to service the greatest number of hair salons around the world, firstly by offering differentiated brands for different individuals and secondly by increasing targeted innovations to improve the quality of services in hair colourants, permanent waves, styling and hair care.

The consumer products are products directed at mass-market retailing channels. The luxury products are premium products directed at customers requiring high quality and service. Luxury products are sold through select retail outlets. The active cosmetics products are derma-cosmetic skin care products, sold through specialist retailers, and pharmacies; pharmacists and dermatologists. Cosmetics sales and profits by these product lines (business units) are shown in Table 8.6.

Table 8.6 Breakdown of cosmetics sales and operating profits by product lines in 2009

	Sales (€million)	%	Operating profit (€million)	Operating profit /sales (%)
Professional products:	2,388	14.7	477	20.0
Hair colourants	847			
Styling and textures	323			
Shampoos and hair care	1,218			
Consumer products:	8,555	52.6	1,577	18.4
Hair colourants	1,582			
Hair care and styling	2,241			
Make-up	2,380			
Skin care	2,023			
Other	329			
Luxury products:	4,080	25.1	617	15.1
Skin care	1,473			
Perfumes	1,654			
Make-up	953			
Active cosmetics:	1,234	7.6	250	20.2
Skin care	969			
Hair care	99			
Make-up	86			
Other	80			
Cosmetics total	16,257	100.0	2,921	18.0
Non-allocated cosmetic branch			–482	–3.0
Total	16,257	100.0	2,439	15.0

Source: L'Oréal, *Annual Report 2009*.

Horizontal expansion strategies

In the meantime, the company has also pursued a horizontal expansion strategy both in new geographical markets and in new market segments through a policy of multiple brands.

In particular, L'Oreal has carried out a geographical expansion, by strengthening its presence or by becoming established in emergent countries, in particular Brazil, Russia, India, Mexico and China. From the eighth place in 1998 revenues, China reached the fourth position in 2008 and Brazil and Russia are now respectively the third and eighth country in revenues.

In the last few years the company has developed its sales especially in Eastern Europe, Asia and Latin America. The growth in these countries largely compensated the reduction in sales in North America, caused by the dollar crisis and the reduction in consumption. The increase in sales in B.R.I.C (Brasil, Russia, India and China) countries and in Eastern Europe has been favoured both by the increase in consumption and by the growth strategy implemented by L'Oreal through acquisitions of firms operating locally.

The growth of L'Oreal in emergent markets is clearly highlighted by the increase in sales obtained in the period 2001–2009 (Table 8.7).

Table 8.7 Cosmetics sales growth by geographical area, 2001–2009

Sales by geographical area	2001 (€million)	2009 (€million)	2001–2009 growth rate (%)
Western Europe	6,581	7,036	6.9
North America	4,257	3,802	−10.7
Rest of the world	2,556	5,419	+112.0
Total sales	13,394	16,257	+21.4

Note: Rest of the world include Eastern Europe, Latin America, Asia Pacific and Africa.

Source: Our elaboration on L'Oreal data from *Annual Reports 2001–2009*.

In the meantime, the company has also pursued an expansion strategy in the different market segments through a policy of multiple brands.

At present, in the professional products business the company operates with four brands: L'Oreal Professional, Kerastase, Redken, Matrix and Mizani. In the consumer product business L'Oreal has successfully utilized the core brand "L'Oreal Paris" which progressively became the foremost beauty brand worldwide. The company also focuses on differentiating and enhancing the value of the sector's product ranges through innovation, while developing blockbuster products to drive market growth. Other leading brands introduced over years in this segment include Garnier, Maybelline, and SoftSheen Carson. In the luxury products business leading brands include Helena Rubinstein, Shu Uemura, Lancome, Biotherm, and Kiehl's, as well as perfume brands such as Giorgio Armani, Ralph Lauren, Cacharel and Viktor & Rolf. Finally, in the active cosmetics sectors L'Oreal brands include Vichy, La Roche-Posay, Inneov and Skinceuticals.

Over the years the company has continually expanded to new market segments to meet consumers' needs in all their diversity. In this context, since the male and seniors market segments are exponentially growing, the company has developed and commercialized new product lines adapted to the specific patterns of these populations.

In developed countries (Western Europe, the USA and Japan), as the market share of ageing populations (over 50) is increasing, more and more care products that prevent ageing are being proposed.

During the period examined, all businesses of L'Oreal have obtained significant growth, with a total increase of 21.4%, as proof of its successful strategies. In particular the active cosmetics products show the most significant increase (88.9%), for the success of new products in the pharmaceutical channel, but also the professional products show a strong growth with a rate of increase in sales of more than 31% (Table 8.8).

Table 8.8 Cosmetics sales growth by product lines in the period 2001–2009

Cosmetics sales	2001 (€million)	2009 (€million)	2001–2009 % growth rate
Consumer products	7,282	8,555	17.5
Luxury products	3,550	4,080	14.9
Professional products	1,811	2,388	31.9
Active cosmetics	653	1,234	88.9
Total Sales (1)	13,394	16,257	21.4%

Note: (1) excluding the dermatology business.

Source: Our elaboration on L'Oreal data from *Annual Reports 2001–2007*.

GROWTH THROUGH ACQUISITION

L'Oreal growth strategies have been realised either through organic development or acquisition of companies already operating in the cosmetics industry. In particular, external growth is part of L'Oreal's long-term strategy, with a goal of 10% annual growth over the long term. This option has been also facilitated by the group's liquidity and low debts. Purchases of more companies also allowed the group to reach the critical size needed for exploiting economies of scale both in R&D activities and in marketing and distribution.

The acquisition of companies also allowed L'Oreal to diversify quickly, expanding its geographical horizon and developing its market segments. The actual portfolio of 25 brands is the result of a series of acquisitions that were begun many years ago (Table 8.9). All acquisitions related to firms already operating in the cosmetics industry and were realised nearly always by maintaining the operative autonomy of the acquired firm. These are the general characteristics of the acquired firms:

- operating in different geographical markets from those in which L'Oreal is already operating;
- operating in geographical markets in which L'Oreal intends to reach a leadership position;
- offering products that complete the portfolio of L'Oreal products or brands;
- having technologies and competences complementary to those of L'Oreal on products or markets segments.

The acquisitions realised by L'Oreal have allowed reinforcement of its presence in the world and being able to maintain its leadership position in the sector. Through acquisitions and mergers L'Oreal has also obtained important objectives, such as:

- reaching a critical size needed for exploiting economies of scale both in R&D and in marketing and distribution, thereby improving its competitive capacity, through the control of larger market shares;
- satisfying local needs through a more direct contact with the market and by adapting products to the local context (multi-domestic policy);
- creating a portfolio of distinctive but complementary products and brands;

- quickly acquiring new resources, competences and technologies, thereby generating synergies;
- overcoming the entry barriers in some markets where normative obstacles and tariff barriers were present.

The most important acquisitions are the following (Table 8.10).

Table 8.9 L'Oreal horizontal acquisitions and expansion in different markets segments

Year of acquisition	Consumer products	Luxury products	Professional products	Active cosmetics
1964	Garnier	Lancome		
1970		Biotherm		
1980		Vichy		
1988		H. Rubinstein		Laboratoires Le Roche Posay
1993			American Redken Laboratories	
1994			Procasa	
1995	Jeda			
1996	Maybelline, Unisa,			
2000	MissYlang			
2001	Colorama			BioMedic
2002			ARTec	
2003	Mininurse			
2004	Yue-Sai	Shu Uemura Cosmetics		
2005	Delial			Skinceuticals
2006				Body Shop, Sanoflore
2007		PureOlogy Research		
2008		YSL brand licenses		

Source: Our elaboration of L'Oreal *Annual Reports*.

- 1964: Acquisition of Lancome. Through this acquisition L'Oreal enters the field of maquillage and perfume and obtained access to the selective channels of perfumeries. In the same year L'Oreal realised the takeover of Garnier, an important consumer brand.
- 1970: Acquisition of Biotherm, a company specializing in biological cosmetics products.
- 1980: Acquisition of Vichy, a luxury brand with a range of products sold in pharmacies.
- 1988: Acquisition of Helena Rubinstein and takeover of Laboratoires Farmaceutical La Roche-Posay, specializing in skin care.
- 1993: Acquisition of the American Redken Laboratoires, producing products for professional hairdressers.
- 1994: Acquisition of Spanish Procasa, producing products for professional hairdressers.
- 1996: Acquisition of Maybelline, an American company specializing in maquillage products.
- 1996: Acquisition of Chilean Unisa. The year before the Group took over the German company Jeda. With these acquisitions L'Oreal became the world leader in the field of large diffusion maquillage. In the same year L'Oreal created a joint venture with the Suzhou Medical College, one of the oldest Chinese universities in medicine.
- 2000: Acquisition of Miss Ylang, leader in large diffusion maquillage in Argentina.
- 2001: Acquisition of BioMedic and of Colorama. The first acquisition was directed to enrich the active cosmetics division, while the second acquisition was directed at growth in the Brazilian market. BioMedic is a firm specializing in products for skin care after plastic and dermatologic surgery; it is present in more than 1500 medical studios in America and it is distributed in 25 countries. Colorama is a Brazilian leader company in the mass-market of make-up and hair care products. The acquisition of Colorama from the competitor Revlon was directed at reinforcing the position on the Brazilian market where L'Oreal was already present with the brand Maybelline. This acquisition allowed production capacity to increase thanks to the Brazilian plant and to the fast expansion of L'Oreal brands on the Brazilian market.
- 2002: Acquisition of ARTec, a firm producing professional products for hair care and colouring. The superior image of ARTec products in American hairdressers allowed the L'Oreal Professional division to develop new products and reinforce its presence in the most prestigious beauty salons of America. The fast increase in professional

products sales and the increase in sales of hair care and hair colour segments in America after the acquisition clearly confirm the success of this strategy.

- 2003: Acquisition of the Chinese Mininurse. This company specializes in skin care products for young women; Mininurse has an excellent image, based on a correct quality–price ratio and it is among the first three companies operating in skin care with a share of 5% of the Chinese market and a distribution in more than 280,000 shops in all country.
- 2004: Acquisition of the Chinese Yue-Sai. This is a cosmetics firm specializing in skin care and make-up products directed uniquely at Chinese women. The Chinese brand benefits from a great reputation and an excellent competitive position. Yue-Sai products are sold in more than 800 iper-markets, located in the largest 240 Chinese towns. The acquisition of the Chinese companies gave great opportunities to L'Oreal; besides the economic benefits, these acquisitions allowed L'Oreal to overcome the high entry barriers and to quickly obtain leadership on the market with its core brands: L'Oréal Paris in hair colour, Maybelline in make-up, Vichy in products sold in pharmacies and Lancôme in selected perfume shops. The acquisition also permitted the extension of knowledge on the particular characteristics of the Chinese customers and finally the expansion of production capacity and increase in productivity. The two acquisitions also produced a rapid increase in sales of Mininurse and Yue-Sai, as a consequence of the relevant synergies produced by the merger.
- 2004: Acquisition of Shu Uemura Cosmetics. This acquisition concerned one of the most famous cosmetic brand in Japan and in other Asian countries. This acquisition enabled L'Oreal to reinforce its position in the luxury segment, accelerating the expansion of the brand in Japan.
- 2005: Acquisition of Delial and Skinceuticals. Delial is a brand which specializes in products for solar protection and it is a leader in this sector in south Europe and particularly in Spain, where it is among the first three brands. This acquisition allowed L'Oreal to reinforce its position in the solar products market and to gain know-how and technological resources developed in Delial laboratories. Skinceuticals is a US firm specializing in professional skin care, with a growth rate among the highest in the USA market. This firm uses a highly specialized distribution network, including plastic surgeons, dermatologists and other professionals. This brand was acquired for enriching the active cosmetics division and increasing the brand

portfolio of American brands (including Ralph Lauren, Redken, Maybelline, SoftSheen-Carson, Matrix and Kiehl's). The sales of Skinceuticals, after the acquisition by L'Oreal, increased by 45.7%, as proof of the important synergies produced by the merger.

- 2006: Acquisition of The Body Shop and Sanoflore. The two acquisitions showed the interest of L'Oreal in responding to the demand from consumers for natural products. As far as The Body Shop is concerned, this is an international distribution chain of body products composed of natural ingredients, with more than 2,100 sales points all over the world. This chain has an important reputation at the international level, thanks to its defence of values in the field of human rights and animal protection; it serves a target of clients who are particularly interested in the chemical composition of cosmetic products. The operation gives evidence for the L'Oreal's commitment regarding ethical themes as well as the will to improve its reputation in terms of social responsibility. The acquisition of The Body Shop has determined the entry into a new type of business, in addition to the cosmetics and dermatology businesses. The acquisition has produced a strong increase in the sales of The Body Shop, as the effect of important synergies with the group. The same can be said for Sanoflore, because this brand also specializes in products made of completely natural ingredients. After the acquisition, Sanoflore became a part of the active cosmetics division.
- 2007: Acquisition of PureOlogy Research. This is a luxury American brand of hair care products. This company was bought because of its high reputation among American hairdressers. With this acquisition L'Oreal aimed at exploiting the enormous potentialities of the brand, reinforcing its position in hairdressing salons. The acquisition was also justified by the strong complementarities between PureOlogy and the brands portfolio of the professional division.
- 2008: Acquisition of operating licenses of the group brands YSL Beauty. Over the last two years the company has also acquired several distributors of professional products in the United States (Beauty Alliance in 2007, Idaho Barber and Beauty Supply in 2009).

ORGANIZATIONAL STRUCTURE FOR IMPLEMENTING GROWTH STRATEGIES

In order to offer consumers its cosmetic products all over the world, the top management of L'Oreal has implemented an organization model based on major geographical poles capable of knowing the specific market needs and autonomously deciding which products to develop, in order to match the different needs of consumers in different countries, on the basis of physical, cultural and economic differences.

It has also been necessary to consider the existing differences among professional clients (for example hair salons) and private consumers and between mass and affluent consumers and between consumers of cosmetics and dermatological products. Therefore an organizational structure has been developed which is characterized by four business divisions: professional, consumer, luxury and active cosmetics. In each division different brands are managed, each of them characterized for matching a specific culture and concept of beauty.

The consumer division operates in the mass market with cosmetic products directed at the mass market using the whole and large retail distribution; the most important brands are: L'Oreal Paris, Garnier, Maybelline and SoftSheen Carson. The products of this division are distributed in 7,600 hypermarkets, 40,000 supermarkets and 74,000 drugstores.

The luxury division operates through selective channels in the highest cosmetics market segment with luxury brand and specialized products. These channels are cosmetic boutiques, other specialist outlets and department stores. Consider that this division is present in 2,500 selected perfumeries with exclusive rights and in department stores with brands like: Lancome, Biotherm, Helena Rubinstein, Giorgio Armani, Guy Laroche, Shu Uemura, Kiehl's, Diesel, Ralph Lauren, Cacharel and Paloma Picasso, Yue-Sai, VictorRolf.

The professional division operates with products directed at hair dressing salons; the most important brands are: Kerastase, L'Oreal Professionnel, Redken, Matrix, Mizani, Pureology. Consider that more than 3 million hairdressers use and sell the brands of this division in their saloons.

The active cosmetics division operates in the derma-cosmetic markets with special products sold through pharmacies. All products of this division derive from the research carried out in scientific laboratories of L'Oreal and the collaboration with international dermatologists. This division operates in the dermo-cosmetic market through 75,000 pharmacies and in spa companies with brands like: Vichy, La Roche-Posay, Innéov, SkinCeuticals and Sanoflore.

The Body Shop has been operating together with these divisions since 2006; this is a cosmetics firm which has specialized in its 30 years of life selling products not tested on animals with a well known brand name in 59 countries and a sales network of over 2,426 shops, offering products of excellent quality at the right price.

Figure 8.2 represents L'Oreal's organization structure at the first managerial level of authority. In turn, each division is organized in business units, each of them responsible for a distinctive brand and with a specific functional structure for pursuing specific objectives. All brand units are supported by specialist staff operating at the division level.

Therefore, there are two levels of divisions within the Group: a series of divisions according to geographical areas or zones (Asia, the USA, Latin America, etc.) and a series of divisions according to business units. At the corporate level a number of staff departments, such as Finance, HR and Legal Affairs help the corporate CEO to run and govern the group and to ensure all activities are coordinated effectively.

Production is organized by geographical areas: 19 factories are located in Europe, eight in North America, three in Latin America, four in Africa and the Pacific Orient and 4 in Asia. All factories specialize in certain products: 22 factories specialize in consumer products, five in luxury products, three in professional products and two factories in active cosmetics (Cogmap.com/loreal, 2010).

This decentralized organization enables the group to seize and exploit opportunities more effectively at any location and to significantly reduce the market access times for the launching of new products in each zone.

To have an idea of the complexity of the entire organizational structure, consider that in Italy the first two product divisions (consumer and luxury products) are part of the same company "L'Oreal Saipo", while the remaining two divisions (professional and active cosmetics) are organized in two distinctive companies. All companies are controlled by an Italian holding company with the mission to coordinate human and financial resources and legal affairs, as well as promoting and developing the image of the L'Oreal Group in Italy and representing the group in Italy at the level of public authorities, associations, political community, information media, etc.

L'OREAL STRATEGIC RESOURCES FOR GROWTH: R&D COMPETENCES AND BRAND REPUTATION

The main strategic resources on which L'Oreal has based its continuous growth are the top level competences of its scientists and product designers and the strong reputation of its brand. In fact, cosmetics is a volatile and turbulent fashion industry, where customers always demand products with innovative characteristics and styles. That requires a continuous flow of new products realised by exclusive physical attributes with top-level quality.

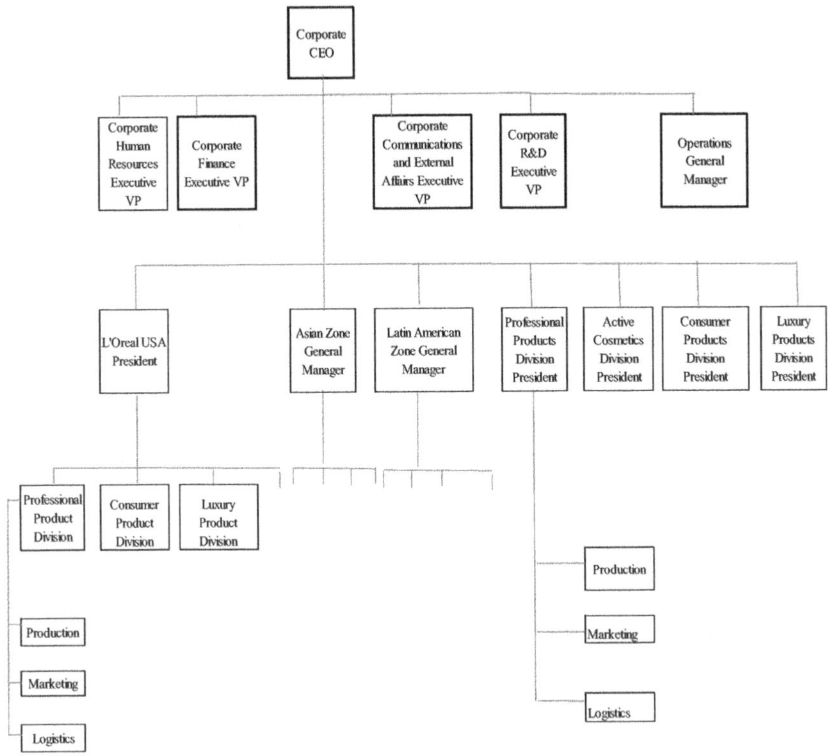

Source: www Cogmap.com/loreal, 2010.

Figure 8.2 L'Oreal organization chart

In addition, the competitors that operate in the mass segment are target fashion followers and they tend to imitate the high performing products of top brands, making the competitive advantage of top brands recede over time and making the product lifecycle short. Therefore, in order to avoid the decline of the product, it is necessary to continuously adapt products to the new demands of customers. In this context L'Oreal decided to innovate regularly so as to achieve the update of roughly 50% of its product line every three years. Such is the importance of new product development for L'Oreal that it tries to grab the maximum market share through the introduction of innovative products that are not only differentiated but also cater to satisfying the different segments of the international market.

The original and distinctive competence of L'Oreal in cosmetics R&D has been reinforced every year by the significant financial means granted to the R&D department. Consider that in 2009 the R&D budget obtained €609 million, equal to 3.5% of the company's total turnover, and L'Oreal registered 674 patents (Table 8.1). L'Oreal's laboratories are mobilized to create innovations capable of covering all price segments, by launching product lines accessible to the greatest number possible, attracting new clients to markets with strong growing potential such as the hairdressing business, body care, or products for men.

L'Oreal's R&D structure is the true key of the competitive advantage of L'Oreal (Table 8.1). R&D at L'Oreal is carried out in 18 research centres and 13 evaluation centres on all continents. In particular, L'Oreal has 11 research centres in France, three in the USA, three in Asia and one in Latin America to ensure that products match consumers' expectations perfectly and provide inspiration for new products. Furthermore, it has over 100 collaboration agreements with academic and research institutions. In these centres, 3,313 scientists operate in R&D with 30 scientific specializations.

The research and innovation laboratories, the number of research employees and the number of patents demonstrate the commitments of the company and the effectiveness of cosmetics and dermatological research (Tables 8.10 and 8.11).

The effects of R&D activity are impressive: consider that half of L'Oreal's annual revenues is determined by new products launched on the market, 20% of products are renewed every year, so that all the product portfolios are renewed after five years on average, and that on average 500 new requests for patent registration are presented each year. R&D resources and competences are reinforced every year by relevant investments, allowing the firm to maintain and improve its leading position in the global market through continuous innovations in products.

The second strategic firm resource for growth is given by L'Oreal's important brand name and reputation. Over the years L'Oreal has strengthened its image of innovative and high quality brand through heavy investment in advertising and promotion (approximately 30%) also by the means of world-famous personalities (Diane Kruger, Patrik Dempsey, Anne Hathaway, Penelope Cruz, Beyoncé, etc.).

Table 8.10 Patents, R&D expenditures and employees at L'Oreal

	2001	2003	2005	2007	2009
Registered patents	493	515	529	576	674
R&D exp. (mill. €)	432	480	496	560	609
R&D employees	2,743	2,921	2,903	3,095	3,313

Source: Our elaboration on L'Oreal data from *Annual Reports 2001–2009*.

The group has spent an ever increasing share of its budget on promotion, reaching $5,389 million in 2009 equal to 30.9% of consolidated sales. Consider that, even though faced with recession and a decline in sales throughout 2009, L'Oreal has decided to keep its promotion-oriented investments at a high level, with the objective of emerging even stronger from the crisis (Table 8.12).

Table 8.11 Investments in R&D of the main cosmetics companies in 2007

Companies	R&D investments (€mill.)	Share of total sales (%)
L'Oreal	560	3.4
Procter & Gamble	447	3.0
Unilever	195	2.5
Estée Lauder	147	2.0
Shiseido	162	2.5
Avon Product	61	1.0
Beiersdorf	127	2.3
Johnson & Johnson	100	2.5

Table 8.12 Advertising and promotional expenditures

€ million	2003	2005	2007	2009
Advertising and promotion	4,177	4,367	5,124	5,389
Sales	14,029	14,533	17,063	17,473
Adv/Sales (%)	29.77	30.05	30.03	30.84

Source: Our elaboration on L'Oreal data from *Annual Reports 2003–2009.*

CONCLUSIONS

In the last decade the growth of L'Oreal in both sales and profits has been constant. The growth has been characterized by simultaneous product diversification and horizontal expansion either by organic development and acquisitions of firms and trademarks.

On one hand, the related diversification strategy allowed L'Oreal to operate in the main cosmetics businesses, hair care, make-up, fragrances and toilet products, exploiting relevant economies of scope, made possible from the intense relationships among these businesses concerning customers and distribution channels, marketing and R&D activities. On the other hand, the horizontal expansion strategy enabled L'Oreal to enter into new geographical markets characterized by high growth rates and creating new segments in traditional markets, through an increasing number of types and models of products and brands, suitable for matching different customer needs and preferences. This strategy allowed L'Oreal to exploit relevant economies of scale, especially in R&D, marketing and distribution activities.

Even in the last decade the L'Oreal business model, based on product innovation, quality and globalization, has kept on showing its outstanding ability to sustain growth and create value for its shareholders.

9. Campari: product diversification and international expansion through acquisitions

COMPANY PROFILE

Campari is a medium sized company operating in the beverage industry and particularly in the spirits, wine and soft drinks businesses. With a secular history it was founded and run by the Campari family. Gaspare Campari invented the famous red aperitif Campari with many other liqueurs, then passed on the activity to his son Davide Campari who opened the new factory in Sesto San Giovanni near Milan in 1904. It remained productive until 2005.

Davide Campari changed the firm policy, limiting the production only to drinks with a strong identity and image: the aperitif Campari and the liqueur Cordial Campari. In addition, he gave an international impulse to the company making Campari products appreciated all over the world. In 1960 Campari products were already wide spread and well known in more than 80 countries and in subsequent years distribution covered 190 countries with leadership in the Italian and Brazilian market and an important position in the USA, Germany and Switzerland. However, it was at the beginning of 90's that Campari made its major transformation, becoming one of the main players in the world market of the beverage industry. Today the group is directed by managers while the majority of shares is owned by the Garavoglia family. As from 6 July 2001 Campari is quoted on the Milan stock exchange.

In 2009 Campari registered net sales equal to €1,008.4 million, an average number of employees of 2,176 and *EBITDA* and net profits respectively equal to €265 million and €137.1 million.

At present the company operates in four businesses: spirits, wines, soft drinks and other (Table 9.1). Spirits are alcohol-based beverages with an alcoholic content either below or above 15% volume; drinks above 15% are defined by law as "spirits". Wines are both sparkling and still wines including aromatized wines such as vermouth. Soft drinks are non-alcoholic beverages. Other products are raw materials, semi-finished and finished products bottled for third parties.

Spirits are the most important business of the group. In this business the company operates today with some key products, such as Campari and CampariSoda, as well as Skyy Vodka, Cynar, Aperol, Glen Grant, Ouzo12, Zedda Piras, Dreher, Old Eight, Drury's and others.

In the wine business the group is present with product brands such as Cinzano, Barbero, Liebfraumilch, Riccadonna, Sella & Mosca, Teruzzi & Puthod and others.

In the soft drinks business Campari is present with aperitifs such as Crodino and fruit-based beverages such as Lemonsoda, Oransoda and Pelmosoda. The main product of the Campari rich portfolio is the homonymous Campari, the alcoholic aperitif obtained by the infusion of herbs and fruits in a mix of alcohol and water with a red ruby brilliant colour and an intense aroma; the image of the product is based on concepts of passion and sexuality, two recurrent themes in Campari brand promotions.

Table 9.1 Campari sales and brands by business areas in 2009

Business Area	Total sales (€million)	%	Campari brands
Spirits	739.6	73.3	Campari, Campari Soda, Cynar, Biancosarti, Glenfiddich, Ouzo 12, Skyy Vodka, Cinzano, Aperol, Dreher, Old Eight, Drury's, Gregson's, Zedda Piras, Aperol, Glen Grant, X Rated Fusion, Cabo Wabo, Destiadora San Nicholas, CJSC Odessa, Wild Turkey
Wines	154.9	15.4	Cinzano, Sella & Mosca, Liebfraumilch, Barbero Mondoro and Enrico Serafino, Riccadonna, Teruzzi & Puthod
Soft drinks	100.3	9.9	Lemonsoda, Oransoda, Crodino
Other	13.7	1.4	
Total	1008.5	100	

Source: Our elaboration of Campari *Annual Report 2009*.

Campari has its headquarters in Sesto S. Giovanni near Milan (Italy) and carries out its production in many areas located in Italy (Novi Ligure, Alghero, Sulmona, Canale, Crodo), Brasil (Jabotao and Sorocaba), the UK, Greece, Argentin and the USA (San Francisco). Campari also owns vineyards in Sardinia and Tuscany. Campari sales in 2009, divided by geographical areas, are shown in Table 9.2.

CAMPARI'S MARKET POSITION

As Campari operates in three fundamental businesses – spirits, wine and soft drinks – it is necessary to refer to these different industries in order to evaluate its position against its competitors.

With regard to the spirits business, the world demand for these products is characterized by the general tendency of consumers to reduce the consumption of alcoholic products. But the dynamics of demand is different in various segments; the demand for white spirits, such as rum, vodka and gin is increasing, while consumptions of grappa, whisky and bitters are in the maturity phase of their cycle and the demand for aperitifs is declining slightly.

In the spirits industry consumption is strongly influenced by fashion and emotional factors. As a consequence, these markets are characterized by intense promotional activities from major competitors, directed at creating immaterial values on products, linked to a convivial life-style. In synthesis, consumption dynamics are characterized by a decrease in quantity and an increase in the quality required.

As far as the wine sector is concerned, world consumption is increasing in the food retail channel, both in value and quantity, because of the tendency to drink better quality wines due to the links to the values of tradition, culture and good living.

Consumption of soft drinks is in a phase of maturity and suffers from strong competition from other beverages such as tea and fruit-based drinks.

With regard to the structure of aggregate supply, over the last ten years the spirits industry has been subject to a very strong process of concentration. Concentration in this sector has been favoured by the particular importance of advertising and promotional expenditures to sustain brand awareness and image. In addition, the high cost of product distribution has favoured concentration, making it convenient to have a large portfolio of brands, with a well known image and reputation, in order to match the needs and preferences of different regional markets. All this has encouraged the most dynamic companies to expand their product lines by buying well affirmed brands and companies, both for entering new markets and consolidating their position in existing markets against incumbent companies and potential entrants. However, in this industry a high number of small firms still operate, focusing on product or market niches.

At present, the most important players are a group of multinational companies such as Diageo, Pernod Ricard, Bacardi, Brown Forman and Fortune Brands. The industry leader is Diageo, a multinational company with $14,898 million in total net sales, after excise duties, operating in closely diversified businesses, such as beer, wine and ready-to-drink products.

The breakdown of Diageo 2009 sales is shown in Table 9.2.

Table 9.2 Diageo sales breakdown by product lines in 2009

Product lines	Sales ($ million)	%
Spirits	9,683	65
Beer	3,277	22
Wine	745	5
Ready to drink	1,192	8
Total	14,898	100

Note: Data originally expressed in £ have been transferred into US$ using the average exchange rate US/Pound sterling in 2009 ($/1£ = 1.60).

Source: Diageo, *Annual Report, 2009.*

In the premium spirits industry, in 2009 Diageo made $9,683 million net sales with a market share estimated at about 28% of the total world market (net total sales estimated as being equal to $34,584 million).

The other big competitors in the premium spirits industry are Pernod Ricard, Bacardi, Brown Foreman and Fortune Brands. All others competitors, among them Campari, hold a total share of 32% (Diageo, 2009; Impact Databank, 2010). Therefore, on the international rank, the Campari Group has reached the sixth position in terms of sales in the premium spirit market, with a market share of about 2% (Table 9.3).

With reference to the wine sector, it is highly fragmented with a large number of niche operators, principally located in Italy, Spain, South Africa, Chile and Australia. In this sector large companies also operate. They have implemented strategies similar to those followed in the spirits sector: regional diversification and multi-brand product diversification. In the wine sector

Campari is the leading company in Italy, but it is a medium-sized firm in the international wine industry.

Table 9.3 Market shares in world premium spirits industry (2009)

Rank	Companies	Net sales ($million)	% sales
1	Diageo	9,683	28
2	Pernod Ricard	6,571	19
3	Bacardi	3,458	10
4	Brown Forman	2,075	6
5	Fortune Brands	1,729	5
6	Campari	740	2
7	Others	10,327	30
	Total industry net sales	34,584	100

Source: Our elaboration on Diageo, *Annual Report 2009* and Impact Data bank, 2010.

Finally, with reference to the soft drinks sector it is characterized by a few global players, such as *Coca Cola*, *Pepsi Cola* and *Cadbury Schweppes* and by a relevant number of local operating companies. Also in this sector, with the exception of the already mentioned multinational companies, the competitive scenario varies according to the markets and the different segments.

Summarizing, with regard to the Italian market, Campari is number one both in the wine and spirits business, while it is still a medium firm with regard to the wine and spirits world markets, even if it is characterized by a high growth rate in the last years.

THE GROWTH OF CAMPARI IN THE PERIOD 2000–2009

In the period 2000–2009, Campari registered a strong and continuous growth in sales, *EBITDA* and investment (Tables 9.4–9.7). In particular, from 2000 to 2009, Campari achieved a 132.8% increase in sales and a 297% increase in invested capital. The growth of sales and investments was especially obtained by acquisitions of companies and well known trademarks.

The growth of sales was accompanied by an increase in *EBITDA* equal to 180%, and an increase in shareholders' equity equal to 159%.

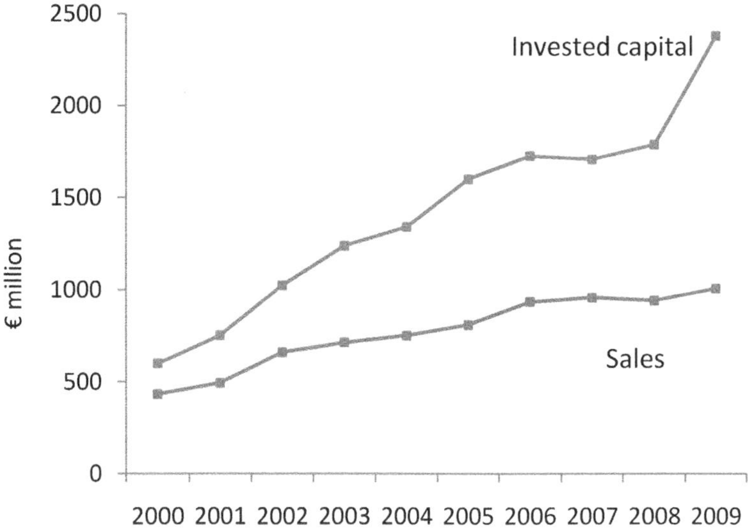

Figure 9.1 Campari sales and invested capital

Table 9.4 Campari consolidated outcomes from 2000 to 2004

€ million	2000	2001	2002	2003	2004
Net sales	434.0	494.0	661.0	714.0	751.0
EBIT	85.3	88.3	115.4	119.6	166.7
Profit before tax	97.5	94.0	109.1	110.6	157.1
Group net profit	52.8	63.4	72.3	52,6	96.9
EBITDA	93.2	100.1	143.2	148.1	184.5
Free cash flow	n.a	n.a	60.3	54.8	98.8

Note: Data according to IAS/IFRS.

Source: Our elaboration on Campari *Annual Reports*.

Table 9.5 Campari consolidated outcomes from 2005 to 2009

€million	2005	2006	2007	2008	2009
Net sales	810.0	934.0	957.0	942.0	1008.0
EBIT	183.9	190.5	200.6	195.4	235.6
Profit before tax	174.2	175.5	183.3	172.5	198.3
Group net profit	118.0	117.1	125.2	126.5	137.1
EBITDA	201.3	209.7	220.1	214.7	261.0
Free cash flow	82.1	93.4	125.3	123.0	184.3

Note: Data according to IAS/IFRS.

Source: Our elaboration of Campari *Annual Reports*.

Table 9.6 Campari assets and liabilities from 2000 to 2004

€ million	2000	2001	2002	2003	2004
Assets					
Net tangible fixed assets	88	91	144	152	144
Goodwill and trademarks	83	153	437	552	576
Others	40	71	60	64	68
Total non-current assets	211	315	641	768	788
Total current assets	388	437	384	472	553
Others					
Total assets	599	752	1,025	1,240	1,341
Liabilities and capital					
Shareholders' equity	404	432	479	548	629
Non-current liabilities	42	46	236	455	460
Current liabilities	153	274	310	237	252
Total	599	752	1,025	1,240	1,341

Note: Data according to IAS/IFRS

Source: Our elaboration of Campari *Annual Reports 2000–2009*.

Table 9.7 Campari assets and liabilities from 2005 to 2009

€ million	2005	2006	2007	2008	2009
Assets					
Net tangible fixed assets	153	146	155	177	284
Goodwill and trademarks	751	816	812	920	1199
Others	50	50	52	47	216
Total non current assets	953	1,013	1 019	1,143	1,699
Total current assets	648	710	687	647	668
Others	0	4	2		11
Total assets	1,601	1,726	1,708	1,790	2,378
Liabilities and capital					
Shareholders' equity	696	798	879	955	1,046
Non-current liabilities	565	472	434	465	992
Current liabilities	340	456	386	385	340
Total	1,601	1,726	1,708	1,803	2,378

Note: Data according to IAS/IFRS.

Source: Our elaboration of Campari *Annual Reports 2000–2009*.

THE GROWTH STRATEGIES OF CAMPARI: PRODUCT DIVERSIFICATION AND INTERNATIONAL EXPANSION

Over time the Campari Group has carried out both a product diversification and a horizontal expansion strategy. The main objective was to reach size and product diversification adequate for obtaining economies of scale and economies of scope, so as to successfully compete with the largest international companies.

Campari adopted a related diversification strategy, starting from the original historic Campari product and enlarging its range of products in the spirits, wine and soft drinks sectors. In each business Campari has incremented the portfolio of products and brands, covering different segments and different geographical markets.

The strategies of horizontal expansion and product diversification have been realised through both internal and external growth. In effect, the history of the last years points out that the robust growth of the group has been achieved mainly through external growth, primarily attributable to selective acquisitions of well-known trademarks and companies with a solid position in their markets (Table 9.8).

The first important acquisition in the spirits and soft drinks businesses was achieved in 1995 when the Italian activities of the Holland Bols Wessanen Group, owner of the brands Crodino, Cynar, Lemonsoda, Oransoda, Biancosarti and Crodo, were bought. With this operation Campari strengthened its position in the spirits business with the trademarks Cynar and Biancosarti, and in the soft drinks business with Crodino, Crodo, Lemonsoda and Oransoda brands.

Table 9.8 Campari diversified acquisitions

Years of acquisition	Spirits	Wines	Soft drinks
1995	Cynar, Biancosarti		Lemonsoda, Oransoda, Codo, Crodino
1996	Glenfiddich, Jagermeister		
1999	Onzo 12, Skyy Vodka, Cinzano, Aperol	Cinzano	
2001	Dreher, All Eight, Drury's, Gregson's		Liebfraumilch
2002	Zedda Piras	Sella & Mosca, Mondoro, Serafino, Riccadonna	
2003	Aperol, Mapo Mapo, Barbieri		
2005		Terruzzi & Puthod	
2006	Glen Grant, Old Smuggler,		
2007	X Rated Fusion		
2008	Sabia, Cabo Wabo, Destiadora S. Nicolas		
2009	CJSC Odessa, Wild Turkey		

Source: Our elaboration of Campari *Annual Reports 2000–2009*.

In 1996 the group continued the expansion in the spirits business by buying the distribution rights on the Italian market of some leader brands in the scotch whisky segment, such as Glenfiddich and Grant's; they joined the production and trading license in Italy (then extended to Brazil) of Jägermeister.

In 1998 the Group accelerated its growth by buying a minority partnership in Skyy Spirits LLC and the world distribution rights (USA excluded) of SKYY Vodka brand, one of the brands with the highest growth rate in the North American market. With this agreement Skyy Spirits LLC became, in turn, the distributor of Campari products in the USA. With this acquisition and strategic alliance Campari strengthened its presence in the spirits business with a leader brand and at the same time strengthened the distribution network of its products in the USA.

In 1999 the Group bought Ouzo 12, an aniseed-based alcoholic Greek beverage, a world leader in this segment and a symbol of Greek lifestyle. In this year Campari also acquired Cinzano, one of the world's leading brands in vermouth and in sparkling wines and one of the most famous worldwide Italian brands.

In 2000 Campari acquired the distribution rights in Switzerland of Henkell Trocken sparkling wine and of Gorbatschow Wodka, from the Group Henkell Söhnlein, leader in sparkling wines.

In 2001 Campari formalized the acquisition of the brands Dreher, whisky Old Eight, Drury's, Gregson's and Gold Cup in the spirits business and Liebfraumilch in the wine business. They were leading brands in the Brazilian and Uruguayan markets, all with a strong growth rate.

In 2002 Campari acquired the company Zedda Piras, owner of the majority of the Sella & Mosca company. By this operation Campari strengthened its presence in the spirits business with another leader brand (Zedda Piras) and in the wine business with the Sella & Mosca wines.

In 2003 Campari carried out a further expansion in the wine and spirits businesses buying Riccadonna, a leading brand in sparkling wines in Italy, Australia and in New Zeland. At the end of 2003 Campari bought Barbero 1891 an Italian company owner of a large portfolio of brands, among them in the spirits business Aperol, Aperol Soda, Mapo Mapo and the liqueurs Barbieri, and in the wine business Mondoro and Enrico Serafino. With this acquisition Campari expanded its supply in some segments of the wine and spirits businesses. Aperol brand completed the supply in the aperitif segments requiring a moderate alcoholic grade, while the Mondoro brand strengthened the group in the premium sparkling Asti wines segment on international markets.

In 2004 and 2005 Campari concluded the acquisition of distribution rights of some important products in the spirits business: Cachaca 51, a famous Brazilian brand, Grand Marnier, the French sweet liqueur exported all over the world and the entire portfolio of spirit products of the American Brown-Forman, with brands such as Jack Daniel's, Southern Comfort, Woodford Reserve and Finlandia Vodka.

In 2005 Campari made a new acquisition in the wine business, buying Teruzzi & Puthod, one of the highest quality wine producers in Tuscany.

In 2006 Campari entered the segment of Scotch whisky, buying from Pernod Ricard the brands of Glen Grant, Old Smuggler and Braemar, in addition to the distillery Rothes in Scotland for the production of Glen Grant, the second leading brand of single malt in the world and leader in the whisky segment in Italy.

In 2007 there was a further acquisition in the spirits business. Campari acquired X-Rated Fusion Liqueur, X-Rated Vodka and the super premium vodka Jean-Marc XO. X-Rated Fusion is one of the trendiest liqueurs in the USA market with a very high growth rate. This is a unique product for its taste and concept especially directed at the female market.

In 2008 Campari entered the Argentinian and Mexican markets, buying the Argentinian company Sabia, operating in Argentina with plants and a distribution structure in the spirits and wine businesses and Destiadora San Nicolas, whose activity includes a distillery and tequila brands like Espolon and San Nicholas and the distribution network for the Mexican market. In the same year Campari purchased Cabo Wabo, an important producer of ultra premium tequila. These acquisitions allowed the group to directly enter the growing Mexican market with a consolidated productive and distribution structure.

In 2009 Campari carried out a further expansion in the whisky segment and in the wine business. In May 2009 the Campari Group finalized the acquisition from Pernod Ricard of Wild Turkey, one of the leading premium brands of Kentucky bourbon worldwide, strengthening its position among the leaders on the US premium spirits market and on some important international markets. The acquisition included the Wild Turkey and American Honey brands, the Wild Turkey distillery in Kentucky (USA) and stocks of product. Wild Turkey is a global brand with sales in more than 60 markets.

In 2009 Campari also completed the purchase of the Ukrainian company CJSC Odessa, a company operating in the sparkling wine business.

In conclusion, from 1995 to 2009 Campari expanded its portfolio of products through the acquisition of a series of brands and companies with the purpose of strengthening its competitive position in the international market.

At present, Campari has a portfolio of products that cover different segments and different countries, either in mature or emerging markets.

The investments made to sustain the growth have been significant, especially those in acquisitions of companies and brands, as shown by the data reported in Table 9.9.

Table 9.9 Investments in acquisitions in the period, 2005–2009

	2005	2006	2007	2008	2009
Investments in acquisitions of companies and trademarks (€ million)	131	179	29	87	441

Source: Our elaboration of Campari *Annual Reports 2005–2009*.

The effects of the growth strategies carried out in the period 2000–2009 are shown in Tables 9.10 and 9.11. Campari principally invested in the spirits business, obtaining a very important increase in sales, from €236 million in 2000 to €740 million in 2009, with an increase of 213.4%. The growth in the wine business has also been important: sales increased from €70.7 to €154.9 (+119.1%). Through acquisitions Campari widened and geographically diversified its portfolio of products and brands, matching customers' needs and preferences in different countries. The growth of sales has mainly been obtained in the spirits business (Table 9.10) and in various geographical areas, in the USA and Latin America (Table 9.11).

Table 9.10 Growth of sales by business in the period, 2000–2009

Sales (in €million)	2000	%	2009	%	2009–2000	% increase
Spirits	236.0	54.38	739.6	73.34	503.6	213.4
Wine	70.7	16.29	154.9	15.36	84.2	119.1
Soft drinks	124.3	28.64	100.3	9.95	–24,0	–19.3
Other sales	3.0	0.69	13.7	1.36	10.7	356.7
Total	434.0	100.00	1008.4	100.00	574.4	132.4

Source: Our elaboration of Campari *Annual Report 2009*.

Table 9.11 Growth of sales by geographical markets, 2000–2009

Sales (in € million)	2000	%	2009	%	2009–2000	% increase
Italy	249.2	57.42	388.1	38.48	138.8	55.70
Europe	127.0	29.26	231.6	22.96	104.5	82.28
The Americas of which:	36.3	8.36	325.3	32.28	289.2	796.69
USA			227.7			
Brazil			65.3			
Others			32.2			
Rest of the World and duty free	21.5	4.95	63.5	6.29	41.9	194.88
Total	434.0	100.0	1,008.4	100.00	574.40	132.25

Source: Our elaboration of Campari *Annual Reports 2005–2009.*

The high growth rate in sales of spirits (213.4%) emphasizes the prominence of this business in the growth strategies of Campari. This is due to the dynamics of demand and higher margins that characterize this sector.

The growth strategies realised in the examined period also created a relevant value for shareholders as Tables 9.12a and 9.12b show.

Table 9.12a Campari share prices and stock market capitalization 2001–2005

	2001	2002	2003	2004	2005
Share price (€)	2.64	3.00	3.85	4.73	6.24
Stock market capitalization (€million)	766	871	1,170	1,372	1,812

Note: Values at the end of period.

Source: Our elaboration of Campari *Annual Reports 2001–2005.*

Table 9.12b Campari share prices and stock market capitalization 2006–2009

	2006	2007	2008	2009
Share price (€)	7.52	6.56	4.80	7.30
Stock market capitalization (€million)	2,183	1,909	1,394	2,118

Note: Values at the end of period.

Source: Our elaboration of Campari *Annual Reports 2006–2009.*

THE ORGANIZATIONAL STRUCTURE FOR IMPLEMENTING GROWTH STRATEGIES

To implement its growth strategies the Campari Group developed a holding organizational structure capable of managing differentiated activities and world-wide businesses (Figure 9.2).

The formal structure is based on an operating holding, Davide Campari Milano S.p.A, controlling a number of subsidiaries, each maintaining its original brand and products. Some of these companies are trading companies operating in different markets (for example Campari Austria, Campari Deutschland, Campari Argentina, Campari Australia, Campari International, etc.), other companies are manufacturing and trading companies (such as Zedda Piras, CJSC Odessa, Old Smuggler Whisky Company, etc.), and others are more sub holdings in turn controlling manufacturing and trading companies (such as Glen Grant Ltd a holding controlling Glen Grant Ltd Distillery Company; Sella & Mosca holding, etc.).

The operating structure is characterized by a corporate office with functional staff and seven business units: five geographical business units, one product line business unit (wine) and one manufacturing business unit:

- global product supply chain business unit;
- Italy business unit;
- North America business unit;
- South America business unit;
- international business unit;
- central Europe business unit;
- wine business unit.

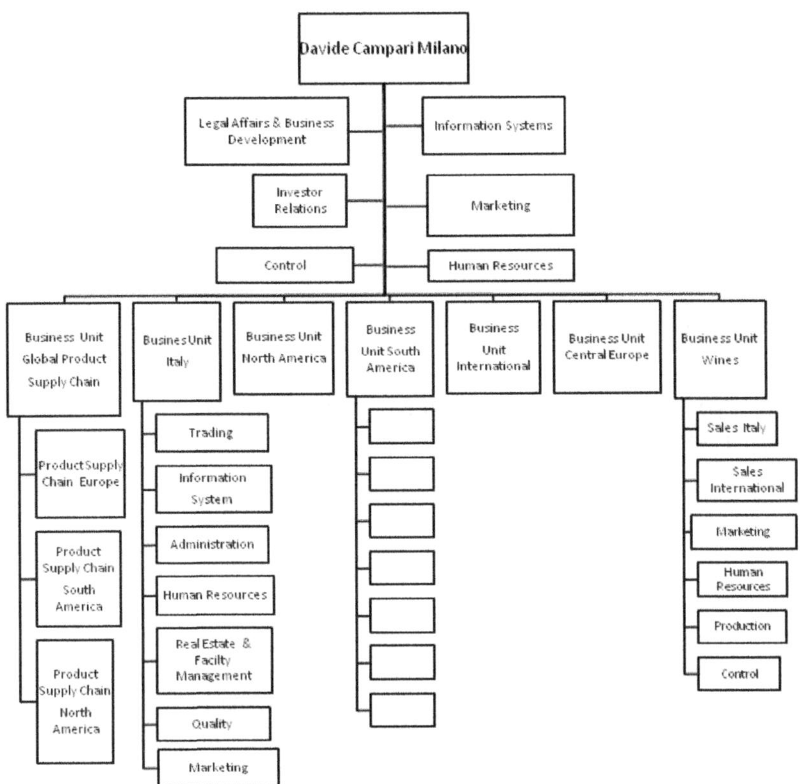

Source: Our elaboration on Campari, "Modello organizzativo, di gestione e controllo" (30 March 2010).

Figure 9.2 Organizational structure of Campari

CAMPARI STRATEGIC RESOURCES FOR GROWTH: DISTINCTIVE COMPETENCES IN MANAGING BRANDS AND MARKETS

To create value, Campari levered on some distinctive firm resources, such as a strong brand image and superior competence in marketing management.

An example is Campari Mixx, a new product launched in 2002 on the market of "ready-to-drink products", a long drink with a sensual packaging, where the 27.5cl bottle is dressed (cap included) with a wrapping in passionate colours with an austere design. This is the most innovative product in recent years, the first ready-to-drink product formulated and realised in Italy.

Over the years, Campari sustained and improved its distinctive resources, brands and image, with relevant promotional investments. With this aim in mind, the role of advertising has been very important for communicating unique sensations and emotions, making every Campari product original and attractive. As image is a key factor to success in the beverage business, Campari imposed a very high standard in creating image and sustaining advertising campaigns. The importance for Campari of creating a strong image is proved by the financial means allocated to brands every year. As shown in Tables 9.13 and 9.14, advertising and promotion expenditures constantly represent 17–18% of net sales.

Table 9.13 Annual advertising and promotional expenditures by Campari

€ million	2000	2001	2002	2003	2004
Net sales	433	494	661	714	751
Advertising and prom. expenses.	80	91	131	144	131
Advertising and prom. exp./net sales (%)	18.4	18.5	19.80	20.12	17.48

Source: Our elaboration of Campari *Annual Reports*.

Table 9.14 Annual advertising and promotional expenditures by Campari

€ million	2005	2006	2007	2008	2009
Net sales	810	932	957	942	1,008
Advertising and prom. exp.	140	163	175	173	172
Advertising and prom. exp./ Net sales (%)	17.25	17.49	18.23	18.34	17.02

Source: Our elaboration of Campari *Annual Reports*.

Know-how and advanced technologies in spirits and wines production also represent strategic resources for Campari. During its life Campari has always maintained high quality in its products and developed important process innovations, constantly increasing the productivity of factors, especially labour. For example, important results in reducing labour costs have been obtained by introducing high precision new technology for bottling sparkling wines.

Levering on distinctive resources, management made it possible to create value for shareholders through coherent growth strategies, carried out in very competitive markets so far dominated by large international companies.

CONCLUSION

In the last decade Campari has achieved a fast growth in sales mainly through a series of acquisitions of companies and brands. Through the expansion in new segments and new geographical markets, Campari exploited relevant economies of scale and economies of scope, particularly as far as distribution and marketing activities are concerned.

For example, through the acquisition of Aperol, Campari integrated its offer with a consolidated brand in the medium alcoholic spirits segment which is experiencing a strong growth in Italy and internationally. Through the acquisition of Skyy Spirits, Campari diversified its product portfolio, acquiring a strong and dynamic brand; the acquisition allowed Campari to strengthen its distribution network in the USA with relevant synergies for the other brands, also obtaining an important geographical diversification of its sales. Furthermore, the acquisition allowed Campari to have new managers with proved success at its disposal.

In the wine business, the Barbero acquisition allowed Campari to acquire the Italian distribution network of Barbero with relevant cost synergies. The merger also gave Campari increasing bargaining power over wholesalers and large retailers and allowed it to exploit the know-how and technology of Barbero in wine production.

At present, Campari has an extensive brand portfolio, well balanced worldwide by products and by market areas. Leveraging on its strong image, very distinctive brands and a global distribution network, Campari can aspire to obtain further success in international markets.

10. Luxottica: a multidimensional growth strategy

COMPANY PROFILE

Luxottica is the world leader in the eyewear business, with net sales reaching €5.1 billion in 2009, approximately 60,000 employees and a strong global presence worldwide (Table 10.1).

Founded by Leonardo Del Vecchio in 1961, the group is a vertically integrated organization that manufactures prescription glasses and sunglasses with a wide-reaching wholesale distribution network and a direct retail distribution network comprising over 6,200 retail locations, mostly in North America, Asia-Pacific and China.

Product design, development and manufacturing take place in six production facilities in Italy, two wholly-owned factories in China and two sunglasses production facilities in the USA. Luxottica also has a plant in India, serving the local market. In 2009, production reached approximately 50 million units.

Luxottica products focus on design and quality and are known all around the world thanks to a strong and well-balanced brand portfolio. House brands include Ray-Ban, one of the world's best known sun brands, Oakley, Vogue, Persol, Oliver Peoples, Arnette and REVO, while its license brands include Bvlgari, Burberry, Chanel, Dolce & Gabbana, Donna Karan, Polo Ralph Lauren, Paul Smith, Prada, Salvatore Ferragamo, Stella McCartney, Tiffany, Tory Burch and Versace.

The group's wholesale distribution, covering 130 countries across five continents, has 23 distribution centres and over 40 commercial subsidiaries providing direct operations in key markets. Wholesale distribution is integrated by an extensive direct retail network, with 6,217 stores, of which 535 are in franchising, mainly located in North America and Asia-Pacific.

Luxottica is a leader also in the prescription glasses business, in North America with its LensCrafters and Pearle Vision chains, and in Asia-Pacific with OPSM, Laubman & Pank and Budget Eyewear chains.

In 2009, Luxottica distributed approximately 19.7 million prescription frames and approximately 35.3 million sunglasses, in approximately 6,400 different styles (Luxottica, *Annual Report 2009*).

LUXOTTICA'S POSITION IN THE EYEWEAR INDUSTRY

Eyewear production worldwide is estimated at over €10 billion in 2007, with a share of high quality and luxury products reaching about 20% of the total market (ANFAO, 2008). The main markets are in North America and Europe, but the Chinese market is increasing rapidly. Eyewear industry products include sunglasses, frames, lenses, protection spectacles and goggles (Table 10.1).

Table 10.1 The structure of the eyewear industry by products (2007)

Products	Market share in %
Sunglasses	32.8
Frames	34.9
Lenses	20.7
Protective, goggles, etc.	11.6
Total	100.0

Source: ANFAO (2008).

As far as the industry structure is concerned, eyewear production is located in South-East Asia and Latin America, where 50% of low segment production is carried out, and in Europe (Italy, France, Germany, Spain, the UK, Austria), North America (USA) and Japan, where medium and high segment products are produced.

On the basis of 2007 data, Italy has a leadership position in the eyewear industry with a share of approximately 27% of total production value equal to

€2,724 million and €2,316 million of exports. Much higher is the Italian share in the highest segments of the market, in which it is present with 154 brands out of a total of nearly 300 worldwide.

In second place is China with a share of 25% of total production value, followed by France, the USA and Germany, each of them with a market share of about 5–6%. In particular, Italy has a leadership position in high added value products and it is appreciated worldwide for style, design, technology and quality. Export represents about 80% of Italy's production and the majority of exports are represented by sunglasses. The main export markets are the USA, Spain and France.

In 2007, 1,040 companies were operating in Italy, of which 185 were industrial firms and 855 craft firms, with about 18,500 employees in total (ANFAO, 2008). They were mainly located in the Belluno district (Veneto region) and characterized by different size and activity: little artisan firms involved in some operations of the glass production cycle, firms producing components and the entire product for other larger firms and for the market, and finally firms producing for the market with their own brands.

The industry is in rapid evolution influenced by globalization processes; it is a global industry characterized by expansion and slowing down phases. It is characterized by a process of continuous concentration led by the need to exploit the economies of scale in production and distribution and the economies of scope emerging by related product diversification and vertical integration. In 2007 a small number of large companies controlled 70% of the market while approximately 1,000 craft firms divided the remaining 30% of the market.

The most important Italian competitors of Luxottica are Safilo, Marcolin and De Rigo (Table 10.2).

Table 10.2 Main Italian competitors of Luxottica (2007)

	Marcolin	De Rigo	Safilo
Sales (€ mill.)	182	558	1,190
Number of models	600	n.a	2,500
House brands	Cebè, Marcolin, Titanio T22	Police, Sting and Lozza	Sàfilo, Oxydo, Blue Bay, Carrera and Smith

Source: Our elaboration of Luxottica *Annual Reports* data.

Among the foreign competitors the most important are: Essilor International, Marchon, The Cooper Companies, Fgx and Fielmann (Table 10.3).

Table 10.3 The main foreign competitors of Luxottica (2007)

	Marchon	The Cooper Companies	FGX International	Fielmann
Sales (€mill.)	525	951	241	1,068
Number of models	200	n.a.	n.a	n.a
House brands	Marchon	CooperVision	Foster Grant; Magnivision Private Eyes Angel	Fielmann

Source: Our elaboration of Luxottica *Annual Reports* data.

THE GROWTH OF LUXOTTICA: SALES, INVESTMENTS AND OPERATING PROFITS IN THE PERIOD 1994–2009

Through the analysis of economic and financial data it is possible to evaluate the great success and the strong growth obtained by Luxottica. Figure 10.1 and Tables 10.4 and 10.5 show the main financial outcomes from 1994 to 2009.

The great growth achieved from 1994 to 1996 is due to the acquisition of Persol in 1995 and of US Shoe, whose optical division LensCrafters represented the largest premium optical retail brand in the US market. The period registered an extraordinary increase of sales from €419 to €1,225 million and an increase of 66% in net income.

From 1996 to 1999, the growth of Luxottica continued constantly at an average annual rate of 16% both in net sales and industrial gross margin, while the operating income registered an increase of 9% and the net income of 14%.

In 1999 Luxottica bought the optical division of Bausch & Lomb and with that the brand Ray-Ban. The success of this acquisition is proved by the outcomes obtained in 2000: an increase in sales of 30% in 2000, an increase in gross profit of 13%, in operating income of 73% and in net income of 68%.

The growth of Luxottica continued in 2001 and 2002, due to the acquisition of Sunglass Hut the world's leading premium specialty sun retailer.

In 2003 Luxottica registered a contraction of sales due to three adverse conditions: the fall of the dollar, the adverse economic situation and the negative effect of the non-renewal of the Armani license.

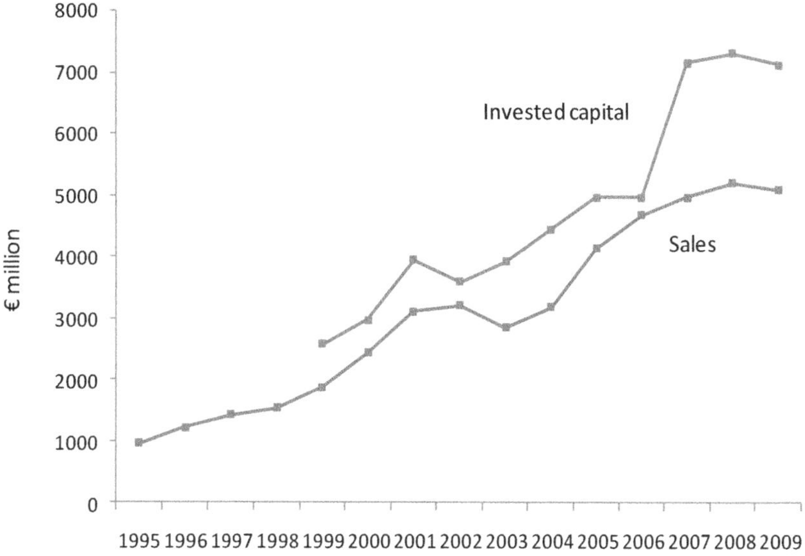

Source: Our elaboration of Luxottica *Annual Reports* data.

Figure 10.1 Luxottica sales and invested capital

In 2004 Luxottica returned to growth following by the acquisition at the end of 2003 of OPSM, the leading optical store chain operator in Asia-Pacific. New brands compensated for the loss of the Armani license: Donna Karan and Dolce & Gabbana. In 2004 Luxottica also acquired Cole National, the second-largest optical store chain operator in North America, with retail brands including Pearle Vision, Sears Optical and Target Optical.

In 2005 Luxottica entered the Chinese optical retail market through the acquisition of two retail chains; the group became a leading player in China's premium optical market segment, with stores in Beijing, Guangdong and Hong Kong. In 2005 sales exceeded €4 billion with an increase of 34% with respect to the previous year and the net income increased by 19%, mainly due to the acquisition of Cole National.

In 2006 the Group expanded its distribution in North America and China through acquisitions in Canada, the Midwest United States and Shanghai; it entered into an agreement to open Sunglass Hut stores in the Middle East.

Table 10.4 Main financial outcomes of Luxottica from 1994 to 2001

€ million	1994	1995	1996	1997	1998	1999	2000	2001
Net sales	419	954	1,225	1,430	1,538	1,874	2,439	3,105
Rate of increase in sales (%)		127.7	28.4	16.7	7.6	21.8	30.1	27.3
Gross profit	n.a	n.a	n.a	n.a	n.a	n.a	1720	2182
Operating income	118	153	179	223	226	238	412	510
Income before taxes	n.a	n.a	n.a	n.a	n.a	n.a	362	441
Net income (1)	64	83	106	129	133	152	255	316
Earning per share (€)	0.14	0.19	0.24	0.29	0.30	0.34	0.57	0.70
Total assets	n.a.	n.a.	n.a.	n.a.	n.a.	2,568	2,968	3,948
Shareholders' equity	n.a.	n.a.	n.a.	n.a.	n.a.	n.a.	n.a.	n.a.

Notes: Data from 1994 to 2001 have been obtained from annual reports in Italian lira converted at a fixed change Lire 1,936.27 = Euro 1.00; ADS = 1 ordinary share; all data in US dollars have been converted at the average change of the reference period.
(1) Attributable to Luxottica Group shareholders.

Source: Our elaboration on Luxottica, *Annual Reports 2000–2009* (Consolidated financial statements in accordance with US GAAP).

Table 10.5 Main financial outcomes of Luxottica from 2002 to 2009

€ million	2002	2003	2004	2005	2006	2007	2008	2009
Net sales	3,201	2,852	3,180	4,134	4,676	4,966	5,202	5,094
Rate of increase in sales (%)	3.1	−11.0	11.5	30.0	13.1	6.9	4.7	−2.1
Gross profit	2,256	1,914	2,127	2,761	3,188	3,390	3,450	3,326
Operating income	601	431	479	581	756	833	750	583
Income before taxes	539	389	445	539	678	781	590	494
Net income (1)	372	267	286	342	424	492	380	315
Earnings per share (€)	0.82	0.60	0.64	0.76	0.95	1.08	0.83	0.69
Total assets	3,586	3,913	4,456	4,973	4,969	7,157	7,305	7,136
Shareholders equity	n.a	1,374	1,495	1,954	2,216	2,495	2,554	2,860

Notes: Attributable to Luxottica Group shareholders.

Source: Our elaboration on Luxottica, *Annual Reports 2000–2009* (Consolidated financial statements in accordance with US GAAP).

In 2007 the acquisition of Oakley provided the group with exceptional potential, due not only to the force and name recognition of the Oakley brand, but, in addition, to its portfolio of seven brands and four distribution chains.

In 2008 sales exceeded €5 billion. The growth of sales was accompanied by a relevant increase in shareholders' equity and in earnings per share. In particular, operating income increased by €118 million in 1994 to €238 million in 1999 and €833 in 2007 (the last year before the recent great recession of 2008–2009) and net income increased from €64 million in 1994 to €152 million in 1999 and to €492 million in 2007. In the same period the net earnings per share increased from €0.14 in 1994 to €0.34 in 1999 and €1.08 in 2007.

In the period considered the total invested capital increased from €2,568 million in 1999 to €3,913 million in 2003 and to € 7,157 million in 2009. The shareholders equity increased from €1,374 million in 2003 to €2,860 million in 2009. The strong creation of value realised in this period, through the extraordinary growth of the company, is clear evidence of the success of strategies adopted.

THE GROWTH STRATEGIES OF LUXOTTICA: HORIZONTAL EXPANSION, PRODUCT DIVERSIFICATION AND VERTICAL INTEGRATION

The company's long-term objective has been expanding and reaching a leading position in the global eyewear market by growing in all its businesses, both organically and through acquisitions. More precisely, the long-term growth of Luxottica has been based on a multi-dimensional strategy characterized by:

- product diversification;
- horizontal expansion in different segments and geographical markets through a wide and balanced portfolio of brands;
- vertical integration of production process and retail distribution.

Product diversification and horizontal expansion strategies (1985–2009)

During the 1970s and the first half of the 1980s the activity of Luxottica concentrated on producing and selling prescription glasses of high quality with its own brands Luxottica and Steroflex. This policy permitted Luxottica to obtain relevant outcomes both in competitive and in financial terms.

In the late 1980s Luxottica decided to diversify its production, entering into the sunglasses business. Luxottica clearly understood the trend of the glasses market: glasses were changing from a medical product and instrument to a fashion product, where the non-material characteristics, such as the beauty, style and image become more and more important. Eyeglasses, previously perceived as mere sight-correcting instruments, began to evolve into "eyewear". This tendency would pull the development of medium–high segments that could be served through design products, interpreting well the new function of glasses. In effect, sunglasses, but also prescription glasses, became not only an instrument, even personalized and functional, but a true fashion accessory, a way of expressing a lifestyle, personality and image. In particular, sunglasses became an element of a total look, able to express a personality. The sunglasses market became of increasing importance and the high segment was completely conquered by stylists' brand products.

The understanding of this market evolution had a clear and immediate consequence for Luxottica: the house brands Luxottica and *Steroflex* could be used also for the sunglasses market (that represented at that time only 5% of sales), but they would not be able to anticipate customers' preferences and needs and even more to impose new fashion tendencies. The management understood that only the introduction of the world's best known fashion brands would determine the radical change in the industry and the success in the market.

So the main objective of Luxottica was to increase its presence in the sunglasses business, with a particular attention to the US market that presented high opportunities for growth. This strategy reflected the right understanding of market dynamics: the sunglasses market presented higher profit margins than the prescription market, not only for the existing competitive forces but also for the possible evolution of medical therapies and optical surgery. Rebalancing the production mix and increasing the share of sunglasses production would increase profits and also reduce the risk of a high presence in the prescription business.

In order to be successful in this new business, style and fashion were of fundamental importance. For this reason in 1988 Luxottica decided to embark on its first collaboration with the fashion industry, by entering into a licensing agreement with Giorgio Armani. Then the company decided to buy some important and well known brands and to define license agreements with other important fashion stylists to achieve different market segments.

The segmentation was enlarged basing itself on specific needs and demands of different targets, even through an increase of advertising pressure. The advertising leverage became more and more important, so that the communication expenditures came to represent 12–13% of sales for sunglasses and 8% for prescription glasses.

In 1990 the brands portfolio was incremented by the acquisition of Fidia, a company licensee of the Valentino brand, and of Florence Line, a trading company owner of the brand Vogue Lunettes. In the same year the license of the Yves Saint Laurent brand was signed.

In 1995 Luxottica acquired Persol. Founded in 1917 in Turin (Italy), Persol specialized in sunglasses and was well known for its quality, innovation and fashion products. It was positioned in the high segment of the sunglasses business. Persol sales were 55% on the Italian market and 45% in foreign markets. Through this acquisition Luxottica enforced its position in the high segment of the market, acquiring a very prestigious and famous brand, well known among the Hollywood stars.

In 1999 Luxottica acquired the optical division of Bausch & Lomb, producers of the famous sunglasses Ray Ban. This was one of the world's best-known sunglasses brands. Through this acquisition, Luxottica also obtained crystal sunglass lens technology and the associated manufacturing capacity and upgraded its portfolio with brands like Arnette, REVO and Killer Loop. Bausch & Lomb was the leader in the American market, in particular in the medium–high segment, with a share of about 36–40%, due to the Ray-Ban brand. For Luxottica the acquisition of Ray-Ban represented a good opportunity to balance its portfolio, reinforcing its position in the medium–high segment of the sunglasses market through a leading brand affirmed and known worldwide. The acquisition also allowed Luxottica to balance the ratio between sales realised with house brands and sales with license brands. Then, this acquisition allowed Luxottica to increase the critical mass of production with a consequent reduction in unit cost, due to the economies of scale. The Ray Ban brand also offered new opportunities for growth in North America and in the original markets of Luxottica, in addition to the opportunities offered by the acquisition of know-how owned by Bausch & Lomb on sun lenses. Thanks to this acquisition Luxottica extended its portfolio to the Ray-Ban, Killer Loop, Rēvo, Porsche Design, Arnette and Suncluod lines. In addition Luxottica also acquired all Ray-Ban factories in Texas, Ireland, Hong Kong and Italy.

In the following years Luxottica continued to pursue a horizontal expansion strategy, extending its product line by acquiring new brands and realizing new license agreements with famous stylists and fashion companies. Enlarging the range of products and the brands portfolio, Luxottica exploited relevant synergies in costs and revenues.

From 1995 to 2009 a number of brands were included in the Luxottica portfolio: Anne Klein, Bulgari (1996), Chanel (1999) and Salvatore Ferragamo (1998). In 2003 other license agreements were signed for the brands Emporio Armani, Sergio Tacchini, Brooks Brothers, in 2004 for Versace and Prada, in 2005 for Donna Karan and Burberry, in 2006 for Dolce and Gabbana, in 2007 for Polo, Ralph Lauren, in 2008 for Tiffany and in 2009 for Stella McCartney and Tory Burch.

In 2007 Luxottica acquired California-based Oakley, a leading sport and performance glasses brand, for $2.1 billion. Oakley, a brand known and appreciated worldwide, owned the Oliver Peoples brand and had a license to manufacture and distribute the Paul Smith brand; furthermore it owned a retail network of over 160 direct stores.

In the last years Luxottica has further extended its brands portfolio, currently owning 26 brands of which eight are house brands and 18 licensed brands.

The long-term objectives have remained the same: focusing on leading brands, balancing house and license brands and avoiding brand dilution. Therefore, the Luxottica portfolio is in a continuous evolution, by the acquisition of new brands, the stipulation of new licensing agreements and the renewal of existing ones and the withdrawal of brands no longer deemed strategic. The Luxottica diversification strategy in the sunglasses business has clearly been successful; the increase in sales has been relevant and since 2002 sunglasses have became the most important business (Table 10.6).

Table 10.6 The evolution of Luxottica businesses from 1990 to 2002

Sales in units by use (%)	1990	1994	1998	2002	2009
Sunglasses	10	24	34.8	59.3	64.2
Prescription glasses	90	76	65,2	40.7	35.8
Total	100	100	100	100	100

Source: Our elaboration of Luxottica *Annual Reports*.

Table 10.7 shows, in chronological order, the main acquisitions made by Luxottica for penetrating the medium–high segments of the sunglasses business.

Table 10.7 Luxottica relevant acquisitions in sunglasses business

Year of acquisition	Company acquired	Brands
1990	Florence Line	Vogue
1995	Persol	Persol
1999	Bausch & Lomb	Ray Ban, Arnette, Rēvo, Killer Loop
2007	Oakley	Oakley, Oliver People, Paul Smith

Source: Our elaboration of Luxottica *Annual Reports*.

Today, Luxottica has a large brand portfolio, with major global brands backed by leading brands both at a regional level and in particular segments and niche markets. It is balanced between house and license brands, combining the stability and volumes of the former with the prestige and high margins of the latter. Consider that in 2002 designer lines represented only 39.5% of total sales, with respect to 60.5% of house brands.

Through house brands Luxottica develops approximately 500 distinct styles, of which 300 are in optical and 200 in sunglasses. Each style is typically produced in two sizes and five colours. The different house brands are positioned to cover different market segments on the basis of characteristics of each brand.

In particular, the presence of Ray-Ban, one of the world's best-selling brands of sun and prescription eyewear, and Oakley, a leader in the sport and performance category, gives the portfolio a strong base on the medium–high market segment, complemented by Persol and Oliver Peoples in the high-end of the market, the Arnette and REVO brands in the sports market, and Vogue in the fashion market.

Alongside the house brands, the portfolio today has over 20 license brands, including some well known and prestigious names in the global fashion and luxury industries. With its manufacturing know-how, capillary distribution and direct retail operations, supported by targeted advertising and experience in international markets, Luxottica is the ideal partner for fashion houses and stylists seeking to translate their style and values into successful premium quality eyewear collections.

Luxottica differentiates each designer's offering as much as possible, meticulously segmenting it by type of customer and geographical market, to produce a broad range of models capable of satisfying the most diverse tastes and tendencies and to respond to the demands and characteristics of widely differing markets. Table 10.8 shows the most important license brands.

Designer lines are produced and distributed through license agreements with major fashion houses. The operating profiles of the license agreements with the different fashion houses and stylists are characterized by a ten-year average duration and consist of obtaining the license for producing and selling glasses with the relative brand with the payment of a royalty of 8–11% on net sales and the sustaining of advertising costs of about 5% on sales.

Designer collections are developed through the collaborative efforts of Luxottica's in-house design staff and the brand designers.

Since the 1970s Luxottica also developed a horizontal expansion entering foreign markets through the opening of commercial branches and agreements or joint ventures with local partners, often wholesalers. Luxottica expanded in Germany, Spain, the UK, France and Sweden, while still continuing to grow in North America.

Table 10.8 Luxottica house and licensing brands in 2009

Type of brand	Brands
House brands	Luxottica, Sferoflex, Persol, REVO, Vogue, Ray-Ban, K&L, K&L, Mosley Tribes, Eye Safety Systems, Oakley
Licensed brands	Brooks Brothers,Paul Smith, Bvlgari, Chanel, Anne Klein, Prada, Burberry, Dolce & Gabbana, D&G, Donna Karan, DKNY, Fox, Miu Miu, Chaps, Ralph Lauren, Ralph, Salvatore Ferragamo, Stella McCartne, Tiffany & Co., Club Monaco, Polo, Ralph Lauren Purple Label, Tory Burch, Versace, Versus

Source: Our elaboration of Luxottica *Annual Report 2009*.

The breakdown of sales by geographical areas, shown in Table 10.9, demonstrates the success of the international expansion strategy.

Table 10.9 Luxottica net sales by geographical area in 2009

Sales (€million)	2009	%
North America	3,056	60
Rest of the World	1,379	27
Asia, Pacific	662	13
Total	5,094	100

Source: Our elaboration of Luxottica *Annual Report 2009*.

In parallel to the expansion of sales, Luxottica has progressively expanded its production capacity. Today Luxottica has six facilities in Italy using advanced technologies; each of them specializes in a particular production technology (metal frames, lenses for sunglasses, etc.) and two facilities in China. The choice of realizing 80% of its production in Italy derives from

Luxottica's will to create a high quality product with the best characteristics of "made in Italy".

Horizontal expansion has also allowed Luxottica to become a cost leader in the industry by exploiting economies of scale in production (through a higher specialization and a larger plant size) and in distribution activities and the exploiting of learning economies through a larger cumulative production of components, parts and products.

Vertical integration strategy in manufacturing (1970–2009)

Luxottica has followed a vertical integration strategy in manufacturing since the first years of its life. Having started out in 1961 as a small workshop, Luxottica operated as a contract producer of dyes, metal components and semi-finished goods for the optical industry until the end of the 1960s. Then, the company gradually widened the range of processes until it had an integrated manufacturing structure capable of producing a finished pair of glasses. In 1971, Luxottica's first collection of prescription eyewear was presented at Milan's MIDO (an international optics trade fair), thus marking Luxottica's transition from contract manufacturer to independent producer.

To day, the group's structure covers the entire chain of value. This situation is the result of a far-sighted choice made by the Company's founder and current chairman, who understood the potential of "vertical" strategy deciding to make entire frames rather than just components.

In terms of manufacturing, the company has vertically integrated all the phases of the production process in order to attain a level of efficiency in line with the quality of products and services it intended to offer. Direct control of the entire production platform makes it possible to verify the quality of products and processes, introduce innovations, exploit synergies and discover new operating methods, optimizing times and costs.

The vertical integration strategy has represented a fundamental and critical factor in Luxottica's success, because it enabled the firm to maintain leadership in costs together with high quality products. It distinguished Luxottica from Italian competitors that generally decentralized production phases and components to other district firms. The vertical integration strategy was based not simply on a comparison of costs between making and buying operations and components, but on a more complex evaluation of consequences in quality of products, guarantee of customer service and market control.

Obviously, the vertical integration strategy requires relevant investments in production capacity, as well as in designing and developing new technologies and products. As a consequence of this strategy, in Luxottica all phases of the production process are integrated and internally managed; in particular the following ones:

- design;
- prototype realization;
- product engineering;
- moulds and frames components production;
- product production of sunglass frames and lenses.

For reducing product costs all facilities are specialized by product technology. Three main manufacturing technologies are involved: metal, acetate slabs and plastic (injection moulding). Plastic frames are made in the Agordo, Sedico, Pederobba and Lauriano plants, while metal frames are produced in Agordo and Rovereto. Certain metal frame parts are produced in the Cencenighe plant. The Lauriano plant also makes crystal and polycarbonate lenses for sunglasses. The Dongguan plants, in China's Guangdong province, make both plastic and metal frames.

In 2009, approximately 46% of the frames manufactured by Luxottica were metal-based, and the remaining were plastic.

Summarizing, the vertical integration strategy in manufacturing permitted Luxottica to obtain:

- economies in transaction costs;
- scope economies in joint production operations;
- scale economies in production, control, coordination and R&D activities.

This strategy also allowed Luxottica to raise greater barriers to entry in the glasses industry and obtain stronger bargaining power towards suppliers and clients, with relevant effects on margins.

Vertical integration strategy in retail distribution (1974–2009)

In the early 1970s, the company sold its frames exclusively through wholesalers. In 1974, after five years of sustained development of its manufacturing capacity, Luxottica decided to distribute frames directly onto the market. The first step was the acquisition of the Scarrone company, which had marketed the company's products since 1971 and which brought with it vital knowledge of the Italian market.

International expansion began in the 1980s with the acquisition of independent distributors, the opening of branches and the forming of joint ventures in key international markets. Having started with the opening of the first commercial subsidiary in Germany in 1981, the company's international wholesale development continued with the acquisition of Avant-Garde Optics Inc., a wholesale distributor in the US market, in the mid-1980s.

Over several decades, Luxottica has also integrated its retail distribution, building a direct distribution network. After having used the consolidated wholesale channel in the beginning, like all companies in the eyewear industry, Luxottica began to use, starting from the domestic market, a direct selling channel for both a stronger control of distribution and a direct relationship with customers. This strategy has represented another constant line in the development of Luxottica right from the beginning to recent years. In this way Luxottica gradually entered the rich retail glasses business that is characterized by higher markup and profit margins, especially in the luxury sunglasses segment.

The vertical integration of retail activities was mainly obtained through some relevant acquisitions. The first acquisition was Avant-Garde Optics Inc. (1982), one of the largest commercial companies in the world operating in the optical industry and based in Long Island (New York).

The strategy was reinforced in 1995 by the acquisition of US Shoe and, within this group, of LensCrafters, the largest retail optical chain operating in the USA market with 600 stores. The American market was the most important market for Luxottica, where the company already exported 39% of its production, and it presented great opportunities for growth. The acquisition of LensCrafters allowed Luxottica to exploit important synergies in product distribution, due to the commercial and marketing strength of the American stores chain and increasing penetration of its products through LensCrafters stores.

In 2001 the Luxottica Group further enforced its leadership with the acquisition of Sunglass Hut International, the largest world retail chain for sunglasses. Sunglass Hut was focused on a high segment of the sunglasses market in North America and in Europe and was a leader in retail distribution with 1962 stores, distributed throughout the USA, Australia, New Zealand and Singapore. The acquisition permitted Luxottica to have a preeminent position on the entire market of glasses distribution in North America, unifying the distribution chain leader in prescription glasses (LensCrafters) with the largest sunglasses distribution chain.

Making leverage on the successful brands in its portfolio, such as Ray Ban, Rēvo, Persol, Killer Loop, Vogue, Arnette and Sunglass Hut, Luxottica largely increased sales in its retailing stores, thus obtaining relevant synergies in costs and revenues.

Moreover, in 2003 Luxottica acquired the retail chain OPSM, operating in Australia, New Zealand, Hong Kong, Singapore and Malaysia, reaching an important market share in this area. OPSM Group was the leader in the retail market in Australia (with 481 stores and three brands), New Zealand (34 stores) and south-east Pacific, in particular Hong Kong with 80 stores and Singapore and Malaysia with 12 each. OPSM Group had three chains: OPSM, Laubman & Pank and Budget Eyewear, each of them operating in a well defined market segment.

This acquisition allowed Luxottica to reinforce its presence in a market area that was not yet covered. The strategy of segmentation and rationalization of OPSM Group brands made the original brands well distinguished: Laubman & Pank for sight care; OPSM for fashion demand; Budget Eyewear for customers more sensitive to price.

Soon after, at the beginning of 2004 Luxottica bought the American Cole National, with its chain of 2,100 shops with brands Pearle Vision, Sears Optical, Target Optical and BJ's Optical. Cole National was the second player in the US market, owner of the historical brands Pearle Vision and of a large net of stores as well as of an optical department managed by licensed brands such as Sears Optical, Target Optical and BJ's Optical. Among these brands the most important was Pearle Vision, present in the US market from more than 40 years with stores specializing in eyesight care and glasses of high quality, elegance and proverbial refinement. At the end of 2004, 1,300 stores were located in diversified department stores such as Sears, Target and BJ's Wholesale Club, each of them with a specific position on the retail market.

In addition to the retail chain, the acquisition of Cole National gave Luxottica the property of seven central laboratories which, together with those of LensCrafters, make Luxottica one of the largest networks in the USA. Finally, the integration of Cole National Managed Vision Care in EyeMed Vision Care, made Luxottica the second manager of agreements concerning companies, public administration and insurance companies.

In 2007, Luxottica acquired California-based Oakley, a leading sport and performance brand, for US$ 2.1 billion. Oakley, a brand which is known and appreciated worldwide, owned the Oliver Peoples brand and a license to manufacture and distribute the Paul Smith brand, as well as its own retail network of over 160 stores.

Table 10.10 lists in chronological order the main acquisitions of distribution chains by Luxottica. The entry into the retail business has been a winning strategy for Luxottica. It allows the company to stay in touch with its end users and understand their tastes and tendencies, directly communicating design and quality and avoiding the price competition of wholesalers. Direct distribution is also perceived as a strength by the stylists and fashion houses because it allows Luxottica to have access to global and widespread markets.

In addition, a worldwide distribution network allows Luxottica to exploit the opportunities emerging in different markets, diversifying risks and activating learning processes at an international level, transferring technical solutions, products and marketing knowledge and value from one country to another. Direct distribution thus enables Luxottica to maintain close contact with its clients and maximize the image and visibility of its brands (Table 10.10).

Table 10.10 Luxottica vertical integration strategy in retail distribution: the main acquisitions

Year	Company	Distribution retail chains
1982	Avant Garde Optics	
1995	US Shoe	LensCrafters
2001	Sunglass Hut International	Sunglass Hut
2003	OPSM Group	Laubman & Pank, OPSM, Budget Eyewear
2004	Cole National	Pearle Vision, Sears Optical' Target Optical*, BJ's Optical*
2007	Oakley	Oakley "O" and Vault, Oliver Peoples

Note: * Licensed brands.

Source: Our elaboration of Luxottica *Annual Reports*.

Furthermore, the group's experience in the direct operation of stores in some of its more important countries gives it a unique understanding of the world's eyewear markets. All this makes it possible, among other things, to achieve tight control and strategic optimization of brand diffusion, both house and license brands. As of December 31, 2009, Luxottica's retail business consisted of 6,251 stores, 535 of which were in franchising (Table 10.12)

Also in the retail business Luxottica developed a horizontal strategy to reach different market segments, offering customers a variety of differentiation points, including the latest in designer and high-performance sun frames, advanced lens options, advanced eye care, everyday value and high-quality vision care health benefits.

Table 10.11 Dynamics of net sales by distribution channels

Sales (€million)	1995	%	2000	%	2009	%
Retail	869	77	1,352	61	3,158	62
Wholesale	266	23	873	39	1,936	38
Total	1,135	100	2,225	100	5,094	100

For example, with regard to optical retail, Luxottica's operations are anchored by leading brands such as LensCrafters and Pearle Vision in North America, and OPSM, Laubman & Pank and Budget Eyewear, which are active throughout Australia and New Zealand. The group also has a major retail presence in China, where it operates in the premium eyewear market with LensCrafters.

In particular, LensCrafters stores offer a wide selection of prescription frames and sunglasses, mostly made by Luxottica, but also a wide range of lenses and optical products made by other suppliers. Points of sale are normally in high-traffic commercial malls and shopping centres and have an on-site optometrist (sometimes a Luxottica employee) so that customers can have immediate eye examinations. Most LensCrafters stores in North America also include a lens finishing laboratory, which improves the customer service level.

Due to the fragmented nature of the European retail market, the company does not operate optical retail stores in Europe outside of the United Kingdom, where in 2008 it increased its stake in the David Clulow chain, which sells both prescription and sun products.

Table 10.12 Luxottica retail stores managed in the world

Business areas and brands	North Amer.	EU	Centre South Amer.	Africa India	South Africa	Asia Pacif.	China	Total Stores
Total stores	4,723	159	10	68	80	963	248	6,251
Prescription								
Lenscrafters	955						243	1,198
Pearl Vision	764							764
Sears Optical	866							866
Target Optical	327							327
The Optical S. of Aspen	23							23
D. Clulow		43						43
OPSM						333		333
Laubman & Pank						104		104
Budget Eyewear						98		98
Oliver People						1		1
Prescription & Sun								
Olivers Peop.	7							7
Sun								
Sunglass Hut	1,634	66		67	78	272	6	2,123
ILORI	25							25
D. Clulow		30						30
Bright Eyes						139		139
Sun Clothing								
Oakley	112	20	10	1	2	16		170

Source: Our elaboration on Luxottica *Annual Report 2009*.

Pearle Vision stores focus on the factors that made the brand a success: customers' trust in the doctor's experience and the quality of service they receive. Pearle Vision stores are mostly located in strip malls instead of the conventional malls where most LensCrafters and Sunglass Hut stores are located. OPSM, the largest of the three optical chains Luxottica operates in Australia and New Zealand, is a leading eyewear retail brand for luxury and fashion-conscious customers. Laubman & Pank is well-known for its high quality assortment and services. Its target segment is for the optical shopper looking for quality eye-care and services.

Budget Eyewear focuses on the price-conscious shopper and offers an easy selection process for frames and lens packages in a bright and modern store environment.

Finally, Luxottica operates through a network of retail locations under the brand names of their respective host American department stores. These "licensed brands" are Sears Optical and Target Optical. These points of sale offer consumers the convenience of taking care of their optical needs while shopping at these department stores. Both brands have a precise market positioning that Luxottica has reinforced by improving service levels while strengthening their fashion reputation by offering brands such as Ray-Ban and Vogue.

With regard to the sunglass retail business, Luxottica operates through leading brands such as Sunglass Hut, ILORI, The Optical Shop of Aspen, Bright Eyes and Oakley, each of them specialized in different retail segments.

Sunglass Hut has focused increasingly on selling premium sunglasses. In 2007 Luxottica developed an exclusive new store concept, which is now being extended to all prime Sunglass Hut locations around the world. This repositioning was made possible by substantial changes to the product mix allowing the chain to focus more on fashion and luxury brands, especially for women, while maintaining a varied selection of lifestyle, sport and performance sunglasses.

ILORI addresses a different, more exclusive clientele than Sunglass Hut, offering a richer purchasing experience in prestige locations, featuring sophisticated luxury collections, exclusive niche brands and a highly personalized service.

The Optical Shop of Aspen is known in the optical industry for its luxury brands for both prescription and sunglasses and its first class customer service in some of the most upscale and exclusive locations throughout the United States.

Oliver Peoples operates in luxury retail stores only offering Oliver Peoples, Mosley Tribes and Paul Smith branded optical products.

David Clulow is a premium optical retailer operating in the United Kingdom and in Ireland, predominantly in London and the South East of the United Kingdom. With 50 years of experience, the brand emphasizes service, quality and fashion; its marketing is targeted to reinforcing these brand values and build long-term relationships with customers. In addition to operating optical stores, David Clulow operates a number of sunglass concessions in upmarket department stores, further reinforcing its position as a premium brand in the United Kingdom.

Bright Eyes, one of Australia's largest and fastest-growing sunglass chains, operated 55 corporate store locations and 84 franchise locations, mostly in tourist resorts and high-traffic areas.

Oakley Stores and Vaults offer a full range of Oakley products including sunglasses, apparel, footwear and accessories in stores designed and merchandised to immerse consumers in the Oakley brand through innovative use of product presentation, graphics and original audio and visual elements. In the United States, Oakley "O" Stores can be found in major shopping centres.

The retail integration strategy produced these significant competitive advantages for Luxottica:

- scale economies in marketing and laboratory activities;
- scope economies in marketing and distribution;
- direct information on market trends and clients;
- a reduction in the bargaining power and opportunistic behaviour of clients (wholesalers);
- stability in orders and delivery of products;
- price control in different markets;
- guarantees in service levels and post selling services;
- a larger capability in differenciating products and brands;
- an increase of entry barriers to the industry.

LUXOTTICA'S ORGANIZATIONAL STRUCTURE

Luxottica is quoted on the Milan stock exchange and New York stock exchange. The major shareholders are Delfin S.r.l. (Del Vecchio family) with 67.7% and Giorgio Armani with 4.9%.

The Luxottica Group's governance system is based on a traditional management and control system with shareholders who vote in ordinary and extraordinary meetings and a board of directors. Amongst its members, it appoints an Internal Control Committee, which also assists the board in its internal control functions, and a Human Resources Committee, which provides consulting and recommendations on compensation for top management positions and incentive plans and the composition of management structures for the main subsidiaries.

A board of statutory auditors is responsible for, among other things, overseeing compliance with the law and with the company by-laws, its principles of governance and organizational model. The board of auditors also acts as an audit committee under the Sarbanes–Oxley Act.

The company's accounts are audited by a firm of accountants registered with Consob and appointed by the shareholders' meeting.

The organizational structure at the end of 2009 is shown in Figure 10.2. It is characterized by three organizational areas, reporting directly to the CEO: central service functions, business units and operating processes departments.

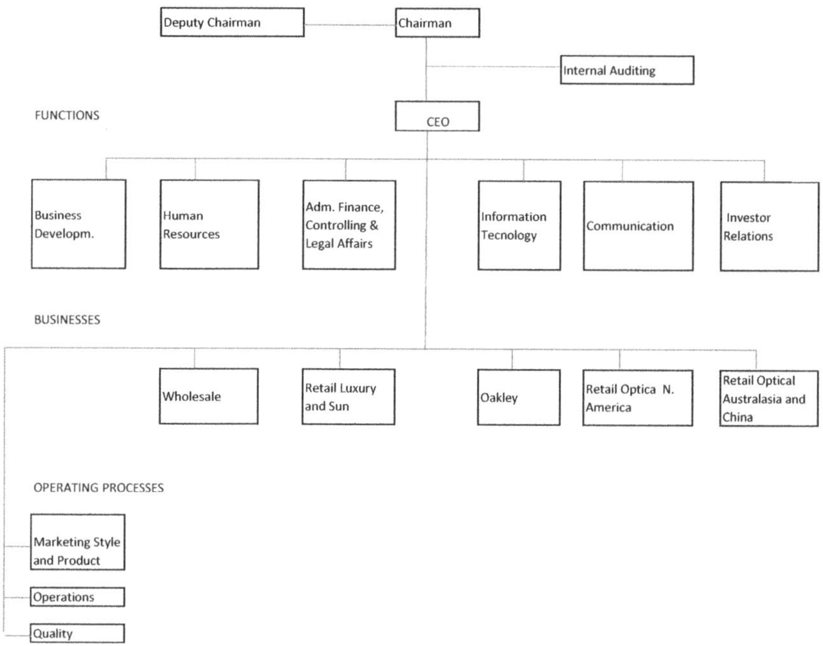

Note: in 2009 Mr Guerra was Group's CEO and director of the Operations department.

Figure 10.2 Luxottica's organizational structure at February 2010

The central service functions are the following:

- Information Technology,
- Business Development,
- Administration, Finance & Controlling,
- Communications,
- Investor Relations,
- Human Resources.

These form a system of services that support the group's businesses and, by applying the group's policies and operating its systems of control, guarantee the framework of governance within which those businesses are authorized to operate.

The Luxottica "business units" are the following:

- Wholesale;
- Retail, luxury and sun;
- Oakley;
- Retail Optical North America;
- Retail Optical Australasia and Greater China.

The retail and wholesale divisions are responsible for establishing commercial presence on the world's markets and developing profitable businesses. They have local sales organizations in their various markets and use centralized structures providing support services.

The operating processes departments are the following:

- Marketing, Style & Product;
- Operations Department;
- Quality Department.

The Marketing, Style & Product Department is responsible for marketing and developing collections. The department has teams in all the main markets to track new styles and trends. The Operations Department, based in Agordo (Italy), is responsible for planning, engineering and product manufacturing and distribution. The Quality Department, also based in Agordo, is responsible for quality and product quality control processes in all of the group's production sites.

In effect the so-called "business units" are not business units specialized on product lines, but organizational structures to manage some relevant sale channels and markets. Luxottica substantially adopts a functional organization structure adapted for managing sales in different international markets and in different channels. The maintaining of a functional structure is due to limited differences in value chain activities of the two main lines of products: prescription glasses and sunglasses.

In 2009 Luxottica adopted a new performance valuation system which considers the company operating in two main businesses:

- manufacturing and wholesale distribution;
- retail distribution.

For the manufacturing and wholesale distribution business, net sales include third-party customers only, while inter-company sales to the retail segment are not included. For the retail distribution business, net sales to the retail customers are included and the costs of acquired goods are estimated at manufacturing cost; therefore the sales of this segment include the so-called "manufacturing profit".

The use of this methodology indicates the interest of the group in monitoring separately the performance of the manufacturing business unit and the retail distribution unit, perhaps preparing the next change in the organizational structure.

LUXOTTICA'S STRATEGIC RESOURCES FOR GROWTH: DISTINCTIVE COMPETENCES IN PRODUCT DESIGN AND MANUFACTURE AND A WIDESPREAD "CULTURE OF QUALITY"

Distinctive capabilities on product design and continuous development of new styles are the strategic resources of Luxottica. Each year, Luxottica adds approximately 2,300 new styles to its eyewear collections. Each collection, each pair of glasses, is the result of an ongoing process of research and development whose aim is to anticipate and interpret the needs, desires and aspirations of consumers all over the world.

Luxottica also has a distinctive know-how in glasses manufacturing, as a leader in product quality and in production efficiency. It continuously invests in research and development activities relating to its manufacturing processes. As a result of such activities, Luxottica operates in its factories with advanced technologies and new plants, thus continuously improving production efficiency and product quality.

Furthermore, the "culture of quality" has always been central to the whole organization, assuming a role of strategic resource. This culture of quality is the underlying principle applied in every process involved in creating eyewear and is the drive behind the continual improvement of products and processes. This characteristic feature covers the entire organization: quality is applied to product development, procurement, the distribution network, analysis of processes and uniform and measurable performance management in the plants.

To achieve this Luxottica continually improves quality in every phase of the production process (and also distribution). That has been the reason for undertaking the full vertical integration of every production phase. Most of the manufacturing equipment used is specially designed and adapted for the manufacturing processes; this helps the company to respond more quickly to customer demand and to adhere to strict quality-control standards.

The achievement of high standards of quality reflects the group's strong technical and manufacturing know-how, the result of 50 years of experience, and its constant commitment to technological innovation, style and design, the study of changing lifestyles and interpretation of fashion trends.

Quality and customer satisfaction also characterize the wholesale and retail distribution networks. Also these structures are organized to offer a high quality after-sales service that is consistent but not standardized, being specially tailored to specific local needs.

CONCLUSIONS

In two decades Luxottica reached world leadership in the high and luxury segments of the eyewear business, with a continuous growth characterized by a continuous creation of value for shareholders.

The company now presents a solid competitive advantage over competitors and a sustainable value principally based on:

- a wide and balanced portfolio of brands;
- the high quality, flexibility and productivity of the production and distribution processes;
- a very large distribution network, wholesale and retail, capable of efficiently serving the world market;
- a high level of customer service.

This is the result of a combination of successful growth strategies: a closely related diversification, a horizontal expansion and a vertical integration strategy both in manufacturing and in retailing. These have been constantly pursued in the last 20 years through both internal development and acquisitions.

Manufacturing excellence and focus on service level with a specialized retail distribution have formed just two of the strengths on which Luxottica leverages to continuously create value for shareholders.

Luxottica can be considered as a model of a company's coherent and successful growth strategies that created value for shareholders in a global world market, characterized by continuous changes in customers' tastes and preferences, innovations in products and processes and strong competitive forces.

11. Geox: horizontal expansion through organic development

COMPANY PROFILE

Geox began its commercial and industrial activity in the 1990s at Montebelluno (Italy) and in a few years became one of the main players in the international footwear market. In 1995 Mr Moretti-Polegato implemented the business idea and founded the enterprise; in 2004 the company went public. In 2009 it is present in 68 countries, has realised €865 million sales and €67 million net income, selling its products worldwide in approximately 10,000 multi-brand stores and in 1000 Geox shops (direct and franchise).

Geox operates in the sector of classic, casual and sport footwear and apparel for men, women and children, in the medium price range. One of its strengths is product innovation; in particular its activity is oriented towards technological solutions that guarantee breathability and impermeability.

Geox is a brand which offers a wide array of products for the entire family; each product is characterized by innovation, comfort and a style in line with the latest fashion trends.

GEOX POSITIONING IN THE FOOTWEAR EUROPEAN INDUSTRY

The footwear industry is in a maturity phase in Europe. Tables 11.1 and 11.2 show the values concerning production, export and import of shoes in Europe, from 2004 to 2008. Data clearly point out the decline in the number of firms and direct employment together with an increase in production value and turnover.

Consumption slowly increases, while production (in quantity) declines, exports increase at a small rate and imports grow at a larger rate. Imports come mainly from China (48% in value and 72.6% in quantities). European exports are mainly directed at the USA (15.9% in value and 11.6% in quantities), Switzerland (15.2% in value and 13.8% in quantities) and Russia

(14.1% in value and 10.2% in quantities). Companies acting in this industry have fragmented market shares and focus principally on differentiation strategies.

Table 11. 1 The structure of European footwear industry

	2004	2005	2006	2007
Number of firms	28,941	27,125	26,624	26,100
Turnover (€mill.)	26,389	25,922	26,233	30,296
Production value (€mill.)	25,072	24,854	24,583	28,927
Value added at factor cost (€mill.)	7,214	6,793	6,944	7,631
Direct employment	443,900	404,500	388,100	368,600

Source: Erostat.

Table 11.2 European footwear industry: production, consumption and external trade

1000 pairs	2005	2006	2007	2008	% change 2005–2008
Production	706,704	684,639	642,386	605,824	−14.3
Exports	161,914	168,495	175,201	177,509	9.6
Imports	1,932,645	2,102,748	2,512,129	2,429,626	25.7
Apparent consumption	2,477,436	2,618,892	2,976,066	2,857,941	15.4

Source: Eurostat.

Italy is the leading shoe manufacturing country in Europe and it holds the fifth place amongst worldwide footwear manufacturing countries and the third among the largest exporters. This is a clear indication of the success of the Italian footwear sector, which, with its 7,570 companies and 113,000 employees, is of considerable importance to the Italian economy and represents one of the leading sectors in the Italian fashion industry.

The success of the footwear sector in Italy is linked to Italian entrepreneurship and to the structure of the sector, which consists of suppliers of raw materials, manufacturers of components and accessories, as well as shoe machinery makers and model designers. This has resulted in a geographic concentration of companies in the so-called shoe manufacturing districts. The main districts are in certain Italian regions: Lombardia, Veneto, Marche, Emilia-Romagna, Toscana, Campania and Puglia.

The leading position of the Italian shoe industry in the international market is due to the high quality of the product and the high capacity of innovation. The characteristics that distinguish Italian production in the footwear sector are: the creative talent of designers, innovation of traditional manufacturing methods, skilled labour, raw materials, accessories and components that are in the forefront in the field of technology and design, and flexibility resulting from the geographic concentration and size of the companies.

For decades, Italian companies (Ferragamo, Magli, Pollini, Fratelli Rossetti, Rossi, Tod's, etc.) have successfully competed by carving out a strategic position characterized by a market niche focus, fashion-based reputation, continuous style innovation, craft-like quality and domestic production. In recent years many Italian companies have lost their edge and even experienced sharp declines in profitability, due to the globalization and the entrance of new competitors. In this situation, Geox has succeeded in defining a new strategic position in the footwear industry, which can be defined as a "blue ocean strategy" (Kim and Mauborgne, 2005). In fact, introducing innovative products, Geox has created a somewhat uncontested market space where competition is less relevant by changing the traditional market segmentation rules.

Though grounded in product innovation, Geox's competitive advantage has not grown out of operational excellence in single activities in the business, but, rather, is derived from a unique and consistent configuration of complementary activities. Due to its product innovation Geox is perceived as unique in the shoe industry, with no direct substitute products.

Thanks to a decade characterized by rapid growth, today Geox holds a leading position in Italy in the sector of classic and casual footwear and it has an increasing presence in some foreign markets, among which are Germany, France, Spain and USA.

THE GROWTH OF GEOX FROM 2001 TO 2009: SALES, INVESTMENTS AND PROFITS

The main financial outcomes in the period 2001–2009 are shown in Tables 11.3 and 11.4.

Table 11.3 Geox key outcomes

Key data (€mill.)	2001	2002	2003	2004	2005	2006	2007	2008	2009
Net sales	148	180	254	340	455	612	770	892	865
Growth rate (%)		29	25	25	26	21	14	16	–3
EBITDA	16	31	50	87	121	153	201	199	166
EBITDA (%)	10.9	17.3	19.7	25.6	26.6	25.1	26.1	22.4	19.2
EBIT	12	24	39	73	103	135	180	170	117
EBIT (%)	8.1	13.3	15.2	21.4	22.6	22.0	23.3	19.1	13.5
Profit before tax	10	20	34	68	106	134	178	166	113
Profit before tax (%)	6.7	10.8	13.3	20.1	23.3	21.9	23.2	18.6	13.0
Net income	7	19	31	53	75	97	123	118	67
Net income/sales (%)	4.7	10.6	12.2	15.6	16.5	15.9	16.0	13.2	7.7

Source: Our elaboration of Geox *Annual Reports*.

As far as net sales are concerned, Geox has registered an outgoing upward trend: from €104.6 million sales in 2001 to €865 million sales in 2009 with an average growth rate equal to 10.2 % per year (Figure 11.1).

Geox outperformed during the period 2001–2009; it obtained an extraordinary increase in *EBITDA* from €16.1 million in 2001 to €199.5 million in 2008; the company also recorded excellent value of return of investment (ROI) reaching an average annual value of 47.1% with values of about 70% in 2005, 2006 and 2007.

The trend of operating cash flow shows the ability of the company to generate cash flow from its operations that enable it to meet its obligation and to reinvest in R&D activities.

The free cash flow conveys the idea of a company that cyclically (about every five years) reinvests its cash to achieve good results later (Table 11.5).

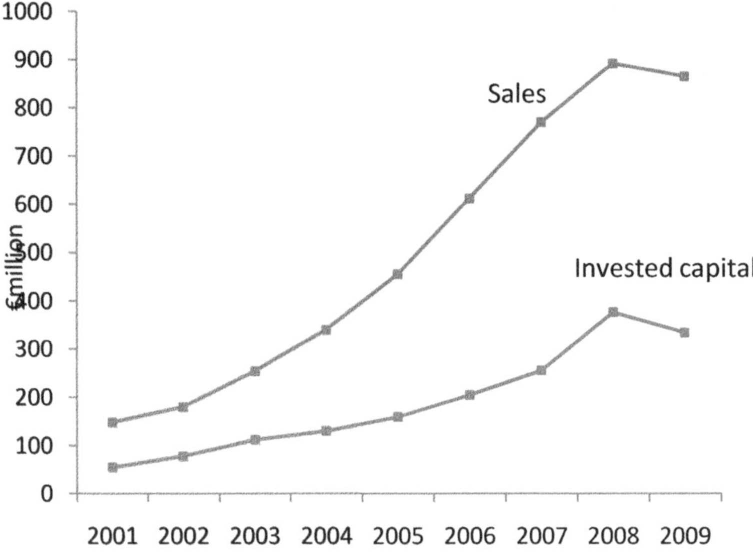

Figure 11.1 Geox sales and invested capital

As data clearly prove, Geox was able to boast an enviable growth track record: sales progressing year after year with millions more pairs of shoes manufactured and sold each season, and profitability indicators showing constant improvement.

When the company went public in 2004 (Geox was listed on the Milan Stock Market), it rewarded shareholders well. The stock prices outperformed over the average of S&P MIB. The earnings per share recorded an increasing trend from €0.2 in 2004 to €0.45 in 2008 and the equity per share increased from €0.56 in 2004 to €1.65 in 2008.

Table 11.4 Geox key assets and liabilities

(€ mill.)	2001	2002	2003	2004	2005	2006	2007	2008	2009
Non-current assets	31	44	61	64	77	86	110	188	190
Working capital	30	32	51	74	98	118	167	204	159
Other net current assets	(7)	2	0.0	(7)	(16)	(1)	(22)	(16)	(15)
Invested capital	55	78	112	130	159	204	255	376	334
Net debt (Cash)	34	37	40	(24)	(48)	(78)	(107	(58)	(104)
Risk fund and other	2	2	2	9	4	6	5	7	10
Equity	19	38	69	146	204	277	357	427	428

Source: Our elaboration on Geox *Annual Reports*.

Table 11.5 Geox operating cash flow, capital expenditures and ROI

(€mill.)	2001	2002	2003	2004	2005	2006	2007	2008	2009
Operating cash flow	7	15	26	54	65	83	117	85	160
Capital expenditure	15	19	29	22	29	26	42.7	94	39
Free cash flow	−8	−3	−3	32	36	57	74	−9	121
ROI (%)	21.8	30.6	34.6	55.8	64.6	66.1	70.3	45.3	35.0

Note: *ROI = EBIT/Invested capital.*

Source: Our elaboration on Geox *Annual Reports*.

GEOX'S GROWTH STRATEGIES

Horizontal expansion strategy

Since the first years of its life, Geox has pursued a horizontal expansion strategy in Italy and all over the world. After having consolidated its first successes in Italy, between 2000 and 2003 Geox expanded its activity internationally, especially increasing the number of customers in Europe, the market share and the loyalty among existing customers, as well as balancing the sales mix by increasing the weight of men's and women's lines compared with the line for children.

From 2001 to 2009 total sales increased by €148 million to €865 million (+584%); sales in Italy increased from €122 million to €326 million (+265%), while sales in Europe grew from €20 to €380 million, sales in North America from €1.5 to €54 million and sales in the Rest of the World from €3.7 to €105 million (Tables 11.6 and 11.7). In the same period the invested capital grew from €55 to € 344 million.

Table 11.6 Dynamics of net sales by geographical areas

(€mill.)	2001	2002	2003	2004	2005	2006	2007	2008	2009
Italy	122.6	136.6	160.2	191.3	230.5	264.7	294.5	333.0	326
Europe	19.7	35.1	71.0	120.5	182.2	273.5	360.3	404.3	380
North America	1.5	2.9	11.5	13.6	13.9	27.4	39.0	49.8	54
Rest of World	3.7	5.6	11.4	14.6	28.4	46.7	76.4	105.3	105
Total net sales	147.6	180.3	254.1	340.1	455.0	612.3	770.2	892.5	865

Source: Our elaboration of Geox *Annual Reports*.

The international expansion of Geox can be interpreted as a result of its capacity to exploit product innovation and Italian appeal. In 2009 over 60% of Geox sales were obtained abroad, particularly in markets which are considered strategic. In particular European countries are the most important contributors to Geox total sales (Table 11.7).

To obtain this extraordinary expansion in sales, Geox has progressively enforced its sales and marketing structure, especially its sales network. It developed a sales organization capable of covering international markets, consisting of a number of independent local agents who handle the distribution of Geox products through over 10,000 multi-brand selling points. Moreover, in just a few years, the group opened many Geox shops in prime shopping locations.

Table 11.7 Breakdown of sales by geographical areas in 2001 and 2009

(€mill.)	2001	% of 2001 total sales	2009	% of 2009 total sales
Italy	122.6	83	326	38
Europe	19.7	13	380	44
North America	1.5	1	54	6
Rest of World	3.7	3	105	12
Total net sales	147.6	100	865	100

Source: Our elaboration of Geox *Annual Reports*.

Vertical integration strategy in retail distribution

Over time, Geox has also developed a vertical integration strategy in the retail footwear business and in the past years has continued its expansion strategy. During 2008 216 new Geox shops were opened, of which 52 were in Italy, 69 in Europe and 27 in North America. In 2009 Geox further incremented the number of Geox shops (68), mainly in franchising, in high volume city centres and key shopping malls. The new openings include, among others, shops in Rome, Venice, London, Cannes, Paris, Berlin, Santa Monica, Miami, Toronto, Tokyo and Hong Kong (Table 11.8).

As a consequence of this strategy today Geox distributes its products through 1008 Geox shops, of which 764 franchising shops and 244 directly operated stores (DOS).

Table 11.8 Geographical distribution of total Geox shops at the end of 2009

Number of shops	Number of shops	Share of total shops (%)
Italy	327	32.4
Europe	306	30.4
North America	56	5.6
Other countries	146	14.5
Countries with licensing agreements	173	17.2
Total	1,008	100

Source: Geox *Annual Report 2009*.

The results obtained by the progressive entry into the retail distribution business are significant: in 2009, 36% of sales were realised through Geox shops against 14.6% in 2001 (Tables 11.9 and 11.10).

Table 11.9 Geox sales by channels

(€mill.)	2001	2002	2003	2004	2005	2006	2007	2008	2009
Whole sale	133	152	207	264	352	462	546	609	554
Franchi-sing	12	20	32	47	65	87	124	143	144
DOS	2	8	15	29	38	64	101	141	167
Total sales	147	180	254	340	455	613	771	893	865

Source: Geox Annual Report (2004 and 2009).

Table 11.10 Breakdown of Geox sales by channels in 2001 and 2009

(€mill.)	2001	%	2009	%
Wholesale	133	90.1	554	64
Franchising	12	8.4	144	17
DOS	2	1.5	167	19
Total net sales	147	100.0	865	100

Source: *Geox Annual Report* (2004 and 2009).

Geox product diversification strategy

Geox's core competence in the technology of membranes permeable to vapour but waterproof was the base of a closely related product diversification strategy realised in the last years. During the period 2001–2009 Geox entered the apparel industry (jackets), exploiting the patent and the know-how obtained in the study of the breathing shoe.

Geox has also grown in this sector, but the percentage of total sales remains quite low even to this day (10.4%) and shoes are still the strongest contributors to Geox's net sales (Table 11.11). That raises doubts about the effectiveness of this strategy.

Table 11.11 Geox sales by product lines

(€million)	2001	2002	2003	2004	2005	2006	2007	2008	2009
Footwear	143	174	247	328	433	578	718	808	766
Apparel	5	6	7	12	22	34	52	84	99
Total net sales	148	180	254	340	455	612	770	892	865
Growth rate (%)		22	41	34	34	35	26	16	–3.1

Source: *Geox Annual Reports*.

The strategy of production outsourcing

With regard to manufacturing, Geox has realised a process of total decentralization of phases and operations. At the end of 2008 it owned two main production units, one in Romania with 1,750 employees and one in Slovakia with 400 employees. In addition to these factories the company owned two operating units in Italy, where R&D, product design and prototyping activities were carried out. However, Geox realised most of its production in factories belonging to third parties in the East Asia.

During the course of 2009 the group has carried out its strategy of optimizing its production sources. For maintaining a maximum degree of flexibility and reducing costs, it has transferred the production activities, historically carried out in Romania and in the Slovak Republic, entirely to third parties. As a consequence of this decision on 31 December, 2009 the Group only had 2,408 employees instead of 4,043 of the end of 2008.

The choice of outsourcing production was made to reach two fundamental objectives: a) improving flexibility and time to market; b) reducing costs. To match these objectives and maintain product quality, Geox organized very close relationships between suppliers and headquarters. These include purchasing of raw materials (both leather and rubber), accessories, as well as plant equipment, while technical specifications are managed centrally. Great care is taken by the group in selecting third-party producers, taking into account their technical skills, quality standards and ability to handle the production volumes they are assigned by the agreed deadlines.

All production phases are closely monitored by the Geox organization, even if they are carried out by third parties. Such monitoring includes the "upstream" phases such as the processing of leather (from raw to tanned hides) and the production of outsoles.

Relations (information, consultancy, exchange of materials) with external business partners (such as suppliers and technical consultants) are all managed centrally. All of the output from these manufacturing locations is consolidated at the group's distribution centres in Italy for Europe, in Edison (NJ) for the USA and Canada, in Tokyo for Japan and in Hong Kong for the rest of Asia. Logistics play a crucial role both for the complex production organization and seasonal peaks in production and selling. Integration of information systems between the headquarters (where R&D and design are carried out), production sites and the distribution network are supported by a company information system.

GEOX ORGANIZATIONAL STRUCTURE

The organizational structure of Geox evolved over years in accordance with the growth of the firm from a typical entrepreneurial structure to a managerial one. At present Geox has a functional organizational structure with a general manager and a series of functional directions. More precisely, at December 2009 Geox had 2,408 employees, split by functions as shows in Table 11.12.

Table 11.12 Geox employees by role at December 2009

Employees role	Number of employees
Managers	28
Middle managers	102
Office staff	639
Shop employees	1,568
Factory workers	71
Total	2,408

Source: Our elaboration from Geox *Annual Report 2009*.

The largest number of employees operate in the retail distribution network and in the office staff, as a consequence of the vertical integration strategy in distribution activities and the outsourcing strategy of production activities.

The organizational chart presented in Figure 11.2 shows the formal organization architecture designed to implement Geox strategies. This is a functional organization structure where the fundamental functions are centrally carried out by specialized units.

A series of controlled companies, directly owned by Geox S.p.A., coordinate the selling activities in different countries. In particular, the organizational structure of the group is split into three macro-groupings: technical companies, EU trading companies and non-EU trading companies (Geox, Annual Report, 2009).

Technical production companies. Notech Kft (Hungary) is the company that heads up the group's production activities in Europe. During the course of 2009 the group has continued its strategy of optimizing its production sources and maintaining a maximum degree of flexibility. In particular it has transferred the production activities that historically were carried out in its plants to third parties. As the manufacturing takes place in third party producers, Notech engages its technical employees for coordinating the manufacturing activities in the factories and checking the quality of the finished products. The company buys its raw materials and manufacturing machinery predominantly in Italy in order to maintain the best quality standard.

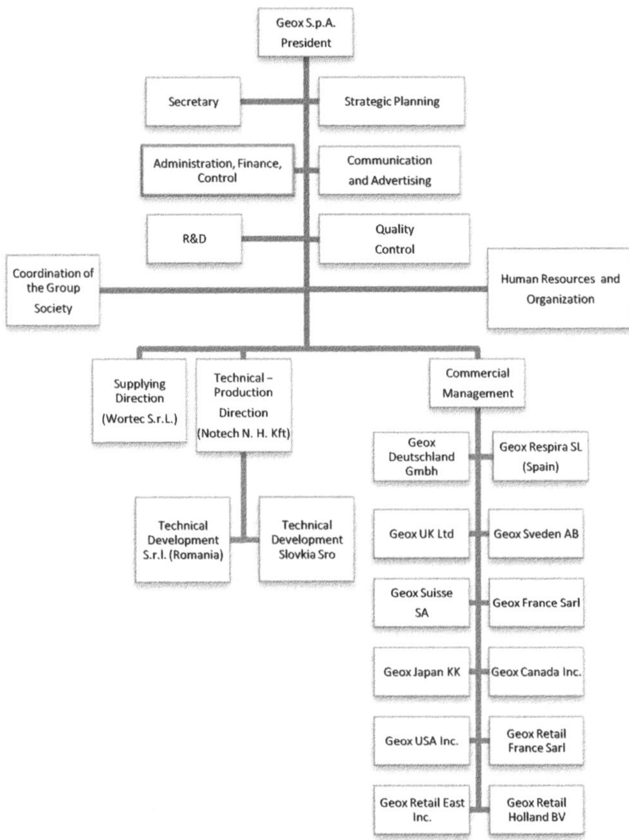

Source: Our elaboration from www.Geox.biz.

Figure 11.2 Geox organizational structure

EU trading companies. The role of these companies is to manage the group's own shops in the various countries of the European Union, as well as to provide customer services and coordinate the sales network in favour of the parent company which distributes the products directly on a wholesale basis.

Non-EU trading companies. The role of these companies is to monitor and develop the business outside the EU. They operate on the basis of licensing or distribution agreements stipulated with the parent company.

With regard to other fundamental elements of organization design, such as human resource management and culture and management style, Geox presents some distinctive characteristics, which are fundamental for successfully operating in its business. From the beginning, top management placed great value on human resources for the company's development: as a matter of fact, 70% of the Geox employees are graduates. Training its personnel is considered an investment of fundamental importance to develop the group's activity.

To promote the training of its human resources, Geox launched the "Geox School" in 2001, a centre designed to prepare new young resources for entry into the group, giving them training in line with company policy, the characteristics of Geox products and the business development needs of the group. The training of the shop assistants is taken into consideration by the company as well because these people represent the link to the consumers and they have to be able to perceive the changing market.

GEOX STRATEGIC RESOURCES FOR GROWTH: PATENTS AND DISTINCTIVE COMPETENCES IN TECHNOLOGICAL RESEARCH AND PRODUCT DESIGN

The founder of Geox, Mr Polegato, and his cognitive skills together with those of closer collaborators represent the true human resources on which the firm has built its success. Product innovation has been the main distinctive feature of Geox from the beginning of its activity and it enabled the company to enter and successfully perform in the footwear market.

Geox has become famous all over the world as "the shoe that breathes". The original Geox patented system is a combination of a perforated rubber sole and an innovative membrane; micro-holes in the rubber outsole which allow perspiration from the feet to be released from the shoes, while the protective breathable membrane keeps water out and the feet dry. This process rests on the fact that the membrane's micro-pores are larger than water vapour molecules, but smaller than water droplets, hence keeping water out and the feet dry. In this way, Geox's shoes offer to customers the benefit of eliminating humidity from the inside of the shoe, since it is natural to sweat through the feet but it is unhealthy to keep the sweat inside the shoes.

With its innovative products Geox has defined a new strategic position in the footwear industry; it has created a somewhat uncontested market space where competition is less relevant by changing the traditional market segmentation rules. It has built a unique configuration of activities, different from the stereotype of the Italian "fashion" footwear manufacturer, but also significantly different from other US and European competitors.

As Geox core competence is technological research, the company has continued to heavily invest in research and development. Geox's Research and Development laboratory is a state-of-the-art facility. In temperature-controlled environments, shoes are tested for different environmental conditions; sweat simulators measure humidity by injecting water into heated shoes, mimicking glands in the feet; flexi meters put Geox patented soles through rigorous tests of tens of thousands of flexions. Experiments and tests are performed on materials, processes and products in disciplines ranging from chemistry to physics, to orthopaedics, to foot ergonomics. Many research activities result from formal cooperation with Italian and European university departments and international research centres.

In 2008, Geox invested €15.7 million in R&D, about 2% of net sales, that is an unusual proportion for a shoe manufacturer. In Geox the R&D organization is articulated, but not bureaucratic: scientists and technicians work in teams, are fully interchangeable and systematically rotate jobs.

The conspicuous research effort has resulted in a stream of patented inventions and innovations related to the original concept, as well as many relating to materials (e.g. plasma applications), products (e.g. the breathable leather shoe), processes (e.g. glue saving assembly and sewing systems allowing improved shoe perspiration and flexibility), equipment and machinery (e.g. for shoe sole moulding and injection). This series of corollary patents which developed around the original patent also have the function to make it impossible for competitors to simply copy the product when the original patent expires. In fact, Geox currently has some 40 patents in addition to the original one which expired in 2009 which is practically unusable by competitors because of subsequent improvements.

CONCLUSIONS

The growth of Geox is characterized by a horizontal expansion strategy in the footwear industry, both in domestic and international markets. This expansion has been carried out without acquisition, but through organic development, characterized by investments in technology, new products and sales networks, as well as in brand and firm image.

The basis of Geox extraordinary success is its distinctive competence in technological research and a unique capability of creating a new market space in the mature footwear industry where competition is less significant, making leverage on product technology and an attractive brand.

In addition to innovative technological solutions developed internally and protected by patents, Geox has based its success on the capability of positioning on the market a vast range of shoes for men, women and children in the medium/high price range. These products are further differentiated by a strong brand obtained thanks to an effective communication strategy.

References

Abell D.F. (1993), *Managing with Dual Strategies. Mastering the Present, Preempting the Future*, New York: The Free Press.

Abell D.F. and J.S. Hammond (1979), *Strategic Market Planning*, Englewood Cliffs, NJ: Prentice Hall.

Adler P.S. and K.B. Clark (1991), "Behind the Learning Curve: A Sketch of the Learning Process", *Management Science*, vol. 37, n. 3, March, pp. 267-280.

Agrawal A. and J. Jaffe (2000), "The Post Merger Performance Puzzle", *Advances in Mergers and Acquisitions*, vol.1, pp. 119-156.

Alchian A. (1963), "Reliability of progress curves in airframe production", *Econometrica*, vol. 31, pp. 679-693.

Ambrosini V., C. Bowman and Nardine Collier (2009), "Dynamic Capabilities: An Exploration of How Firm Renew their Resource Base", British Journal of Management, vol. 20, pp. 9-24.

Amram M. and N. Kutilaka (1999), *Real Option*, Boston: Harvard Business School Press.

Andrade G., M. Mitchell and E. Stafford, (2001), "New Evidence and Perspective in Mergers", *Journal of Economic Perspectives*, vol. 15, n. 2, Spring, pp. 103-120.

ANFAO (2008), Associazione Nazionale Fabbricanti Articoli Ottici, *Studio di settore*, www.anfao.it.

Ansoff H.I. (1968), *Corporate Strategy: An Analytical Approach to Business Policy for Growth and Expansion*, New York: McGraw-Hill.

Ansoff H.I. (1988), *New Corporate Strategy*, New York: J. Wiley.

Arrow K.J. (1974), *The Limit of Organization*, New York: Norton.

Bain J. (1956), *Barriers to New Competition*, Cambridge, MA: Harvard University Press.

Baden Fuller C. (1983), "The Implications of the Learning Curve from Strategy and Public Policy", *Applied Economics*, vol. 15, pp. 541-551.

Baden Fuller C. and J. Stopfor (1992), *Rejuvenating the Mature Business*, London: Routledge.

Baloff N. (1971), "Extension of the Learning Curve: Some Empirical Results", *Operational Research Quarterly*, vol. 22, n. 4, pp. 329-340.

Barney J.B. (1991), "Firm Resources and Sustained Competitive Advantage", *Journal of Management*, vol. 17, pp. 99-120.

Barney J.B. (1996 and 2002), *Gaining and Sustaining Competitive Advantage*, Upper Saddle River: Pearson/Prentice Hall.

Barney J.B. (2001), "Is the Resource-Based View a Useful Perspective for Strategic Management Research? Yes", *Academy of Management Review*, vol. 26, n. 1, pp. 41-56.

Bellandi, M. (1995), *Economie di Scala e Organizzazione industriale*, Milano: FrancoAngeli.

Berger P.G. and E. Ofek (1995), "Diversification's Effect on Firm Value", *Journal of Financial Economics*, vol. 37, pp. 39-65.

Berry C.H. (1975), *Corporate Growth and Diversification*, Princeton, NJ: Princeton University Press.

Besanko D., D. Dranove and M. Shanley (1996), *Economics of Strategy*, New York: Wiley.

Boari C., A. Grandi and G. Lorenzoni (1989), "Le Organizzazioni a Rete: Tre Concetti di Base", *Economia e Politica Industriale*, n. 64.

Bohn R.E. (1995), "Noise and Learning in Semiconductor Manufacturing", *Management Science*, vol. 41, n. 1, pp. 31-42.

Boston Consulting Group (1972), *Perspective on Experience*, BCG.

Brealey R.A. and S.C. Meyers (1996), *Principles of Corporate Finance*, New York: McGraw-Hill.

Campari (2000–2010), *Annual Report*.

Campbell A. and K. Sommers Luch (eds) (1998), *Strategic Synergy*, London: International Thomson Business Press.

Capron L., W. Mitchell and A. Swaminathan (2001), *Strategic Management Journal*, vol. 22, pp. 817-844.

Capron L. and N. Pistre (2002), "When do Acquirers Earn Abnormal Returns?", *Strategic Management Journal*, vol. 23, pp. 781-794.

Ceccanti G. (1996), *Corso di Tecnica imprenditoriale*, Padova: Cedam.

Chandler, A. (1962), *Strategy and Structure. Chapters in the History of the American Industrial Enterprise*, Cambridge, MA: The MIT Press.

Chandler A. Jr. (1990), *Scale and Scope. The Dynamics of Industrial Capitalism*, Cambridge, MA.: Harvard University Press.

Christensen H.K. and C.A. Montgomery (1981), "Corporate Economic Performance: Diversification Strategy versus Market Structure", *Strategic Management Journal*, vol. 2, pp. 327-343.

Colipa (2008), *The European Cosmetics Association*: www.colipa.com.

Collis D.J. and C.A. Montgomery (2005), *Corporate Strategy. Resources and Scope of the Firm*, New York: McGraw-Hill (2nd ed.).

Copeland T. and J.F. Weston (1988), *Financial Theory and Corporate Policy*, New York: Addison Wesley.

Copeland T., T. Koller and J. Murrin (1995), *Valuation. Measuring and Managing the Value of Companies*, New York: Wiley.

Daft R.L. (2001), *Organization Theory and Design*, London: South-Western College Publishing.

Day G.S. (1990), *Market Driven Strategy. Processes for Creating Value*, New York: The Free Press.

Damodaran A. (1994), *Damodaran on Valuation*, New York: J. Wiley & Sons.

Dess G.G., A. Gupta, J.F. Hennart and C.W. Hill (1995), "Conducting and Integrating Strategy Research of the International Corporate and Business Level: Issue and Directions", *Journal of Management*, vol. 21, pp. 357-393.

Diageo (2009), *Annual Report*.

Dierickx and Karel Cool (1989), "Asset Stock Accumulation and Sustainability of Competitive Advantage", Management Science, vol. 35, n.12, December, pp.1504-1514

Dixit A.K. and R.S. Pyndick (1994), *Investment Under Uncertainty*, Princeton, NJ: Princeton University Press.

Dixit A.K. (1995), "The Option Approach to Capital Investment", Boston: *Harvard Business Review*, May–June, pp.105-115.

Dringoli A. (1973), *Modelli Decisori della Spesa Pubblicitaria*, Milano: Franco Angeli.

Dringoli A. (1995), *Struttura e Sviluppo dell'Impresa Industriale*, Milano: McGraw-Hill.

Dringoli A. (2000), *Economia e Gestione delle Imprese. Modelli e Tecniche per la Gestione*, Padova: Cedam.

Dringoli A. (2006), *La Gestione dell'Impresa*, Padova: Cedam.

Dringoli A. (2009), *Creating Value through Innovation*, Cheltenham, UK and Northampton, MA, USA: Edward Elgar.

Edwards J., I.Kay and C. Meyer (1987), *The Economic Analysis of Accounting Profitability*, Oxford: Oxford University Press.

Eisenhardt K.M. and J.A. Martin (2000), "Dynamic Capabilities: What are They?", *Strategic Management Journal*, vol. 21, pp. 1105-1121.

Easterby-Smith M., M.A. Lyles and M.A. Peteraf (2009), "Dynamic Capabilities: Current Debates and Future Directions", *British Journal of Management*, vol. 20, pp. 1-8

Ferrucci, L. (2000), *Strategie Competitive e Processi di Crescita dell'Impresa*, Milano: FrancoAngeli.

Forrester J.W. (1961), *Industrial Dynamics*, Cambridge, MA: The MIT Press.

Galbraith J.R. (1977), *Organizational Design*, Reading, MA: Addison-Wesley.

Gary M.S. (2005) "Implementation Strategy and Performance Outcomes in Related Diversification", *Strategic Management Journal*, vol. 26, n. 4, July, pp. 643-664.

Geox (2001–2009), *Annual Report*.

Gerloff E.A. (1985), *Organizational Theory and Design*, New York: McGraw-Hill.

Ghemawat P. (1985), "Building Strategy on the Experience Curve", *Harvard Business Review*, March–April, pp. 143–149.

Ghemawat P. (1991), *Commitment. The Dynamic of Strategy*, New York: The Free Press.

Gort M. (1962), *Diversification and Integration in American Industry*, Princeton, NJ: Princeton University Press.

Grant R.M. (1991), "The Resource-Based Theory of Competitive Advantage. Implications for Strategy Formulation", *California Management Review*, Spring, pp. 119–135.

Grant R.M. (1998), *Contemporary Strategy Analysis*, Malden, MA: Blackwell.

Grant R.M., A.P. Jammine and H. Thomas (1988), "Diversity, Diversification and Profitability among British Manufacturing Companies", *Academy of Management Journal*, vol. 31, n. 4, pp. 771-801.

Gregory A. (1997), "An Examination of the Long Run Performance of UK Acquiring Firms", *Journal of Business, Finance & Accounting*, vol. 24, pp. 971-1002.

Gruber H. (1992), "The Learning Curve in the Production of Semiconductor Memory Chip, *Applied Economics*, vol. 24, pp. 885-894.

Guillart F.J. and J. Kelly (1995), *Business Transformation*, New York: McGraw-Hill.

Hamel G. and A. Heene (1994), *Competence Based Competition*, New York: Wiley.

Hamel G. and C.K. Prahalad (1994), *Competing for the Future*, Boston: Harvard Business School Press.

Harrigan K.R (1986), *Managing for Joint Venture Success*, Lexington: Lexington Books.

Haspeslagh P.C. and D.B. Jemison (1987), "Acquisition: Myth and Reality", *Sloan Management Review"*, vol. 28, n. 2, pp. 53-58.

Hatch N.W. and D.C. Mowery (1998), "Process Innovation and Learning by Doing in Semiconductor Manufacturing", *Management Science*, vol. 44, n. 11, pp. 1461-1477.

Hatch N.W. and J.H. Dyer (2004), "Human Capital and Learning as a Source of Sustainable Competitive Advantage", *Strategic Management Journal*, vol. 25, pp. 1155-1178.

Hax A.C. and N.S. Majluf (1984), *Strategic Management*, Englewood Cliffs, NJ: Prentice Hall.

Hay D.A. and D.J. Morris (1979), *Industrial Economics. Theory and Evidence*, Oxford: Oxford University Press.

Helfat C.E. and M.A. Peteraf (2003), "The Dynamic Resource-Based View: Capability Lifecycles", *Strategic Management Journal*, vol. 24, pp. 997-1010.

Helfat C.E., S. Filkestein, W. Mitchell, M. Peterlaf, H. Singh, D. Teece and S. Winter (2007), *Dynamic Capabilities: Understanding Strategies Change in Organizations*. Oxford: Blackwell.

Hitt M.A., R.D. Ireland and R.E. Hoskisson (1997), *Strategic Management*, St Paul, Minneapolis: West Publishing Company.

Hill C.W. and R.E. Hoskisson (1987), "Strategy and Structure in the Multiproduct Firm", *Academy of Management Review*, n. 12, pp. 331-341.

Hill C.W., M.A. Hitt and R.E. Hoskisson (1992), "Cooperative versus Competitive Structures in Related and Unrelated Diversified Firms", *Organization Science*, vol. 3, n. 4, pp. 501-521.

Hofer C.W. and D. Schendel (1978), *Strategy Formulation: Analytical Concepts*, St Paul, Minneapolis: West Publishing Co.

Hull J. (1997), *Options, Futures and Other Derivatives Securities*, Englewood Cliffs, N.J: Prentice Hall.

Impact Databank, *Top 100 Premium Spirits*, February 2010.

Jensen M.C. (1986), "Agency Costs of Free Cash Flow, Corporate Finance and Takeovers", *American Economic Review*, vol. 76, pp. 323-329.

Jensen M. (1988), "Takeovers: Their Causes and Consequences", *Journal of Economic Perspectives*", n. 2, pp. 21-48.

Jensen M.C. and W.H. Meckling (1976), "Theory of the Firm: Managerial Behavior, Agency Cost and Ownership Structure", *Journal of Financial Economics*, Oct., pp. 305-360.

Jensen M.C. and K.L. Murphy (1990), "Performance Pay and Top Management Incentives", *Journal of Political Economy*, vol. 98, pp. 225-264.

Johnson R.A., R.E. Hoskisson and M.A. Hitt (1993), "Board of Director Involvement in Restructuring: the Effects of Board versus Managerial

Controls and Characteristics", *Strategic Management Journal*, vol. 14, pp. 33-50.

Johnson P. (2006), "Strategy and Valuation", in Faulkner D.O. and A. Campbell (eds), *The Oxford Handbook of Strategy*, Oxford: Oxford University Press.

Karim S. and W. Mitchell (2000), "Reconfiguring Business Resources Following Acquisitions in the US Medical Sector 1978–1995", *Strategic Management Journal*, vol. 21, n. 10–11, pp. 1062-1081.

Kim W.C and R. Mauborgne (2005), *Blue Ocean Strategy. How to create Uncontested Market Space and Make Competition Irrelevant*, Boston, MA: Harvard Business School Press.

Kitching J. (1974) "Winning and Losing with European Acquisitions", *Harvard University Review*, n. 52, pp. 124-136.

Klein B., R.A. Crawford and A.A. Alchian (1978), "Vertical Integration, Appropriable Rents and the Competitive Contracting Process", *Journal of Law and Economics*, vol. 21, October, pp. 297-326.

Kogut B. and N. Kulatilaka (2006), "Strategy, Heuristic and Real Option", *The Oxford Handbook of Strategy*, Oxford: Oxford University Press.

Kumar S., C. Massie and M.D. Dumonceaux (2006), "Comparative Innovative Business Strategies of Major Players in the Cosmetics Industry", *Industrial Management & Data System*, vol. 106, n. 3, pp. 285-306.

Larsson R. and S. Finkelstein (1999), "Integrating Strategic, Organizational and Human Resource Perspectives on Merger and Acquisitions: a Case Survey of Synergy Realization", *Organization Science*, vol. 10, n. 1, pp. 1-26.

Leiblein L.M.J. and D.J. Miller (2003), "An Empirical Examination of Transaction and Firm-Level Influences on the Vertical Boundaries of the Firm", *Strategic Management Journal*, vol. 24, pp. 839-859.

Levy H. and M. Sarnat (1986), *Capital Investment and Financial Decisions*, Englewood Cliff, NJ: Prentice Hall.

Lieberman M. (1984), "The Learning Curve and Pricing in the Chemical Processing Industries", *Rand Journal of Economics*, vol. 15, Summer, pp. 213–228.

Lins K. and H. Servaes (1999), "International Evidence on the Value of Corporate Diversification", *Journal of Finance*, vol. 54, pp. 2215-2239.

L'Oreal (2000–2009), *Annual Report*.

L'Oreal International (2008), Home page, www.loreal.com.

L'Oreal Italia (2008), Home page, www.loreal.it.

Lorenzoni G. (ed.) (1992), *Accordi, Reti e Vantaggio Competitivo*, Milano: EtasLibri.

Lorenzoni G. (1990), *L'Architettura di Sviluppo delle Imprese Minori*, Bologna: Il Mulino.

Luffman G.A and R. Reed (1984), *The Strategy and Performance of British Industry 1970–1980*, London: MacMillan.

Luxottica, (2000–2009), *Annual Report*.

Markides C.C. (1995) "Diversification, Restructuring and Economic Performance", *Strategic Management Journal*, vol. 16, pp. 101-118.

Marris R. (1964), *The Economic Theory of Managerial Capitalism*, London: Macmillan.

Marris R. and A. Wood (eds.) (1972), *The Corporate Economy. Growth, Competition and Innovative Potential*, London: Macmillan.

Michel A and I. Shaked (1984), "Does Business Diversification Affect Performance?", *Financial Management*, vol. 13, n. 4, pp. 18-24.

Milgrom P. and J. Roberts (1992), *Economics, Organization and Management*, Englewood Cliffs, NJ.: Prentice Hall.

Miller D.J. (2004) "Firm's Technological Resources and the Performance Effects of Diversification: a Longitudinal Study", *Strategic Management Journal*, vol. 25, pp. 1097-1119.

Mintzberg H. (1983), *Structure in Five: Designing Effective Organizations*, Englewood Cliffs, NJ: Prentice Hall.

Modigliani F. (1958), "New Developments on the Oligopoly Front", *Journal of Political Economy*, vol. 66, June, pp. 215–232.

Monteverde K. and D.J. Teece (1982), "Supplier Switching Costs and Vertical Integration in the Automobile Industry", *Bell Journal of Economics*, vol. 13, pp. 206-213, reprinted in J. Birkinshaw (ed.) (2004), *Strategic Management*, vol. 1, Cheltenham, UK and Northampton, MA: Edward Elgar Publishing.

Montgomery C.A. (1985), "Product-Market Diversification and Market Power", *Academy of Management Journal*, vol. 28, n. 4, pp. 789-798.

Moomaw R.L. (1974), "Vertical Integration and Monopoly: A Resolution of the Controversy", *Rivista Internazionale di Scienze Economiche e Commerciali*, Milano, vol. 47, n. 1, pp. 267-293.

Nelson R. and S. Winter (1982), *An Evolutionary Theory of Economic Change*, Cambridge, MA: Harvard University Press.

Nelson R. (1994), "Why Firms Do Differ and How Does it Matter? Rumelt P., D. Schendel and D.J. Teece (eds), *Fundamental Issues in Strategy*, Boston, MA: Harvard University Press.

Nelson R. (1995), "Recent Evolutionary Theorizing About Economic Change" *Journal of Economic Literature*, vol. 33, n. 1, pp. 87-112.

Nerlove M. and K.J. Arrow (1962), "Optimal Advertising Policy under Dynamic Conditions", *Economica*, May, pp. 129-142.

Norman G. (1979), "Economies of Scale in the Cement Industry", *The Journal of Industrial Economics*, June, pp. 317-337.

Norman, R. (1977), *Management for Growth*, New York: J. Wiley & Sons.

Ollinger M. (1994), "The Limits of Growth of the Multidivisional Firm: A Case Study of the U.S. Oil Industry from 1930-90", *Strategic Management Journal*, vol. 15, pp. 503-520.

Pammolli F. (1996), *Innovazione, Concorrenza e Strategie di Sviluppo nell'Industria Farmaceutica*, Milano: Guerrini Scientifica.

Panzar J. and R. Willig (1979), "Economies of Scope", *American Economic Review*, Conference supplement.

Penrose, E.T. (1959), *The Theory of the Growth of the Firm*, Oxford: Oxford University Press.

Perry M.K. (1980), "Forward Integration by Alcoa: 1888–1930", *Journal of Industrial Economics*, n. 29, pp. 37-53.

Peteraf M.A. (1993), "The Cornerstones of Competitive Advantages: A Resource Based View", *Strategic Management Journal*, vol. 14, pp. 179–191.

Peters T. and R. Waterman (1982), *In Search of Excellence*, New York: Harper & Row.

Pisano G., W. Shan and D. Teece (1988), "Joint Ventures and Collaboration in the Biotechnology Industry", in D.C. Mowery (ed.), *International Collaborative Ventures in US Manufacturing*, Cambridge, MA: Ballinger.

Pisano G.P. (1994), "Knowledge, Integration and the Locus of Learning: an Empirical Analysis of Process Development", *Strategic Management Journal*, Winter, Special Issue, vol. 15, pp. 85-100.

Porter M.E. (1980), *Competitive Strategy*, New York: Free Press.

Porter M.E. (1985), *Competitive Advantage*, New York: Free Press.

Porter M.E. (1987), "From Competitive Advantage to Corporate Strategy", *Harvard Business Review*, vol. 65, n. 3, pp. 43-59.

Prahalad C.K. and Y.L. Doz (1998), "Evaluating Interdependences Across Businesses", in A. Campbell and K. Somers Luchs, *Strategic Synergy*, London: International Thomson Business Press.

Prahalad C.K. and Y.L. Doz (1986), *The Multinational Mission: Balancing Local Demands and Global Vision*, New York: The Free Press.

Pratten C.F. (1971), *Economies of Scale in the Manufacturing Industry*, Cambridge: Cambridge University Press.

Rappaport A. (1986), *Creating Shareholder Value. The New Standard for Business Performance*, New York: The Free Press.

Ravenscraft D.J. and R.M. Scherer (1987), *Mergers, Sell Off and Economic Efficiency*, Washington, DC: Brookings Institute.

Rajan R., H. Servaes and L. Zingales (2000), "The Cost of Diversity: the Diversification Discount and Inefficient Investment", *Journal of Finance*, vol. 55, pp. 35-80.

Rispoli, M. (1998), *Sviluppo dell'Impresa e Analisi Strategica*, Bologna: Il Mulino.

Roberts E.B. (1999), *Managerial Application of System Dynamics*, Portland, Oregon: Productivity Press.

Ross S.A., R.W. Westerfield and J. Jaffe (1999), *Corporate Finance*, Boston: McGraw-Hill.

Rovenscraft and D.F.M. Scherer (1987), *Mergers, Selloffs and Economic Efficiency*, Washington: Brookings Institution.

Rumelt R.P. (1974), *Strategy, Structure and Economic Performance*, Boston, MA: Harvard Business School Press.

Rumelt, R.P. (1982), "Diversification, Strategy and Profitability", *Strategic Management Journal*, n. 3, pp. 359-369.

Saloner, G., A. Shepard and J. Podolny (2001), *Strategic Management*, New York: John Wiley.

Scherer R.M., A. Beckenstein, E. Kaufer and R.D. Murphy (1975), *The Economics of Multi-Plant Operation: An International Comparisons Study*, Cambridge, MA: Harvard University Press.

Scherer R.M. and D. Ross (1980), *Industrial Market Structure and Economic Performance*, Boston: Houghton and Mifflin.

Seth A., K.P. Song and R. Petit (2002), "Value Creation and Destruction in Cross Border Acquisitions: An Empirical Analysis of Foreign Acquisitions of U.S. Firms", *Strategic Management Journal*, vol. 23, pp. 921-940.

Simon, H. (1981), *The Sciences of the Artificial*, Cambridge, MA: The MIT Press.

Shleifer A. and R.W. Vishny (1994), "Takeovers in the 1960s and 1980s. Evidence and Implications", in R.P. Rumelt, D.E. Shendel and D.J. Teece (eds), *Fundamental Issues in Strategy*, Boston, MA: Harvard Business School Press.

Sloan A.P. (1963), *My Years with General Motors*, New York: Doubleday and Co.

Spence A.M. (1981), "The Learning Curve and Competition", *Bell Journal of Economics*, vol. 12, n. 1, Spring, pp. 49-70.

Stigler G.J. (1951), "The Division of Labour is Limited by the Extent of the Market", *Journal of Political Economy*, vol. 59, n. 3, June, pp. 185-193.

Sylos Labini P. (1964), *Oligopolio e Progresso Tecnico*, Torino: Einaudi.

Teece D.J. (1980), "Economies of Scale and Scope of the Enterprise", *Journal of Economic Behaviour and Organization*, n. 1.

Teece D.J. (ed.) (1987), *The Competitive Challenge. Strategies for Industrial Innovation and Renewal*, Cambridge, MA: Bollinger.

Teece D.J., G. Pisano and A. Shuen (1997), "Dynamic Capabilities and Strategic Management", *Strategic Management Journal*, vol. 18, n. 7, August, pp. 509-533.

Teece D.J. (2007), "Explicating Dynamic Capabilities: the Nature and Microfoundations of (Sustainable) Enterprise Performance", *Strategic Management Journal*, published online in Wiley Interscience.

Telser L. (1962), "Advertising and Cigarettes", *The Journal of Political Economy*, vol. 70, pp. 471-499.

Tosi H.L., S. Werner and J.P. Katz (2000), "Analysis of CEO Pay Studies", *Journal of Management*, vol. 26, pp. 301-339.

Thompson A.A. and A.J. Strickland (1998), *Strategic Management Concepts and Cases*, Boston, MA: McGraw Hill.

Unipro (2008), *Associazione Italiana delle Imprese Cosmetiche*, http://www.unipro.org.

Utton, M.A. (1979), *Diversification and Competition*, Cambridge: Cambridge University Press.

Vaccà S. (1986), "L'Economia delle Relazioni tra Imprese: dall' Espansione Dimensionale allo Sviluppo per Reti Esterne", *Economia e Politica Industriale*, n. 51.

Wernerfelt B. (1984), "A Resource-Based View of the Firm", *Strategic Management Journal*, vol. 5, n. 2, April–June, pp. 171-180.

Weston J.F. K.S. Chung and S.E. Hoang (1990), *Mergers, Restructuring and Corporate Control*, Englewood Cliff: Prentice Hall.

Weston F.J. (1994), "Divestiture: Mistakes or Learning?", in P.A. Gaughan (ed.), *Reading in Merger and Acquisitions*, Oxford: Blackwell.

Williamson O.E. (1975), *Markets and Hierarchies: Analysis and Antitrust Implication*, New York: The Free Press.

Williamson O.E. (1981), "The Economics of Organization: the Transaction Cost Approach", *American Journal of Sociology*, vol. 87, n. 3, pp. 548-577.

Williamson O.E. (1986a), *The Economic Institutions of Capitalism: Firms, Markets, Relational Contracting*, New York: The Free Press.

Williamson O.E. (1986b), "Vertical Integration and Related Variations on a Transaction-Cost Theme", in J.E. Stiglitz and F. Mathewson, *New Developments in the Analysis of Market Structure*, Proceedings of a conference held by the International Economic Association in Ottawa, Houndmills, Canada: MacMillan Press.

Winter S.G. (1987), "Knowledge and Competence as Strategic Assets", in D. J. Teece (ed.), *The Competitive Challenge. Strategies for Industrial Innovation and Renewal,* Cambridge, MA: Bollinger.

Winter S.G. (2003), "Understanding Dynamic Capabilities", *Strategic Management Journal*, vol. 24, pp. 991-995.

Wright T. (1936), "Factors Affecting the Cost of Airplanes", *Journal of Aeronautical Sciences*, vol. 3, n. 4, pp. 122-128.

Zollo M. and S.G. Winter, (2002), "Deliberate Learning and the Evolution of Dynamic Capabilities", *Organization Science*, vol. 13, pp. 339-351.

Index

Printed and bound by CPI Group (UK) Ltd, Croydon, CR0 4YY

23/04/2025

14660958-0003